WILLIAM TEMPLE
AND CHRISTIAN
SOCIAL ETHICS TODAY

For   JENNY

WILLIAM TEMPLE
AND CHRISTIAN
SOCIAL ETHICS TODAY

ALAN M SUGGATE

T & T CLARK
EDINBURGH

Copyright © T. & T. Clark Ltd, 1987.

Typeset by C. R. Barber and Partners (Highlands) Ltd,
Fort William,
printed by Billing & Sons, Worcester,

for

T. & T. CLARK LTD
59, George Street, Edinburgh EH2 2LQ.

First printed in the U.K. 1987.

British Library Cataloguing in Publication Data

Suggate, Alan M.
William Temple and Christian social ethics today.
1. Temple, William, *1881–1944*
2. Christian ethics   3. Social ethics
I. Title
241′.092′4   BJ1275

ISBN 0–567–09455–3 (cased)
ISBN 0–567–29140–5 (paperback)

CONTENTS

PREFACE

My debts in writing this book are innumerable, but I particularly wish to thank those friends who read it in draft and made many helpful suggestions: Miss Margaret Kane, Professor Ronald H. Preston, Professor Stephen W. Sykes, the Rev. Fr. Ian D. Hoskins, and Dr. James Y. Muckle. The faults that remain are of course my own responsibility.

I also wish to record my gratitude to the Deutscher Akademischer Austauschdienst for a very generous grant for a study visit to West Germany in May 1984, and to all those Germans who were so welcoming and gave me so much of their time and counsel. I also thank the Librarian, Dr. E. G. W. Bill, and the staff of Lambeth Palace Library for their assistance.

I am more than grateful to my parents for all their encouragement, especially to my mother, who performed wonders transcribing numerous tapes into a typescript. My daughters have been very tolerant of my absences on travels and in my study. Above all, they and their friends have simply been themselves—the very best way of reminding me that there is far more to life than theology. My greatest debt is to Jenny, who for so many years has given me such marvellous support in every way. The least I can do is to dedicate this book to her.

Abbey House,   A.M.S.
Palace Green, .   December 1986
Durham, DH1 3RS.

ACKNOWLEDGEMENTS

I gratefully acknowledge the permission of the Executor of William Temple to quote from his many published works, and also the permission of the following publishers to quote certain extracts from the respective works. In some cases I have not been able to track down the copyright holder.

Macmillan, London and Basingstoke: E. G. Sandford, ed., *Memoirs of Archbishop Temple* by Seven Friends (1906); *Foundations* (1912); W. Temple, *The Nature of Personality* (1911), *Studies in the Spirit and Truth of Christianity* (1914), *Church and Nation* (1915), *Mens Creatrix* (1917), *The Kingdom of God* (1912), *Christus Veritas* (1924), *Christianity and the State* (1928), *Thoughts on Some Problems of the Day* (1931), *Nature, Man and God* (1932–4), *Readings in St. John's Gospel* (1939–40), *Thoughts in War-Time* (1940), *The Church Looks Forward* (1944).

Oxford University Press: W. Temple, *Christianity and War* (1914); F. A. Iremonger, *William Temple* (1948); G. M. Young, *Portrait of an Age* (1936, 1953); E. R. Norman, *Church and Society in England, 1770–1970* (1976) and *Christianity and the World Order* (1979); W. Temple, *Some Lambeth Letters* (edited by F. S. Temple) (1963).

Longmans: W. Temple, *Personal Religion and the Life of Fellowship* (1926), *Essays in Christian Politics* (1927); *The Pilgrim; The Proceedings of COPEC* (1924); *Malvern 1941.*

SPCK: W. Temple, *The Preacher's Theme Today* (1936); *Doctrine in the Church of England* (1938); G. C. Binyon, *The Christian Socialist Movement in England* (1931).

Shepheard-Walwyn: W. Temple, *Christianity and Social Order* (1942, rep. 1976).

SCM Press: W. Temple, *Christianity in Thought and Practice* (1936), *The Hope of a New World* (1940), *Christ and the Way to Peace* (1935); R. Niebuhr, *An Interpretation of Christian Ethics* (1941); J. Macquarrie, *Three Issues in Ethics* (1970); G. Outka and P. Ramsey, eds., *Norm and Context in Christian Ethics* (1967); I. T.

Ramsey, ed., *Christian Ethics and Contemporary Philosophy* (1966); R. H. Preston, *Church and Society in the Late Twentieth Century* (1983).

The Editors of *Theology*: W. Temple, 'Theology Today', November 1939.

Epworth Press: W. Temple, *Social Witness and Evangelism* (1943); *Christian Faith and Political Hopes* (1979).

Cambridge University Press: *Men Without Work* (1938).

Hodder and Stoughton: H. H. Henson, *Quo Tendimus?* (1924).

Allen and Unwin: W. Temple and R. Niebuhr in Vol. IV of the Oxford Conference of 1937 on *Church, Community and State* (1938).

The Contemporary Review: articles by Temple July 1920 and April 1932.

The Spectator: article by Temple 24 January, 1941.

Geoffrey Chapman, a division of Cassell Ltd: W. M. Abbott, S.J. and J. Gallagher, eds., *The Documents of Vatican II* (1966).

Martinus Nijhoff: Jack F. Padgett, *The Christian Philosophy of William Temple* (1974).

Victor Gollancz: R. Craig, *Social Concern in the Thought of William Temple* (1963).

Charles Scribner's: R. Niebuhr, *The Nature and Destiny of Man* (1941, 1943).

The Editor of *New Blackfriars*: W. Temple, 'Thomism and Modern Needs', in *Blackfriars*, March 1944.

INTRODUCTION

This book is a critical study of William Temple's Christian social thought and action, leading to proposals for a framework for Christian social ethics today.

William Temple (1881–1944) is an obvious choice. He is chiefly remembered for his spirituality and his leadership in the Church. Yet he was a remarkably unified person, and it is impossible to separate his spirituality from his philosophy or social thought, and his leadership always expressed a deep concern not just for the Church but also for the world.

Temple never claimed to be original in his social thought. He once remarked that greatness of mind is primarily a matter of receptivity, and his instinct was always to preserve in a synthesis the best in previous thought. For the most part he drew on a long tradition of social thought in England and became its most famous exponent. He believed that historically it reflected the dominant tradition of the Church as a whole. It had suffered an eclipse in England in the eighteenth century, but had been revived by a small number of Christians in the nineteenth, notably Thomas Arnold and F. D. Maurice.

For most of his working life Temple reflected this tradition as he grappled with the problems of his day. He developed his own Christian philosophy which undergirded the principles of his social ethic. However, in the last ten years of his life, under the pressure of national and international events and the shifting currents of theology, Temple was adjusting his thought to cope with its weaknesses. He became very interested both in Roman Catholic thought, with its accent on natural law and natural order, and in the thought of the American Reinhold Niebuhr, who came from a Lutheran background. Temple was still searching for a new framework when death prematurely intervened. He is therefore interesting both because he lucidly represented a long-standing tradition of social thought, and also because he himself became dissatisfied with it, and was widening his theological horizons and deepening his sensitivity to world events in the effort to find new foundations for his theology and social ethics.

Part I gives an overall view of the background and development of Temple's Christian social thought and action. It provides a context for the more detailed accounts of specific areas in later chapters. It also notes in a preliminary way some of the difficulties of Temple's Christian social ethics. Chapter 5 is an extensive account of Temple's Christian philosophy, which he developed from about 1908 to 1934. This is included for two reasons. First, it is the matrix of his chief approach to social ethics. *Christianity and Social Order* (surely Temple's best known and most accessible work on social ethics) presents this approach, but quite reasonably gives only a limited indication of the matrix. A greater knowledge of the foundations of Temple's social ethics is necessary if we are searching for foundations ourselves. Secondly, the significance of Temple's later experimentation with other frameworks is lost if we do not have some appreciation of the philosophy. Since Chapter 5 is inevitably demanding, I have broken it up into short sections to ease digestion.

In Part II Chapters 7 to 9 provide an analysis, with some critical comment, of Temple's thought and action on industry, unemployment and economics. As far as possible he is allowed to speak for himself. We find here that two approaches are used – principles and natural law – to relate the Christian faith to such areas. Chapter 10 tackles the question of natural law, which holds that God created the world with a certain empirical and moral structure, accessible to human reason independently of the Christian revelation. It considers the assessments of natural law offered by Temple and others, and looks at how Catholics and Anglicans have been working towards a radical revision of natural law. This exploration enables us to define the enduring insights of the natural law tradition which must be part of any framework of Christian social ethics. Chapter 11 carries forward the search for an adequate Christian social ethics by considering Temple's approach through principles. It first spells out Temple's ethical stance as part of his Christian philosophy, and compares it briefly with the situation ethics of Joseph Fletcher and with recent Roman Catholic thought. It then shows how there are signs of a growing convergence of thought on an ecumenical front over how principles arise, which ones are indispensable for society, and what contribution the Christian faith can make to their elucidation. A central claim is that the dialectical method of oscillating between theory and fact, which Temple inherited from the British Hegelian Edward Caird, is a valid method, subject to certain corrections. Examples from Catholic, Protestant and Anglican writing show what it could mean to practise the dialectical method. Finally we see to what extent Temple himself implemented the method he professed in the spheres of industry, unemployment and economics. We find that he is variable in his practice, and we decide to follow up a clue that he was much better in his handling of international relations.

Part III therefore investigates how Temple handled the themes of pacifism, war and peace (Chapters 12 to 14). Here we find him extensively using an approach through the concepts of love and justice. In Chapter 15 his position on love and justice is summarised and compared with that of Reinhold Niebuhr, to whom he was greatly indebted. Our conclusion is that Temple is at his best when he uses this approach, but that he found it difficult to adjust from a rather comfortable position, rooted in British Hegelianism, the Anglican tradition and his own particular interpretation of St. John's Gospel, to a more rugged stance with emphases drawn from St. Paul and from Lutheran and Reformed Protestantism. Niebuhr's position is more co-ordinated and more thoroughly dialectical than Temple's ever was, and it basically meets Temple's own perception of 1937 onwards of the need for a modification of his philosophy and social ethics which would take greater account of the doctrine of redemption.

In Part IV I gather together our findings in order to make some proposals about a framework of thought for Christian social ethics today. I try to achieve internal coherence and an adequacy both to the fundamental motifs of the Bible and to our experience of the world. In particular I commend the dialectical method, and also clarify the biblical basis for a Niebuhrian understanding of the relationship of love and justice.

The book ends with three appendices. The first belongs closely to the last chapter and might have been a part of it. The material is put in an appendix not as an afterthought but simply to avoid overloading the last chapter. The purpose is to comment on certain other explicit or implicit understandings of the relation of the Christian faith to social order.

Appendix II develops the point that the primary place for the implementation of the dialectical method is at the local level, where people can come together to help each other live their faith in society with greater confidence. It makes suggestions about how such faith and life groups can best be constituted and function.

Appendix III returns to the specific areas of social concern considered in Chapters 7–9 and 12–14. It does not attempt to state what Temple should have thought, or what we should think in the changed circumstances of today. Rather it is restricted to suggesting a number of questions about these areas which I believe are prompted by the framework.

The focus of this book is the approaches which Temple used in his Christian social thought, with a view to suggesting a framework for today. The urgency of the task of clarifying and criticising different approaches to social ethics is undeniable. There is still very wide disagreement among Christians about the connections between the Christian faith and social order. Controversy in this field is inevitable, and we might as well face that fact with equanimity. However, matters are made more difficult by those who rush to speak as if truth were self-evident and betray ignorance of the history of Christian social thought and a threadbare theology. I hope that this book will bring a little light in spite of a widespread preference for heat!

For clarity's sake some comment should be made on the term 'dialectical', which is used in two quite different contexts. First, it is used with reference to a *method* of developing an understanding of reality. Temple describes the method as one of oscillation between theory and fact. 'Theory' denotes our overall understanding of reality hitherto. 'Fact' refers to data and events we experience concretely in our daily lives. We use our understanding to interpret the facts, but conversely our reading of the facts reshapes our understanding of reality. The dialectical method is handled chiefly on pp. 17, 134ff. and 207ff. We shall see that the term 'reciprocal method' is better. Secondly, 'dialectical' is used to describe the *relationship* of love and justice, which in turn is grounded in the relationship of God and man. The point here is that the Christian faith does not suggest that a neat, logically coherent 'map' can be made of these relationships. Rather, because of man's fall it portrays a dramatic tension where God says both 'yes' to man as his merciful Redeemer, but 'no' to him as his Judge. This dialectical relationship is dealt with mainly in Chapter 15 and on pp. 211ff. If it be asked how the dialectical method and the dialectical relationship are connected, we can say briefly that the dialectical method would be appropriate even without the factor of man's fall, simply because man is finite and historical, and must therefore build up his understanding of God and the world in and through his historical experience. The dialectical relationship of God and man, however, sharpens the need for the dialectical method, because fallen man can so easily settle down to a sub-Christian understanding of God and blind himself to the signs of the times in the situation before his eyes. This should become clearer as the book proceeds.

The dialectical method is not novel. Readers may find on reflection that they have been practising something like it most of their lives, or that one of the earliest practitioners was the Old Testament figure of Job. Nor is it a panacea. No method ever is, least of all one which entails repentance.

Concentration on the approaches and a framework has dictated the forms of selection of material and topics. There is almost nothing about Temple's major interest in education. This is because the other areas raise the central issues more effectively, and to have included education would have made the book unjustifiably longer. I have also selected among the more recent literature examples which tackle my central concern, and especially some which are unknown to English readers. I am particularly glad to have had the opportunity of reading high-quality work in West Germany, Catholic and Protestant, and of having discussions there during a study visit, in some cases with the authors. I am sure we have much mutual ignorance to dispel and much to learn from one another.

The framework in Chapter 16 (taken with Appendix I) should therefore have the merit of being worked out in the light of the dominant motifs of the Bible and the pressures of the world, and of being thoroughly ecumenical. Nonetheless I am still very conscious of its limitations. There are many other positions taken by eminent writers whom I scarcely mention. For instance, much

attention has been given recently to the significance of the fact that
narrative is the literary form of much of the Bible, and centrally of
the Gospels, and also to the Church as the community which lives
in response to those narratives. I would not wish to deny the capital
importance of these developments. I refer myself from time to
time to narrative. And I accept that if the Church is to make society
more just, it must be a community which sustains and develops the
characters of its members in response to the story of God's
revelation of Himself. I am, however, not persuaded that this
approach offers adequate tools for grasping problems of an
institutional and corporate kind in the world today. Christians
must develop out of their experience of living in the Church and in
the world some guidelines which, albeit in summary form, express
the dramatic dealings of God with his world.

The framework I offer is only a working model. It is the result of
prolonged thought, but it is certainly capable of modification.
Indeed the requirement of modification is in-built. The word
'framework' is not meant to suggest rigidity. It is chosen to
emphasise that we do need some guidelines if we are to respond
constructively and faithfully to the world from a Christian
perspective. In fact I am sure that we all do have guidelines of some
sort, and one function of my proposal is to provoke readers to a
little more self-conscious reflection about the guidelines they
actually use. If this framework is superseded by a better one, it will
have served its purpose.

I have tried to write this book for a wide audience, because the
subject is one in which we are all entangled willy-nilly. I have
completely recast what was a doctoral thesis, and it is not written
simply or even primarily for the universities. Nor is it primarily for
clergy. It is above all for the laity. I have restricted the number of
notes, often preferring to gather in a single note the sources of a
paragraph. They all come at the end of the book. (A more detailed
matching of passages to sources is available from me.) The
bibliography is almost entirely confined to those books actually
cited, and followed by some suggestions for further reading. The
structure of the book requires a good system of cross-referencing,
so I have supplied an extensive composite index of people and
subjects referred to in the text.

The word 'man' is almost invariably inclusive of both genders.

Quite often I avoid it, but I retain it in direct and indirect quotation and where it is simpler to do so.

At the end of his life William Temple wrote: 'There is scarcely any more urgent task for the Church than that this whole complex of problems should be thought out afresh, and it is obviously a task which can be successfully undertaken only in the closest relation with the experience of those who are exposed to the daily pressures of the economic and political struggle.' Many have responded to that challenge in the last forty years. I hope this book will bring illumination and encouragement to those who already shoulder the task, and entice many others to join them in a demanding but exciting venture.

PART I

THE DEVELOPMENT OF
WILLIAM TEMPLE'S SOCIAL THOUGHT

CHAPTER 1

TEMPLE'S HOME BACKGROUND

When William Temple was enthroned as Archbishop of Canterbury in 1942, he acknowledged in his sermon that his father, Frederick, 'was and is, among men, the chief inspiration of my life.'[1] The influence is most evident in three spheres: theology, education, and social affairs.

Frederick Temple was born in 1821 in the Greek Ionian Islands, where his father Octavius was a major in the British protecting force. Later Octavius resigned his commission and became a rather unsuccessful farmer in Devon, who incurred unpopularity by publicly criticising the bad conditions of agricultural labourers. In the face of poverty his wife Dorcas maintained the family tradition of culture by educating her growing sons at home. Rote learning alternated with physical work on the farm. To repair his fortunes Octavius became Lieutenant-Governor of Sierra Leone, where death soon carried him off in 1834. In that year Dorcas secured a place for Frederick at Blundell's School, Tiverton. 'Freddy, don't argue; do your work,' was her frequent advice. He took it, won a leaving scholarship to Balliol College, Oxford in 1839, a double First in Classics and Mathematics, and a Lectureship and Fellowship at his old College. He was ordained by Bishop Samuel Wilberforce of Oxford in 1846-7.[2]

Frederick was brought up in a home of simple pieties. At Oxford he was plunged into the theological ferment caused by the Tractarians. He was repelled by their habit of pushing arguments to extremes. Yet there was much that he admired. Pusey impressed him with the power of his preaching, Newman with his belief that the way to truth lies only through constant spiritual growth. He studied the early Church fathers for himself, and for the rest of his life bore many of the marks of the Oxford Movement: a deep sense of awe in worship; a conviction that the Church is not a man-made convenience but the creation of Christ Himself; a strong hold on the world beyond the grave and the Communion of Saints; a belief in the objective truth of the Christian faith and in the importance of the sacraments.[3] At the end of his life he said, 'If I did not believe that Christ had by His Incarnation raised my whole life to an entirely higher level – to a level with His own – I hardly know how I should live at all.'[4]

His deep sense of fairness was offended by Christians who attacked other Christians (and especially Roman Catholics) without being certain what they really maintained, and who seemed afraid of finding the slightest agreement between them. He deplored the wild prejudice against Newman when he produced Tract Ninety, which argued that in spite of the Thirty-nine Articles the doctrine of the Church of England had not been fundamentally changed at the Reformation. Moreover, when the Tractarian W. G. Ward, a colleague and close friend, was arraigned before Oxford University Convocation for his book *The Ideal of a Christian Church*, Temple voted firmly against the censure motion. This was partly because in his view only Newman and Ward were capable of offering effective resistance to the flood of rationalism pouring into Oxford.[5]

Above all, however, Temple was swayed by his understanding of the way we arrive at truth. Here Coleridge, inspired by Kant, influenced him to stress the role of conscience and of the will in the life of faith, and to see practical reason as the surest foundation for religion. The best proof of Christianity was not external evidence but the correspondence of its doctrines with the deepest things in human life. Furthermore Coleridge inspired him to avoid a narrow creed and to recognise that there were limits to human knowledge. There was a place for honest doubt; Christians had to wait on God, trusting He would give them light.[6] Coleridge also maintained the close connection of morality and religion, whereas Christians Temple met at Oxford struck him as revealing 'a very high tone of morality, distinctly disjoined from any *religious* feeling; it looks excessively like most determined Heathenism.'[7]

Frederick Temple was to remark of Newman that his 'initial mistake was that he began by searching for the true Church rather than for the truth – he inverted the right order.'[8] In discussing the question of authority himself Temple set the highest value on freedom of enquiry. Liberty in the Church of England had saved valuable schools of thought from extinction and given it a more truly catholic character than any other body of Christians. Liberty alone had made the Church national, and he feared that disestablishment, if it came, would hand the Church over to narrow-minded dogmatists. In the 1850's Temple had lamented with his Balliol friend Benjamin Jowett a widespread reticence over religious views and the unwillingness of people honestly to state their opinions on points of doctrine. Both men were certain that Christians had to face up to the intellectual challenges to their faith. Temple agreed to write an essay on 'The Education of the World' as part of a volume called *Essays and Reviews*, which would encourage free discussion of biblical topics. It provoked a storm of criticism. Though rather dismayed by the degree of liberalism shown in some of the other essays (none of which he saw before their publication in 1860), Temple was undeterred in upholding the necessity of free enquiry. His only regret was that, since he was by then Headmaster of Rugby School, some of the pupils might read it before they were mature enough to cope. His own essay merely traced the supposed analogy between the life of the individual and the history of the human race. Childhood corresponded with the period of the external authority of the law before Christ; youth and early manhood with the period of the example set by Christ in His ministry; full manhood with that of the Holy Spirit speaking to succeeding generations through conscience. Temple consistently maintained that the Essays caused more good than harm, and when in 1869 Gladstone nominated him Bishop of Exeter he withstood the combined assault of the Evangelical Shaftesbury and the Tractarian Pusey. In the name of religious liberty he refused to withdraw his essay before consecration, or to accede to the demand for a declaration of his opinions: 'Those who now ask for it might live to find their own weapons turned against themselves with fatal effect.'[9]

It has been said that Frederick Temple became theologically less liberal in the forty years after *Essays and Reviews*. His Bampton Lectures of 1884 on *The Relations between Religion and Science* were certainly more acceptable to the public. This was partly because they were more positive and constructive, and were plainly the product of a man of deep Christian faith. But also the very effect of *Essays and Reviews* itself had been to make believers more open to new learning.[10] Charles Darwin himself was by now interred in Westminster Abbey. If there is a lessening of the spirit of enquiry, it can be traced to two causes. First, he thought that the freedom with which he wrote depended on his office; a bishop had to be more cautious than a headmaster. As his episcopal career took him to London in 1885 and Canterbury in 1897, so the caution increased. Secondly, Temple was always deeply concerned with practical religion. He himself in 1839 criticised the Bampton lecturer for treating 'religion as a science, not as a duty or a blessing', and for failing to make 'even a moral much less a religious deduction from it, as far as concerns practice.'[11] The longer he lived the more he trod unrelenting the path of simple duty. For him doctrine was tested in life, and he did not care much for pure speculation. 'The danger of your speculation,' he once told his son William, 'is that if you do not take care you will lower your idea of God.'[12]

Frederick Temple's interest in the education of the nation went back at least to the years when he was a Fellow of Balliol. He took to heart Shaftesbury's revelations that over a million children received no education at all, and the fact that Sir James Graham's Bill of 1843 for general education through Church schools failed because of denominational differences. At a more local level he supported the work of Edmund Hobhouse at the Oxford Diocesan Training College for masters in elementary schools. Temple shared the widespread fear of a repetition of the French Revolution in England. He accepted aristocratic government, but was wise enough not only to support popular education but also to insist that corrupt political institutions had to be reformed, if that education was not to generate revolution.[13]

In 1848 Temple left Oxford for a post as Examiner under the Committee of the Privy Council on Education, and soon became first Principal of Kneller Hall, Twickenham, a college for training school-masters to teach workhouse boys. The experiment was dogged by misfortune. There was no school of pauper children where teaching practice could be done. The conditions for the new teachers in workhouses were very depressing, and the salaries were cut below a tolerable minimum. There was talk of setting up district schools for pauper children outside the workhouses, but this remained a dream. The government starved the Hall of resources, partly through lack of interest in education and partly because of the prior claims of the Crimean War. Furthermore there was opposition in Church circles from both high and low churchmen. This was largely because Temple practised a double principle: that religion ought to be integral to the national system of education, but that the rights of the individual conscience should be respected. Thus at Kneller Hall Temple made religion according to the Church of England 'the centre of all the teaching', and taught it himself, whilst welcoming members of all denominations. Yet no student was required to learn any religious formulary to which he had a conscientious objection. Temple even contemplated letting Dissenters go to their own meeting house. He consistently rejected two positions. The first was the 'combined' system, which gave education to all sects together but excluded religious education. The second was 'denominationalism', where each sect educated its own children. The foolish insistence of churchmen in 1839 that all children in Church schools must be taught the catechism had led to denominationalism in 1840. Temple could not accept that the Church of England was a sect; and in any case he knew the government would never give money to the enthusiasts for a sectarian system. For Temple the only valid system was the 'comprehensive', which brought children of different denominations together and taught them religion, but avoided controversial points wherever they were non-essential.[14]

Temple resigned as Principal of Kneller Hall in 1855 in a state of considerable depression, but this was relieved by his appointment as Headmaster of Rugby in 1857, just fifteen years after the death of his great predecessor, Thomas Arnold. After government restrictions the freedom given him by the Trustees of the school was an elixir. Hopes were expressed that he would be another Arnold. He signalled a vigorous regime by walking from the station to the school carrying his own bag. Rugby became 'a nursery of the strenuous life'.[15] English language and literature were introduced throughout the school. Music and drawing rose in status, and in particular Temple greatly strengthened the study of the sciences.[16] Yet for him education was above all a moral and religious affair. Mathematics and science could make a man more intelligent, he maintained, but not more human. All true education came from contact with other minds. Historical examples of noble thoughts and deeds were indispensable. He encouraged in his pupils a sense that history yielded moral principles, a reverence for conscience, and a sympathy with the conditions of the poor. He taught them to look at both sides of a question before making up their mind, and then to stand by their convictions, whilst remaining aware of areas of doubt.[17] Temple had a strong sense of justice, especially towards the less gifted, to whom he gave much attention and sympathy. He was a severe though often unconventional disciplinarian, but followed the Arnold tradition of trusting boys and relying on moral influence and force of character rather than punishment. He similarly trusted his staff, giving them considerable freedom, consulting them regularly and accepting criticism. 'Of course Temple's a beast,' one boy wrote home, 'but he's a just beast.' The moral force of Temple's teaching was rooted in the school chapel, where even on Saturdays he could hold the attention of boys hot from the rugby field with powerful sermons adapted to their religious understanding.[18]

In his approach to social, economic and political questions Frederick Temple predictably warned against the absorption of the things of the other world by the things of this world; but even more did he deplore their separation. He claimed to have difficulty in defining their true relationship, but 'it is unquestionable that it is intended that our religion should penetrate into all our ordinary conduct.'[19] As usual he was quite definite in his opinions on specific matters. In some ways he was attractive to the working class. His own upbringing and rugged appearance gave him an advantage. He impressed the working-men of Rugby so much that they persuaded working-men of Westminster to drop in on Temple's consecration as bishop in the Abbey in 1869 as a tribute to him.[20] He advised his clergy never to preach down to working-men, but to treat them as intelligent beings. Yet in the 1840's he had a poor opinion of the Chartists, and in 1901 dubbed the working class prone 'to apathy, to a false contentment . . . with bad surroundings, which drags them down in spite of every effort you may make to draw them up'; they seemed perversely to resist all attempts to do them good. Temple's watchwords were self-help, self-control and self-sacrifice – not surprising in a man of his career. His sympathy for the poor was born of religious conviction, and expressed itself strictly along the line of the development of individual character. He won a reputation for lecturing working-men on temperance, and would have liked to give himself full-time to the cause.[21] He distinguished sharply between the voluntary and involuntary unemployed, and stressed the need to keep a 'moral hold' on such people, lest the misfortune spread. Similarly he said that any poor relief which acted on men's circumstances without affecting their character was not merely wasted but mischievous; it was impossible to lift people up without their own co-operation. Quiet and sympathetic performance of Christian duty was far more valuable than schemes to transform the condition of whole classes.[22]

This preoccupation with character is also apparent in his dealings with Stewart Headlam, the swashbuckling Anglo-Catholic priest whose incarnational theology led him to an enthusiastic championing of the arts. When Temple became Bishop of London in 1885 Headlam invited him to a meeting of his Church and Stage Guild. Temple refused, declaring, 'My own personal experience of young men is very considerable, and I have no doubt whatever that a very large number of spectators of the ballet, even if they are quite able to prevent impurity from going into act, are nevertheless led into most disastrous sins of imagination.' In an interview Temple quoted to Headlam the verse: 'If thy right eye offend thee, pluck it out.' 'Quite true, my Lord,' retorted the waspish Headlam, 'but the scriptures do not say that you should pluck out other people's eyes.'[23] In response to the Guild's claim that they wanted the Church to recognise the good in the stage and by that means gradually oust the evil, Temple merely demanded that ballet dancers had better first be properly clad.[24]

Frederick Temple showed his cast of mind twice in 1889. When he was asked to join an Anti-Sweating League in its crusade against economic exploitation of workers, he could not accept the clause in the objects of the League which read: 'by which the worker is oppressed and deprived of the legitimate fruits of his labour.' The phrase 'legitimate fruits' seemed a misleading and mischievous one. 'The choice is constantly this: Shall a man get wages on which he cannot live, or no wages at all?' Better no wage at all, he said, than an inadequate wage, because then the worker would be driven to transfer his labour to some place where he could get a living wage. A man should indeed receive enough to live on; but businesses would collapse if this principle were universally adopted.[25] Temple's view reveals a commitment to liberty in theory but no understanding of the workers' lack of economic liberty in a free market economy. His son was to be far more perceptive.

Also in 1889 there occurred the great London Dock Strike. Temple was persuaded to come back from a holiday in North Wales to serve on the Lord Mayor's Mansion House Committee of Conciliation. When the strike leaders, Ben Tillett and John Burns, failed to persuade the strike committee to accept a compromise formula, Temple resumed his holiday, leaving the credit for settling the strike to accrue to Cardinal Manning. Temple's conduct is partly to be understood by his persistent wish to do his duty unobtrusively and make no religious capital out of the strike. In any case he was not nearly so much the diplomat as Manning. But much more potent is the fact that he applied rigid standards of individual moral integrity, and thought Tillett and Burns had shown bad faith. This ignored the problem of relations between groups and their representatives, but Temple was on unfamiliar ground here. It is clear that he also viewed strikes with great distaste, as they often involved various forms of intimidation to prevent people working. This offended against Temple's conviction of the sovereignty of a free conscience.[26] Here too he showed that he did not appreciate the realities of trade union life. In contrast William could understand the importance of group solidarity.

Frederick Temple was devoted to his mother, and it was only ten years after her death that at the age of 54 he married Beatrice Lascelles, grand-daughter of the Earls of Harewood and Carlisle. They had two sons, Frederick (born 1879) and William (born 15 October, 1881). It is perhaps mostly from his mother that William derived his basic poise and assurance. He observed that she was never *taught* anything; she acquired a spaciousness of mind through simply living in houses which were frequented by leading figures like Gladstone and Disraeli. She also tempered William's precocious intellect. She once terminated an argument with him by saying, 'You know more than I do, William, but I know best.' William's respect for her was unbounded. He wrote to her every day from school, and she presided over his domestic life until her death in 1915. Only then did he marry.[27]

It is impossible to exaggerate the influence of William's parents upon him. In particular his father mediated his profound sense of the Incarnation, of worship and sacrament, of the Church and the Communion of Saints. Frederick's understanding of how we arrive at truth reappeared in William: the importance of conscience, will and practical reason; the need to act with conviction, yet live with doubt; the integral connection of religion and morality. William showed his father's deep concern for education and society, especially for the development of character. The chief difference is that William was much more sensitive to the influence of social forces upon character and to the claims of labour for social justice. There is also a difference of temperament. Though capable of much gentleness and humour Frederick appeared rather forbidding. In spite of his marriage into the aristocracy, which meant that many peers became his cousins, he was treated, as Archbishop E. W. Benson noted, with indifference by the House of Lords, because of his slightly harsh provincial accent, his square figure and rough hair. He was also 'horribly vigorous', as one West Country clergyman unfortunately put it. Yet his old-fashioned integrity and simplicity were also attractive in the worldliness of the later Victorian age. It was little wonder that he was called 'granite on fire'.[28] By contrast William was more genial and polished. He was also more radical. Perhaps it is true that the father suffered from social insecurity, whereas the son could afford the radicalism of one to the manner born.[29]

CHAPTER 2

TEMPLE'S EDUCATION

Inevitably William was educated at Rugby (1894–1900) and imbibed the Arnold ethos for himself. It was to influence him for life in several ways. He once wrote approvingly to his wife that Thomas Arnold 'first clearly put character before brains as the aim of education.'[1] Here was another curb on any intellectual bumptiousness in William, and it was his lifelong concern that all should have opportunities to develop character. Moreover, Arnold was an important source of William's impulse to ecumenism. In his *Principles of Church Reform* (1832) Arnold wanted to open the doors of the Church of England to Dissenters and create a broad church by allowing a variety of opinion and ceremony and by keeping dogmatic articles to a minimum. It is no surprise that William Temple advocated non-dogmatic religious instruction, and strove throughout his life for as much agreement as possible with Nonconformists.

Furthermore, though Temple could never quite follow Arnold in identifying Church and state as aspects of a single society, he remained an establishment man, believing in the complementarity of Church and state, not their contradiction or separation. He never equated social progress with the Kingdom of God, but he did believe with Arnold that the kingdoms of the world were destined to become provinces of the Kingdom of Christ. Arnold held that without an establishment, though the majority of Englishmen might still be Christians individually, yet England would not be a Christian nation, its government no Christian government, and we should be 'wholly a kingdom of the world, and ruled according to none but worldly principles.'[2] William Temple similarly thought that a nation was more than an aggregate of individuals, and that the Church had a mission to it and could offer it Christian principles.

Here the debt to Arnold the social reformer was incalculable. 'I cannot understand what is the good of a National Church,' Arnold had written, 'if it be not to Christianize the nation, and introduce the principles of Christianity into men's social and civil relations.'

He had inveighed against the free market economy advocated by Adam Smith. Whereas the protagonists of *laissez-faire* largely blamed the poor themselves for their poverty, Arnold remarked that 'their physical distresses, their ignorance, and their vices are the true fruits of the system of "letting alone" '; the strong penalised the weak for their inferiority. He had criticised industry for wanting 'hands' – of men's heads or hearts or eternal destiny it cared nothing. He had also censured the Church for the perversion of its responsibilities: she 'has never dared to speak boldly to the great, but has contented herself with lecturing the poor.'[3] Ideas like these became part of Temple's mental furniture. Rugby School itself in his day ran a club which enabled the pupils to do social work among the poor. We shall see Arnold's influence at every turn.

It required considerable effort for Temple to escape certain weaknesses of Arnold. First, there is a class moralism, and here Temple was largely successful. Like so many Victorian churchmen Arnold was certainly anxious to bridge the gap between the classes, but took a very negative view of working-class movements. His approach is very much *de haut en bas*. The wage-earners needed to be led by gentlemen. Moreover Arnold's concept of reform is spiritual and moral. He is not nearly so interested in social, political and economic analysis and reform.[4] Temple too remained weak on empirical analysis compared with moral zeal. G. M. Young beautifully captures the ethos Arnold diffused in his vignette of the new type issuing from the universities and public schools in the 1840s, 'somewhat arrogant and somewhat shy, very conscious of their standing as gentlemen, but very conscious of their duties, too, ... passionate for drains and co-operative societies, disposed to bring everything in the state of England to the test of Isaiah and Thucydides ... These are the Arnoldians.'[5]

Just as inevitably William moved on to Balliol. Oxford was to be his home for ten years (1900–1910), initially as Exhibitioner, and then, after a First in Greats, as Lecturer in Philosophy and Fellow of Queen's. Years later he was to say that the three continuously formative influences on his mind were Plato, Robert Browning and St. John.[6] The first two held him spellbound from his Oxford days. Classical philosophy suited him much better than the minutiae of grammar or history, and Plato permeated Temple's thinking about education, and encouraged him more generally to interpret the world as grounded in a purposive Mind, as we shall see in Chapter 5. In 1916 he produced *Plato and Christianity*, which so harmonised the two that Plato fell short of Christianity only in his failure to appreciate the excellence of sacrificial love.[7]

In Browning Temple found a poet who was 'the greatest product of the nineteenth century and with Shakespeare the greatest figure in our literature'; he was thoroughly Christian, said Temple in 1904, since his poetry conveyed not only the joy of comedy, but also the joy of work and workship too. Temple saw a prevailing optimism in Browning. All that exists has good in it, and all, even the worldling and the liar, stand in direct relation to God and trust confidently in Him. Browning is also 'the greatest of all realists', in that he sees everything as brimming with significance. He can raise the everyday to the highest vision, or find fundamental religious truth in a sordid segment of human life. This is so because 'to Browning the climax of history, the crown of philosophy, and the consummation of poetry, is unquestionably the Incarnation.' Temple was to give a vital place to the arts in the construction of his own incarnational and sacramental Christian philosophy.[8]

Temple once said that Browning's *A Death in the Desert* was the best commentary on St. John. His own devotional and scholarly *Readings in St. John's Gospel* (1939–40) were to be hailed as a classic. They were the fruit of thirty and more years of meditation and exposition to all manner of people, Repton schoolboys, Blackpool holiday-makers, and ordination candidates among them. St. John was his own spiritual mainstay for a lifetime. 'With St. John,' he said, 'I am at home.'[9] His worship, his philosophy, his ecumenism and his social thought were all saturated with St. John. In Iremonger's biography of William Temple, Dorothy Emmet wisely closes her chapter on Temple the Philosopher by quoting his meditation on the words 'The Light shineth in the darkness, and the darkness did not absorb it.'[10] And Leonard Hodgson noted how after a stormy ecumenical committee meeting Temple led them into a chapel for closing devotions and read from Isaiah 40 and St. John 15, whereupon 'the whole atmosphere changed ... There was no mistaking the fact that in heart and soul we were being lifted up into the realm where he habitually dwelt. We knew then whence came the courtesy, the patience, the love of justice, and the calm strength with which he had led us into order out of the chaos of our controversies.'[11] Behind Temple's social thought lies his conviction of the Incarnation of the Word (John 1.14), the self-giving love of God (3.16) and Christ's patient drawing of the human race to Himself (12.32).

William Temple can be understood only if we know something about the dominant philosophy at Oxford in the generation before the First World War. Rugby sent many of its brightest pupils to Balliol, and none had more influence on Temple than the philosopher T. H. Green (1837–82). Green performed the remarkable feat of popularising the German philosopher Hegel by developing a distinctive form of his philosophy which was attuned to the Arnold ethos. One of Temple's mentors, Henry Scott Holland, once said of Green, 'He gave us back the language of self-sacrifice and taught us how we belonged to one another in the one life of organic humanity. He filled us again with the breath of high idealism.'[12]

Green restored these ideas of self-denial and self-sacrifice through his criticism of utilitarianism. He believed that all utilitarians were involved in a conflict between the logic of the various theories of utility and their impulses to philanthropy. In practical terms it was vain to suppose that selfish pursuit of pleasure could somehow become altruistic. Green substituted a doctrine of self-sacrifice. He was passionately concerned with social reform, and highly sensitive to the needs of his contemporaries. Their problem was that their Christian faith was crumbling in an age of critical questioning, and they were looking to secular outlets for those impulses to altruism and sacrifice which their Christian parents had instilled into them. Green's own convictions seemed to resolve the conflicts of faith and of utilitarianism and provide new certainty. He believed that his philosophy could articulate Christianity without loss of content and show that there was no inherent conflict between religion and science. He heavily stressed God's immanence. In society God is immanent in human institutions, aspirations and customs. In individuals He is immanent in the sense of being the principle of reason and morality. Green noted people's awareness of the difference between their actual self and their higher self, or conscience. The latter he identified with God.[13]

Green understood the self, society and God in a teleological sense, that is, as moving towards a goal. God realises Himself progressively in men and in society. This takes place through the development of character to perfection by a process of asceticism, self-sacrifice and devotion to a noble cause. Conversely the essence of sin is selfishness. It is hardly surprising that once Green had identified God with the higher self, he had considerable difficulty with the idea of sin. He found the notion of original sin barbaric, and once remarked of a man who was feeling an acute sense of being wicked: 'Poor fellow, the sense of Sin is very much an illusion. People are not as bad as they fancy themselves.' He was highly optimistic about the possibility of social and individual progress, and had a touching confidence in the potency of ideas. He claimed that the higher resolve and discipline of life would gradually neutralise or transmute harmful passions. 'Where the selfishness of man has proposed, his better reason has disposed,' he wrote.[14]

The very fact that the same principles of reason operated both in man and in society meant that ultimate conflict between them was impossible. Indeed, at the heart of Green's philosophy is the belief that reality is rational. It has no room for paradoxes. Green accepted Hegel's view that the purpose of philosophy is to synthesize and reconcile all aspects of human life by showing its ultimate purpose and goal. Though he criticised utilitarianism, he wanted to incorporate its partial truth into a higher synthesis. His method was always to include rather than to exclude. Of Christianity itself he wrote that its glory 'is not that it excludes but that it comprehends; . . . it is the expression of a common spirit, which is gathering together all things in one.'[15]

Green is one of the chief representatives of the philosophical idealism, as it was called, which was highly influential up to the outbreak of the First World War, the very period when William Temple grew to manhood. It was a reaction against two trends. The first sharply distinguished theology and philosophy by accentuating the transcendence of God, the authority of Scripture, and the salvation of individual souls. The other trend was towards a hard empiricism which excluded religion itself from consideration. Men like Green, Edward Caird, F. H. Bradley and

Bernard Bosanquet insisted that art, morality, religion and science suggest by their very existence that reality is more than sense data. There are religious values to be discovered in this world. For Caird and Green value is located principally in self-conscious personality and the organism of society. Against Bradley and Bosanquet's impersonal Absolute Idealism they maintained the personal nature of God, and so can be called personal idealists. All were constructive metaphysicians, that is, they sought to work out a coherent intellectual map of the world.

It was to the memory of Edward Caird, the Master of Balliol, that Temple was to dedicate his Gifford Lectures of 1932–4, *Nature, Man and God*. Temple was Caird's debtor in both his philosophy and his social concern. In philosophy he unashamedly took over Caird's dialectical method of acquiring knowledge. It is sketched by Temple in 1914 as a way of overcoming the inadequacy of both the deductive and the inductive method, namely, that they never represent the way we think in real life. 'All actual thinking proceeds in circles or pendulum swings. We approach a group of facts; they suggest a theory; in the light of the theory we get a fuller grasp of the facts; this fuller grasp suggests modifications of the theory; and so we proceed until we reach a systematic apprehension of the facts where each fits into its place. In the end we have not one universal and unquestioned proposition with other propositions deductively established from it, but a whole system – a concrete universal – in which each element is guaranteed by the rest, and all together constitute the whole which determines each.' Temple approvingly cites Caird's dictum that there is no harm in arguing in a circle if the circle is large enough.[16] This dialectical method, oscillating between fact and theory within the process of actual living, will play an important role in our enquiry.

Caird was thereby committed to the apprehension of the facts and values before us in individuals and in society. It is therefore no surprise that he was passionately concerned with social reform. This began when he was a lecturer in Glasgow, and at Oxford he encouraged his pupils to go down to the East End of London to study first-hand the problem of poverty in the midst of plenty. W. E. Beveridge and R. H. Tawney, two of Temple's close friends, were notable respondents. This was the era of the great investigations into poverty by Charles Booth in London and B. S. Rowntree in York, and of the University Settlements inspired by men like Canon Samuel Barnett of Whitechapel. Temple himself sampled the settlements. At the Oxford Medical Mission at Bermondsey he risked his ample frame on a rickety bed and passed the night in the company of vicious bugs.[17]

The impact of philosophical idealism is pervasive in Temple's writings right up to his death in 1944. It is, however, important to realise that whilst he used Caird's dialectical method in the search for syntheses, Temple's philosophy was, as we shall see in Chapter 5, very much a Christian philosophy; for his unifying ideas came from the tradition of Christian faith. To be more precise, Temple's Christianity obviously reflects the tradition of the Church of England. As Joseph Fletcher has written, 'The plain truth is that Temple was every inch an Anglican, standing in between Romanism and Protestantism in the *via media* or bridge-church position.'[18] Temple himself said he was more interested in mastering the great stream of classical theology than bothering with the polemics of the Reformers and Counter-Reformers. His theological position has been correctly characterised as 'critical classicism'. A. E. Baker wrote of him: 'There was in his thinking a notable balance between traditionalism and independence, the former stemming from his sensitive awareness of the value of fellowship, the latter expressing his profound conviction of Christ's careful respect for each individual soul and its value and freedom.'[19]

A potent influence, contemporary with philosophical idealism and responsive to it, was liberal catholicism, epitomised by the volume of essays entitled *Lux Mundi* (1889). Subtitled 'A Series of Studies in the Religion of the Incarnation', it was an attempt, as the editor Charles Gore said, 'to put the Catholic faith into its right relation to modern intellectual and moral problems.' The writers stressed the category of personality to clarify the relationship of human beings to God and to each other. They understood God as both transcendent over the world and immanent in it, and spoke of a general revelation given by God preparatory to the coming of Christ, as well as the special revelation recorded in the Bible. Gore himself depicted the social character of the work of the Holy Spirit. He was an immense influence on Temple. In 1914 Temple dedicated *Studies in the Spirit and Truth of Christianity* to Gore, saying he was one 'from whom I have learnt more than from any other now living of the Spirit of Christianity and to whom more than to any other . . . I owe my degree of apprehension of its truth.'

Green, Caird and Gore were not the only sources of William Temple's social concern. He always claimed to stand in a long tradition of Christian social thought, which, after an untypical eclipse in the eighteenth century, was revived in the 1840s by Frederick Denison Maurice, John Malcolm Ludlow and Charles Kingsley, and then developed by men like Bishop Westcott, Charles Gore and Henry Scott Holland. This has been called by G. C. Binyon 'the true line of Christian social theology', a phrase which contains some truth but also a generous masking of difficulties.[20] Temple himself adopted the movement's general stance, but never really investigated its endemic problems. We need to know something of both.

It was the economic distress of the 1840s which occasioned the first phase of Christian Socialism in England (1848–54). Like Thomas Arnold and Coleridge before them, Maurice and Ludlow were keen to relate Christianity to the thought of the day, and were convinced that all life rested on a Christian foundation and should reflect that fact in practice.[21] The free market (*laissez-faire*) economy was a prime target of criticism, on the grounds that it was a denial of man's spiritual capacities and his need for brotherhood. Both men were well aware of the chasm between the classes, which *laissez-faire* had widened, but their solution was typical of the nineteenth century and problematical. For they looked to the upper and middle classes to help the lower, especially by providing them with education. Both were therefore rather hostile to genuine working-class movements such as Chartism and the Trade Unions.

The differences between Maurice and Ludlow escaped their own notice for a long time, but Ludlow eventually arrived at a state of despair over Maurice, tempered by an admiration which made him take the blame for the misunderstanding. Maurice was basically a theologian, who developed the concept of a Divine Order.[22] In creating the world God had sent up a Divine Order in which all people everywhere and at all times stand. The Incarnation, Death and Resurrection of Jesus Christ only clarify this fact. The Divine Order is identical with the Kingdom of Christ. Christ is the Head of every person, and thus His Kingdom is a universal fellowship. A renegade Unitarian, Maurice believed that the Church of England was the best equipped church to testify to this Order. Maurice's aim was basically to 'socialise Christians'. Church members should break out of their individualistic understanding of Christianity and grasp its social dimensions. If only the world could be educated to acknowledge the truth of God's Order, then its problems would vanish. Ludlow on the other hand had no such elaborate theory. He was brought up in France, saw the 1830 and the 1848 revolutions, and wanted to 'Christianise socialism', that is, to make sure that political movements were put on a Christian foundation. His philanthropic work in the slums around Lincoln's Inn in London led him to remark, 'It seemed to me that no serious effort was made . . . to help a person out of his or her misery, but only to help him or her in it.'[23] In other words charity was not enough. There had to be legislation and fresh institutions which would lift the poor out of their economic and social degradation. Ludlow had a vision of the Church playing a leading role in this process, but no illusions about the moribund state of the Church of his day. He hoped for a brotherhood of Christians who would spearhead the reform of society and of the Church. A small brotherhood was created around Maurice for Bible study, prayer and discussion. The tension between Maurice and Ludlow was apparent whenever Ludlow enthusiastically urged the creation of institutions for social reform, such as producers' co-operatives or a National Health League. Maurice had a phobia of any kind of sect or party, mainly because it could easily cut across his idea of the Divine Order already existing. It was Ludlow who was the inspiration and the brains behind the setting up of small producers' co-operatives in London. Maurice agonised long over their compatibility with his first principles, and never accepted Ludlow's idea of diffusing the principles of co-operation as the practical application of Christianity to trade and industry. Eventually he let the co-operatives die, preferring to found a Working Men's College. 'I cannot be interested,' he said, 'in the mercantile part of the business till I feel that it has a moral basis; and I am satisfied that nothing but direct teaching will give it that character.' Ludlow was left to remark, 'So Mr. Maurice had his way, and the comparatively broad stream of Christian socialism was turned into the narrow channel of a Working Men's College.'[24]

As the Golden Age of British Capitalism (c. 1850–75) came to an end, so the second wave of Christian Socialism arose, lasting from 1877 to c. 1924. Though there were Nonconformist groups, the most prominent societies were exclusively Anglican, and of a Catholic orientation. This wave also was largely middle-class; the problem of bridging the chasm between the classes remained. The history of the groups which sprang up in this period shows a prolongation of the disagreement between Maurice and Ludlow. Stewart Headlam, who founded the Guild of St. Matthew in 1877, was a devotee of Maurice.[25] But his strong personality and the legacy of two generations of the Oxford Movement led him to develop an aggressive sacramental socialism. This meant that he could not appeal widely even to his fellow-Anglicans, let alone to other Christians or the population at large. He had none of Maurice's inhibitions about the practical application of Christianity. In the name of Jesus, the Incarnate Son and Carpenter of Nazareth, he supported all manner of causes, including a sweeping tax on profits from land, universal suffrage, and the abolition of the House of Lords. On the other hand he looked on the founding of the Independent Labour Party in 1893 as an absurdity. The Guild members found themselves implicated in the waywardness of their leader. A steadier and more respectable body was called for, and it came in 1889.

It is not surprising that the socially-minded Gore, in the very year of the publication of *Lux Mundi*, joined with several of his friends, including Bishop Westcott and Henry Scott Holland, to found the Christian Social Union, whose main aim was to study in common how to apply the moral truths and principles of Christianity to the social and economic difficulties of the time.[26] During its early years the Christian Social Union was taken up with self-education and the attempt to convert the Church from guilty neglect to an interest in social reform, that is, to socialise Christians. The Christian Social Union was far more cautious than Headlam about specific issues, though it did draw up a 'white list' of approved firms which had adopted acceptable Trade Union wage rates, and also urged relatively concrete measures during the

London County Council elections of 1892, such as sanitary dwellings, pure and cheap water, and fairer taxation. The President was the saintly Bishop Westcott of Durham. In 1892 he acquired an aura for settling the Durham miners' strike, but he had scarcely an inkling of the economic situation which prompted the strike in the first place.[27] His speeches were filled with opaque rhetorical antitheses, such as socialism and individualism, which were morally uplifting at the price of contact with the real world of politics and economics. One observer crossly remarked in 1910 that the Christian Social Union 'glories in its indefiniteness, and seems to consider it a crime to arrive at any particular economic conclusion ... Its leaders arrive at no clear dogma in theology or politics.'[28] Indeed Peter Jones has claimed that of all the Christian reform groups of the period, perhaps the Christian Social Union exhibited the widest gap between its critical rhetoric and its cautious policy. It was successful in disseminating its ideas among the leadership of the Church of England, partly perhaps because its own leaders belonged to the same privileged elite, partly because of the very harmlessness of the Christian Social Union, wedded as it was to Westcott's view that it would be disastrous if the Church itself were to be identified with a party or a class. Insofar as it had a programme it was radical liberal. It spoke strongly for labour but fell far short of any genuine socialist economic policy.[29] Like Headlam the leadership did not recognise the importance of the rise of the Independent Labour Party.

It was small wonder that people like F. L. Donaldson, who in 1904 made a protest march with hundreds of unemployed men from Leicester to London, became exasperated and looked for a society with a greater commitment to the cause of labour. He was quick to join the Church Socialist League when it was founded in 1906, for it explicitly backed economic socialism, the principle 'that the community should own the land and capital collectively and use them co-operatively for the good of all.'[30] It aimed for a wide spectrum of membership among Christians. Yet it was also strongly sacramental, notably through its connection with members of the Community of the Resurrection at Mirfield, which had been founded by Charles Gore in 1892. It did commend itself to the largely Nonconformist leadership of the rising Independent Labour Party as the Guild of St. Matthew and the

Christian Social Union had never done. Yet there was division of opinion from the start, and when in 1909 the President, G. A. West, tried to persuade the League to affiliate with the Labour Party, the cry went up that the League must not identify itself with any wing of the social reform parties. 'We are a society of socialists of various shades of socialist opinion, and our common platform is not that of the Independent Labour Party or the Social Democratic Federation [a Marxist group] but that of the Church of God. Our business is to convert Churchmen and make them socialists, but the particular tint which may colour their socialism is no concern of the League.' The speaker, A. T. B. Pinchard, succeeded West as President. But there was another group within the Church Socialist League, led by Percy Widdrington, which agreed with the policy of non-alignment, but approached the matter differently. They thought the Church Socialist League was not theological enough, and wanted to work out a Christian sociology, that is, a social theory deduced from Christian dogma, by which medieval catholic Christendom could be reborn in modern form. Eventually in 1923 they transmogrified the Church Socialist League into the League of the Kingdom of God, which was thereafter active mainly through a small body called the Christendom Group.[31]

Peter Jones has concluded from a study of Christian Socialism of the period 1877–1914 that it is an enigma.[32] The various groups were torn by dissension and never found a satisfactory way of relating the two terms so that justice was done both to the Christian faith and to the social and political situation. Nor could they break out of ecclesiastical sectarianism or overcome their paternalistic approach to the gap between the classes. It is hardly surprising, given his background, that William Temple joined the Christian Social Union at Oxford, and eventually became Chairman of the Westminster branch, where he met and married the secretary, Miss Frances Anson, in 1916. He never suffered from sectarianism, and he largely overcame any paternalism, but the search for an adequate way of relating the Christian faith and social order was lifelong, and became increasingly restless towards the end of his life.

CHAPTER 3

TEMPLE THE EDUCATOR

As an Oxford don (1904–10) Temple eagerly extended his experience of philosophy, theology and social affairs. He studied twice in Germany. In spite of much enjoyment and benefit he preserved a critical distance. A master of lucid expression himself, he showed an amused distaste for professorial rhetoric. When Professor Wendt claimed St. Paul for individualistic morality, Temple claimed the saint's doctrine of the Body of Christ for social morality. On another visit Evangelical services offended Temple's sense of worship and of biblical criticism. They were, he said, almost devoid of liturgy and exalted the Bible to a level of uncritical idolatry.[1] In spite of his professed adherence to the dialectical method, Temple virtually bypassed continental giants like Friedrich Schleiermacher and Søren Kierkegaard.

He revelled at this time in English liberal Christianity, and within its terms he did allow a critical interplay between his understanding of the Christian faith and contemporary thought. In *The Faith and Modern Thought* (1910) he was satisfied that the Christian faith met the requirements of both reason and experience. *The Nature of Personality* (1911) is an early sketch of parts of his Christian philosophy. Then he joined with half a dozen friends to produce *Foundations* (1912), subtitled 'A Statement of Christian Belief in Terms of Modern Thought'. When R. A. Knox retorted that it scaled down the Gospel to an irreducible minimum so that even 'Jones' could swallow it, Temple replied that he was himself Jones asking what there was to eat. Robert Craig suggests that *Foundations* was the high point of Temple's theological exploration; later he fell back on uncritical orthodoxy. Thus in *Foundations* he explains how our twentieth-century understanding of the world-process predisposes us to accept the concept of the Incarnation, in which Christ is fully man and yet God also; by *Christus Veritas* (1924) however he prefers to accept the credal affirmation 'truly God and truly man' simply as authoritative.[2] Other critics, as we shall see, have similarly held that Temple muted the operation of the dialectical method and

24

settled for apologetics and the exposition of Christianity.

The tension between the believing mind and the critical mind was also evident in the story of Temple's ordination. In 1906 Francis Paget, Bishop of Oxford, refused to ordain him since he had intellectual reservations about the Virgin Birth and the bodily Resurrection of Christ. Yet Temple never doubted the truth of the Christian faith in the depths of his personality, and Archbishop Davidson was soon content with his orthodoxy and conducted the ordination himself.[3]

In social affairs Temple spread a liberal idealism. He reflected the confident optimism of the Edwardian era. The rise of the Independent Labour Party and the introduction of welfare schemes by the Liberals in 1906 heralded a morally superior social order. The considerable waves of domestic strife seemed to be an incentive rather than a threat to idealism; the world outside Britain gave no hint of menace. Typical were Temple's article 'The Church and the Labour Party' and his contribution to the Pan-Anglican Congress, both of 1908.[4] He uncritically saluted the latest social force, the Labour Movement, drawing the analogy between its ideal of brotherhood and the Pauline doctrine of the Body of Christ. The Church, alas, blind to its own doctrine of the Incarnation, had ignored labour's concern with material conditions and preached a purely spiritual gospel. It had to repent and recognise the social dimension of sin, and 'the justice, the essential Christianity of the Labour Movement'. The Church needed the Labour Movement, but the Labour Movement needed the Church too, for the Church alone, especially through its Communion Service, could point in Jesus Christ to an embodied ideal and standard of personal effort and sacrifice powerful enough to move men's minds. The choice was between socialism and heresy, between Christ and selfish individualism.

In 1909 Temple chaired the Student Christian Movement's Matlock Conference. It was important for his future directions. He was reinforced in the view that churchmen needed educating about the social problem. The upshot was the Collegium, a small interdenominational group, chaired by Temple, which shared a common life of prayer and considered social problems. It produced a well-balanced study in *Competition* (1917). The idea of small study groups and larger conferences was fixed in Temple's mind. He was also able to develop his remarkable skills as a chairman. The Student Christian Movement also brought him his first major experience of ecumenism at the Edinburgh Faith and Order Conference of 1910, followed by a lecture tour of Australia.[5]

Education became a dominant interest for Temple in these years. Following his father and Thomas Arnold he argued for a religious understanding of education as a whole, whilst wishing to spare young children controversial points of doctrine.[6] In the 1920's Temple modified his position and began to stress the distinctive importance of Church schools. However, he always cared more about Christian support for general education. The clearest example is his devotion to the Workers' Educational Association, which he joined in 1905. He rapidly became President (1908), an honour which he genuinely thought the greatest of his life. The inventive brain behind the W.E.A. was Dr. Albert Mansbridge, who shrewdly spotted his man. 'As a merely personal matter . . . he invented *me*,' said Temple.[7] The W.E.A. suited his outlook perfectly: here was another movement Christianity could wholeheartedly endorse. The elevation of the worker through education had been a persistent theme of Christian Socialism. Here was a movement which sought the spiritual and not merely the material advancement of the working class. It is little wonder that Temple decked the ideals of the movement with the aura of the theological virtues of faith, hope and love. At last he was really meeting members of the working class, even if only those who accepted the movement's ideals. He was also spurred to think further about the outlook of the working class and the problems of communicating the faith – a clear advance on the patronizing Maurice. His experience removed any lingering danger of ecclesiasticism. Indeed, Temple found the atmosphere of the W.E.A. more genuinely Christian than much Church life.[8]

William Temple followed again in his father's footsteps by accepting an invitation to be a headmaster. He went to Repton School in 1910. In some ways he was a success. Like his father he brought intellectual vitality to the school and was popular, especially with the sixth form. But he had none of his father's disciplinary flair. At the end of his first term, and during a general election campaign, the local *Daily News* reported with relish how

300 boys from the school had made an attack on the Liberal Party candidate's rooms, pelting the occupants with apples, kippers, eggs, potatoes, and even stones. Temple's stern predecessor, Lionel Ford, returned from Harrow to a reunion in 1912, and dolefully remarked in an after-dinner speech that he believed the school continued to flourish – or at any rate to exist.

Nor was Temple successful in his broader aim to reform the public schools through the Headmasters' Conference, especially by widening the social base of admission. He valued the public schools far too much to consider abolishing them: they excelled in educating pupils as members of a community, and in giving them standards of judgement and criticism through studying outstanding figures of history. He wanted to stop them reproducing class divisions in accentuated form, by diffusing their benefits over a broader public. However, by the time he left Repton in 1914 his revolution had not even started. He remarked later that institutions could not turn in a wholly new direction and be able to use their running powers as before; they had to run on their own lines or be scrapped.

It was with some relief that Temple was able to enter a larger public life. He nearly left Repton at the end of 1912, when he was offered the living at St. Margaret's, Westminster and a Canonry at the Abbey. But the Prime Minister, the Archbishop of Canterbury and the Dean of Westminster were all thrown into confusion by the discovery that Temple had not been ordained long enough to be eligible for a canonry. Temple appeared as usual at Repton in January 1913, looking for all the world, as one wit remarked, 'like a runaway wife who had missed her train'. Another year elapsed before he moved to be Rector of St. James's, Piccadilly.[9]

CHAPTER 4

TEMPLE THE SOCIAL REFORMER

In July 1914 Lloyd George remarked that in external affairs the sky had never been more perfectly blue. A month later came consternation. Few Christians had read the signs; few could therefore respond theologically. On the Continent Karl Barth was writing, 'The unconditional truths of the Gospel are simply suspended for the time being and in the meantime a German war-theology is put to work, its Christian trimming consisting of a lot of talk about sacrifice and the like ... It is truly sad!'[1] It was no better in England. The word sacrifice became a frantic catchword for bellicose and bereaved alike. The jingoist Bishop Winnington-Ingram of London compounded it with Tennysonian images of knightly chivalry as he called for a Holy War. The liberal Christian Socialist R. J. Campbell thought the war demonstrated that sacrifice was a catalyst of the co-operative ideal of the Kingdom of God. The Anglo-Catholic Paul Bull stressed the congruence of the sacrifice of the soldiers in war with the sacrifice of the Mass. As Alan Wilkinson rightly says, three major modes of nineteenth century thought were all weighed in the balances between 1914 and 1918 and found wanting. Chivalric romanticism perished at the Somme and Passchendaele. Liberalism, confronted with the evil and irrationality of man, feebly declared that the war was a temporary setback; only the Germans were corrupt, and this was a war to end all wars. Moreover it treated Christ's death merely as an example and identified the self-sacrifice of the soldiers with that of Christ. By contrast evangelicalism tended to work with a simple antithesis of good and evil. Lacking a firm theology of the Incarnation of the Word, it treated secular life as a hostile world from which individual souls were to be saved. It therefore could make no sense of the mixed multitude of soldiers capable of both heroism and degradation. Apart from distinguished work on the significance of the Cross by P. T. Forsyth, it was the war poets like Wilfred Owen, not the theologians, who created a new language of ambivalence and tragedy.[2]

During the war Temple was frenetically busy preaching,

speaking and publishing. He edited the Church of England weekly *The Challenge* from 1915 to 1918 and contributed to a series of *Papers for War-time*. Airy rhetoric gave way to plain tough realism in his thinking about the war. He went straight to the heart of the matter: a defective understanding of God. To those who spoke of God punishing men with war for Sabbath breaking he opposed the teaching of St. John's Gospel: men bring judgment upon themselves by choosing darkness and flouting God's moral order; the love of God is not mere amiability; it will be hard against men's self-indulgence. Against self-righteous talk of reprisals against Germany he preached Britain's own need of repentance and purity of motive.[3] The issue of pacifism forced him to ask fresh questions about the state and the individual citizen. An individual might embrace costly self-sacrifice, but could a government commit a whole community to it? If not, what was the individual Christian to do? As a legatee of T. H. Green Temple emphasised human sociality and citizenship. He recognised as a consequence our entanglement in sin, and the necessity of compromise in the Christian practice of love in a sinful world. He therefore rejected pacifism.[4] Nevertheless he had a high regard for the rights of the conscientious objector who was personally witnessing to a higher standard.[5]

When, however, he came to the practice of citizenship within Britain Temple remained very much the idealist. He believed the sacrifice of the soldiers had to be matched by a rigorous sacrifice at home in the interests of a better society. He even spoke for the total prohibition of alcohol. Above all he held that the Church had to confess its social guilt, if it was to lead the social reconstruction. Temple served on a commission on Church and State, which recommended greater autonomy for the Church. He was also caught up in the National Mission of Repentance and Hope and in the Life and Liberty campaign, both of which were geared to reform in Church and society. The Mission was a failure: the note of repentance did not appeal to a nation with its back to the wall. Plainly religious revival was not in the offing. The Life and Liberty campaign involved Temple himself in great financial sacrifice, when in 1917 he resigned St. James's and took a large cut in salary. It was mainly through his efforts that the Church of England acquired an Assembly which had a measure of independence of

Parliament, and Parochial Church Councils, which at least in theory gave greater scope for all baptized members of the Church of England to shape the future of the Church and the social order.[6] Though Temple was not unduly surprised at the failure of the Mission, he continued energetically to propound ideals and urge people to will their realisation. 'The world is plastic now,' he confidently remarked in 1918, revealing how little he had imbibed the wartime poets, or reflected on the implications of the Cross.

The mood of the country at the end of the war was an unpropitious mixture of euphoria and rancour. On the one hand men and women had defended their way of life at great cost, and there was an optimistic determination that British society should be reconstructed beyond the achievements of the Liberal administration of 1906. Lloyd George exploited his politician's sense of public opinion to call a quick election with the promise of 'a fit country for heroes to live in'. He also encouraged the lust for vengeance on Germany. As J. M. Keynes said, 'A vote for a Coalition candidate meant the Crucifixion of Anti-Christ and the assumption by Germany of the British National Debt. It proved an irresistible combination.'[7]

In foreign affairs Church comment varied from vindictive demands that in the name of justice Germany should pay heavy indemnities, to the view that justice was sterile if it offered no hope of redemption.[8] We shall see that Temple himself took the latter view, adding the practical consideration that to cripple Germany would damage the British economy too. Right from 1918 he could see that a vindictive peace could foreshadow another war. The other major issue was the League of Nations. Almost all churchmen supported its creation. The critical question was its powers. Idealists favoured reliance on religious and moral influence only and rejected all talk of military sanctions. Others recognised that in the political climate the moral authority of the League should be backed by armed force in the last resort.[9] This division of opinion, which so bedevilled Church thinking between the wars, was presently to force Temple to carry much further his ideas about Christianity and international politics. As we shall see in Chapters 12–14, it was above all in the international arena that he encountered a fatal challenge to his ethical idealism.

In domestic affairs Temple's idealism was only tardily modified.

He largely shared the euphoria of 1918. This was fed by the reports of five Committees set up by the Archbishops as a sequel to the National Mission. The fifth, on *Christianity and Industrial Problems* (Gore, Tawney and Mansbridge were all members, but not Temple), insisted that Christian moral teaching applied to industry and economics, and stressed the importance of personality: the high regard for the individual in Christianity is complemented by insistence on the duty of service in man's corporate life. The Report therefore deplored a system which gave rise to deficiencies such as the treatment of workers as 'hands', excessive emphasis on the motive of self-interest, the co-existence of extreme poverty and riches, the evils of insecurity and unemployment, and antagonism between employers and workers. Constructively the Report defined the proper function of industry as service and its method as association (that is, harmonious co-operation), and called concretely for a living wage and adequate leisure, both generously defined, and for protection against unemployment. Associated with this comes the call for a vigorous housing programme and better educational opportunities for all, not just the few – in W.E.A. terminology a highway not a ladder. Public expenditure must be increased even to the point of extravagance. A cleavage of opinion was evident in the Report itself between those who in the interests of economic progress and efficiency favoured the retention of strong powers of decision at the top in industry, and those who wanted a radical redistribution of power towards the creation of producers' co-operatives.[10] Here the Report was in part influenced by Guild Socialism, which was enjoying a considerable vogue. Its supporters, disenchanted with the prospects of collectivist government and with the performance of the Labour Party, looked to radical change through the creation of self-governing industrial guilds. Christian supporters of Guild Socialism were largely those rebels within the Church Socialist League like Widdrington who were searching for a Christian sociology. The notion of guilds fitted well with the idea of refurbishing mediaeval Christendom.

Critics of the Fifth Report thought it misread both Christianity and economics. Some, like A. C. Headlam, Professor of Divinity at Oxford, believed it was making State Socialism integral to the faith. W. Cunningham, Archdeacon of Ely and a trained economist, advocated the growth of a Christian sense of responsibility within existing industry rather than structural change. Some thought the Report ignored the factor of costs and the need for material progress as a prerequisite for social welfare schemes.[11] In the event the great plans for reconstruction quickly ran into the sand. The brief post-war boom lured people into chasing higher wages and profits rather than into financing reconstruction. The ambitious housing scheme of Addison, Minister of Health, had collapsed by 1921. Unemployment was growing fast. The next year government spending felt the Geddes axe.[12] As the recommendations of the Fifth Report looked less and less feasible the tension grew between Christian calls for working the present system and those for creating a new order.

In 1918, the year when the Labour Party formulated a clear socialist policy, Temple became a member of it for a few years, acknowledging in Convocation that he shared its ideals. Two years later Lloyd George offered him the See of Manchester. At his enthronement he made clear the basis for all his work: 'Pray for me chiefly that I may never let go of the unseen hand of the Lord Jesus and may live in daily fellowship with Him.' He continued the practice of conducting missions on Blackpool sands. His preaching, especially on St John's Gospel and Revelation, drew large crowds even on August Bank Holiday Monday.[13] The titles of his books reflect his central concern: *The Universality of Christ* (1921), *Christus Veritas* (1924), *Christ in His Church* (1925). In 1920 he undertook the editorship of *The Pilgrim*, a quarterly 'Review of Christian Politics and Religion'. Characteristically he wrote in it: 'A religion which offers no solution to world-problems fails to satisfy; a scheme of reconstruction, apart from religion, strikes cold and academic. Our effort is to bring home to men the claim of Christ that He is the Way, the Truth, and the Life.'[14] The problematical nature of the phrase 'Christian Politics' was not yet apparent. Indeed, in 1919 the idea was conceived of a large-scale conference on Christianity and social order, which came to be known as the Conference on Christian Politics, Economics and Citizenship, COPEC for short. Temple's headed notepaper declared that the Christian faith gave the vision and power essential for solving social problems, not merely for the regeneration of the individual. Twelve committees worked to produce twelve

volumes covering every facet of social life. In his address to the
delegates in 1924 Temple justified the scale of the exercise by
saying that since problems interlock and human life is one, the
whole field had to be surveyed synoptically.[15]

During the years of preparation for COPEC Temple slowly
modified his idealism under the pressure of events. In 1920 he
pleaded for 'moral opportunism', which would seek to maintain
an ideal whilst being realistic about the steps calculated to lead
towards it. However, by 1921 the phrase had become unusable:
'Opportunism is triumphant. Political life is directed according to
no intelligible principles and towards no distinguishable goal.'[16]
By 1923 he had substituted a distinction between ideals and
principles. In an article in *The Pilgrim* called 'Principles or Ideals?'
Temple sketches three possible attitudes of the reforming mind.[17]
The first stresses the organic nature of society and warns that all
changes of system are from the known to the unknown. It will try
to remedy evils which the general conscience of decent citizens
condemns. The state may do much to check evil; but it can do little
positive good. Thus it was right to pass legislation to protect
children from employment in mines and factories; but
nationalisation would be wrong, because ' "public control" would
diminish "private initiative", and it is at best doubtful if any
equally effective incentive to enterprise in industry could be
discovered.' Now Christianity, says Temple, does have some
affinities with this safe and dull method; it is at least true that Christ
did not instigate revolution or agitate for the abolition of slavery.
But Temple finds this attitude far too unadventurous.

The second attitude thinks up an ideal system and then sets out to
realise it. This is very attractive, but its defects are that the ideal is
sure to be seriously defective, and that the idealist creates havoc
because he is very impatient of considering what dull
improvements can be achieved in the immediate future. Temple
agrees that Christianity does have its idealistic hope for the
Kingdom of God. However, he insists that it gives us no detailed
account of the Kingdom as a social order. Temple therefore looks
for another attitude which will mediate between the first two.

This third attitude rests on the belief that there are ascertainable
principles of conduct which are always valid and should be applied
in every phase of life. This method is idealist in that it goes beyond

the negative activity of remedying admitted evils, and suggests positive relationships to be established; but it is realist, in that it is always concerned with the application of principles to what is, rather than with dreams of what might be. This method is more risky than the conservative one, but it is also more hopeful, for it deals with the root causes of social evils. It is less risky than the idealist method: if a mistake is made, the situation can be retrieved before great harm is done. Beyond question, Temple writes, Christianity's own method is that of principles (and also, and fundamentally, a gift of power to implement them). 'The Gospel, being a proclamation of the true nature of God and Man, and of the true relationship between them, necessarily consists of principles from which some others may with perfect security be deduced ... [The precepts of the Sermon on the Mount] are explicitly based on the unchanging character of the eternal God and the unchanging relationship of His children towards Him.'

Temple then for the first time co-ordinates into a set of four the social principles which he (and many other churchmen) had already been using: freedom, or respect for personality; fellowship; the duty of service; and the power of sacrifice. On the fundamental principles he thinks there is universal agreement, and his hope for COPEC is this: 'There is now a danger that constant reiteration of them may lead to their being regarded as pious phrases not intended to be taken seriously. Our need is to work out the form in which they become specially applicable to our own circumstances. That does not mean the fashioning of a Programme or the forming of a Party ... Christian men and women must exercise their own judgement on all matters of expediency. But it is at least conceivable that Christianity may have much to say, in general terms, about the right of wage earners to be consulted on all decisions of the management affecting their own lives, about the quantity of leisure to be rightly claimed by a man engaged in purely mechanical work ... Our aim therefore must be to work out the primary principles of the Gospel into those secondary principles which may make them effective guides to action in the world of our own time, yet without seeking to determine the details to which judgement of practical expediency is always relevant.' These secondary principles, because of their intermediate position between the four primary social principles and programmes, were often known as middle axioms. The whole procedure must have looked perfectly clear and straightforward to Christians whose excited anticipation of COPEC still reflected much of the optimism of 1918. The 1500 delegates from almost all denominations (the Roman Catholics withdrew a few weeks before the conference) used the principles of the Christian faith to expose the deficiencies of the current system and passed a veritable cavalcade of middle axioms. For example, workers were to have an increasingly effective voice in the management of industry; there was to be a living wage sufficient to maintain the worker and his family in health and dignity; unemployment was to be eliminated; wealth was to be more justly distributed.

The unanimity was remarkable. There was little criticism. The most telling was that by Sir Max Muspratt, Vice-President of the Federation of British Industries, who said, 'I think the ideal has been allowed to obscure the practical.' The Ninth Report of COPEC, on Industry and Property, 'states the problems rather than suggests the solutions,' he said, because of 'the complexity of the subject.' Muspratt evidently recognised that a knowledge of industry and its technicalities was indispensable. The Conference was plainly having trouble finding the middle ground it sought.[18]

Outside the Conference Hensley Henson was by far the most barbed critic. In his *Quo Tendimus?* he declared that the Conference had felt itself 'free to indulge the luxury of programme-framing without reference to those obstinate facts which a responsible statesman, tied to the necessity of carrying his policies into practice, must needs consider.' The Conference had, he complained, in no way considered the cost of its social reforms. He protested that the critics of industrialism were obsessed with its darker features. He shared with Cunningham an appreciation of its merits. He claimed to expose the paradox of seeking to appropriate the wealth of industrialism for social schemes whilst destroying its wealth-producing qualities. Henson also challenged what he took to be the main assumption of COPEC, that the Christian revelation included adequate direction on political and economic matters. COPEC seemed to be establishing the Kingdom of God on earth according to plan, as if the Gospel provided the Christian with the solution of all the problems involved in our earthly life. To this Henson opposed his basic belief: 'It is fundamental in Christ's religion that the redemption of the world must be effected through the redemption of individuals.' He also touched on a major problem when he noticed that COPEC's programme was proposed 'for acceptance as the policy of a nation, the majority of whose citizens are in no effective sense Christian, that is, lack the essential condition of applying Christian ethics in the life of society.'[19] Some of Henson's criticisms were scarcely fair. COPEC had sought to frame middle axioms, not to deduce programmes, and had also itself spoken of the transformation of the individual without which no change of policy or method could succeed. Yet there were undoubtedly unresolved problems about the relation of principle and policy, of individual and society, and of Christian community and civil community, which COPEC had glossed over.

Another problem was the format of the Conference. Temple won golden opinions for his handling of committees and conferences. It was said at Manchester that he always had a thorough grip of the agenda and the pertinent questions; gave full scope for opinions from all sides and welcomed criticism; could keep everyone in a good temper; sensed intuitively when to put a matter to the vote; and could draft the common mind of a conference (he called it his 'parlour trick' and it reflected his instinct for synthesis). His chairmanship at COPEC was described as superb.[20] Nevertheless Henson regarded the Conference as 'the worst conceivable method of arriving at the truth.' The format mainly consisted of speeches introducing each debate, and votes on resolutions. There was certainly little opportunity for real discussion; rarely was the wording of resolutions changed at the Conference. One explanation is that the selection process brought together birds of a feather. COPEC was an amalgam of liberal protestant and liberal catholic thought. Moreover, though this was not the only theology at that time, it was in the ascendancy. Temple himself was later to note that when the Church of England Doctrine Commission began its deliberations in 1922 theologians were taking up the prosecution of the task which the war had compelled them to lay aside; their problems were still predominantly set by the interest of pre-war thought. The influence of Westcott and Lux Mundi, with their theology of the Incarnation rather than of Redemption, was still dominant.

Temple's *Christus Veritas*, which appeared in the same year as COPEC, was in this mould. As Charles Raven was nostalgically to point out years later, for a brief while it seemed possible to 'formulate a coherent interpretation of a creative-redemptive theology and a consequently Christ-centred ethic.' The First World War and the acids of the post-war years had not yet eaten away the optimistic consensus among the intelligentsia of English churchmen. Nor had the continental theology of crisis under Karl Barth's leadership yet impinged upon them. As a reflex the format of COPEC thus militated against searching theological and empirical enquiry as a prerequisite for the recommendations.[21]

Certainly COPEC, as E. R. Norman points out, provided a more systematic and coherent statement of social radicalism, spread it down to the parish level, at least among the clergy, and marked the rise of William Temple to ascendancy over the social teaching of the Church of England. COPEC's findings also had international circulation in that they became the British contribution to the ecumenical Stockholm Conference of 1925 on the Life and Work of the Church. Yet COPEC faltered very rapidly. There was very little continuation work; the only notable success was *Studies of Industrial Tyneside* by H. A. Mess, whose judgements really were based on solid empirical investigation. It was not until 1929 that a permanent Christian Social Council was set up to develop COPEC's work, and then it was too much influenced by the Christendom Group with their deductive sociology, and lacked the necessary empirical expertise to give it weight. Perhaps the very euphoria of COPEC was in part responsible for this delay. Perhaps too, as J. Oliver says, COPEC itself was not quite sure where it stood, what it wanted, or what its next move should be, and the quest of an authentically Christian sociology, eventually undertaken by the Christian Social Council and the Christendom Group, was fraught with difficulty and controversy. In any case not only did the theological climate change, but a succession of industrial, economic and political events cruelly exposed the gap between COPEC's enthusiastic visions and harsh reality.[22]

The first blow was dealt by the coal crisis, culminating in the General Strike and the Miners' Strike of 1926. This will be dealt with in more detail in Chapter 7. Temple, probably inspired by the aura (rather than the reality) of Westcott's achievement in the Durham miners' strike of 1892, joined a group which sought to mediate in the dispute. Though much of the criticism which fell upon them was unjust, their attempt had some questionable features, which will be faced in an assessment of Temple's way of principles in Chapter 11. In particular, they accentuated the moral dimensions of the problem, supported arbitration as the industrial counterpart of fellowship, and assumed it was bound to provide the solution in the end. This raised the question whether the technical issues did not require much more attention, and whether the group was sensitive to the alignments of power, in this case the stance of the government and coal owners. Charles Raven, one of Temple's closest colleagues over COPEC, hit the mark when he said in 1926, 'Some of my friends, not least the Bishop of Manchester, are very fond of talking about industrial problems as if all you had to do was to speak of them as vocation, and the whole spirit in which they were undertaken was changed.'[23] As we shall presently see, Temple's belief in the power of vocation to generate solutions is integral to his Christian philosophy.

Though Iremonger is not justified in saying that there was a gradual movement to the right in Temple's thinking, he certainly became more cautious. Gone is the crusading cry 'socialism or heresy'; after 1926 Temple is almost as depressed by the Labour Movement as by its opponents. He made a careful exploration of the respective roles of the Church and state in *Christianity and the State* (1928). Here he stressed that the prime concern of the Church is with the fundamental reality of God, not with political programmes, and that it was the failure of the mediaeval Church that it corrupted both politics and itself by usurping political authority.[24] In the same year, when Parliament rejected a proposal for the revision of the Book of Common Prayer, which had very wide backing throughout the Church of England, Temple disappointed many friends by declining actively to pursue disestablishment in order to give the Church the freedom to manage its own affairs. He had certainly come round to a higher doctrine of the Church, and a clearer distinction of Church and state: in this sense he had ceased to be an Arnoldian. Yet he firmly believed that Church and state had complementary roles, and favoured partnership as long as the state was willing.[25] His support for the dual system of Church schools and state schools reflects these convictions and culminated in the provisions of the Education Act of 1944.

After the 1926 strikes the T.U.C. also became more cautious. It found itself threatened by a retaliatory Trades Dispute Bill and suspended its visions of a reconstructed industrial order in favour of co-operation with a group of industrialists, led by Sir Alfred Mond, to improve industrial relations and organisation.[26] But this was only a prelude to greater catastrophe.

In 1929 Temple moved to Bishopthorpe as Archbishop of York, where he stayed for thirteen immensely active years. His responsibilities for the developing Ecumenical Movement grew rapidly. His performance at the Lausanne Faith and Order Conference (1927) led to his appointment as Chairman of its Continuation Committee, and then as Chairman of the Edinburgh Faith and Order Conference (1937). It was here, and at the corresponding 1937 Oxford Conference on Church, Community and State, that the decision was taken to form a single ecumenical body, and Temple inevitably went on to become Chairman of the Provisional Committee of the World Council of Churches. At home he distinguished himself in the approaches to the Nonconformist Churches. He became increasingly concerned with Church unity, not merely because of the words of Christ in St. John's Gospel (17.21), but because he believed that only a Christian Church speaking with a united voice could offer effective resistance to Marxism, Fascism and secular Humanism.

In the early years at York, as we shall see, Temple continued to cross swords with various opponents over the Versailles Treaty, the League of Nations and pacifism. His opposition to pacifism grew; the depressing weakness of the League only underlined for him the necessity for military sanctions. Shortly after Hitler came to power in 1933 Temple began his vigorous action on behalf of the Jews, and he had no illusions about the nature of the Nazi regime. It was the challenge presented to the Christian faith by secularism and totalitarianism which was the focus of the 1937 Oxford Conference. Temple played only a modest role because of his commitments at Edinburgh a fortnight later, but he did write a paper and draft the final message of the Conference. Most importantly, the preparations for Oxford brought him into much closer contact with many shades of theological opinion on both the European and American continents. The driving force here was Joseph H. Oldham, a Scotsman with much experience in the mission field, who masterminded the research and process of consultation in preparation for Oxford. He secured a full-time staff who had the leisure to make personal contact with many leading Christian thinkers, arrange small-scale consultations, and circulate well over a hundred essays for critical comment. Oldham, Emil Brunner, Pastor Marc Boegner and the Greek Orthodox Archbishop Germanos of Thyatira, all leading figures of the Ecumenical Movement, enjoyed Temple's hospitality at Bishopthorpe. It was surely these contacts which impelled Temple even further away from the optimistic social idealism of COPEC and into the restless explorations of his last ten years. The most influential of all in his thinking about international affairs was very probably Reinhold Niebuhr. The two had met for the first time in 1923 and came to have a very high regard for each other. Both wrote papers called 'The Christian Faith and the Common Life' for the Oxford Conference. We shall see in Chapter 15 how Temple responded to Niebuhr's swingeing criticisms of the sentimentalities of the American Social Gospel.

At home the dominant questions were the economy and unemployment. The crisis of 1929–31 provoked much comment from churchmen. In the forefront was V. A. Demant, who wrote an analysis of the coal industry in 1929 and *This Unemployment: Disaster or Opportunity?* in 1931. Temple was quick to reflect his thought. Demant was Director of Research for the Christian Social Council and in the Christendom Group, and was strong in his insistence that Christians should not fall in with the popular ideologies of the day, but work out a social order from a dogmatic Christian base. His watchword was 'from ethics to sociology'. It was superficial, he claimed, to proclaim ethical ideals and then try to drum up the will to realise them. What was crucial were people's fundamental dogmas or presuppositions, and if the ideals rested on presuppositions which could not support them, the task was plainly to correct the presuppositions. Demant severely criticised liberalism, in that it proclaimed the ideal of the worth of each individual human being, yet held to the dogma that man is to be accounted for in purely historical terms of becoming and has no permanent core of being. Liberalism could therefore be no match for Marxism and Fascism, since, however laudable its ideals, it shared their basic presupposition.[27] Ideas like these had a growing effect on Temple's approach to the problems of his day, and explain in part why, in spite of certain reservations, he was to give the Christendom Group a major opportunity to commend their views at a conference he convened at Malvern in 1941. Problematical with the Group was their knowledge of economics. They had the misfortune to swallow a misguided scheme for social credit devised by a Major Douglas, and repeatedly suggested that the economic problems of the day were due to the conspiracy of financiers. Temple certainly was very suspicious of the profit-motive, and increasingly reflected on the inadequacy of the economic system itself, including the problem of the distribution of purchasing power. However, as early as 1922 he declared that the Douglas ideas were still at the stage of incomprehensibility to all but a few, and he seems on the whole to have favoured the ideas of the economist J. A. Hobson,[28] and refrained from accusations of conspiracy.

One of Temple's most significant ventures in social ethics in the 1930s was his initiative over long-term unemployment, which we shall consider in Chapters 8 and 11. Its importance lies in two directions. First, he employed a method of tackling issues which was a great advance on COPEC. For it started out from a very careful empirical investigation of long-term unemployment in selected areas, relying on a team of investigators who really had expertise in their several disciplines. Secondly the investigation was undergirded by the conviction that what was at stake was not economic or statistical units, but living persons. The investigation both presupposed and pointed to the social principles of freedom, community and service which had been so prominent in the thinking of Temple and COPEC in 1923–4. Temple played a crucial but very discreet role, and the approach paid dividends: the report *Men without Work* (1938) was well received even in Whitehall for its competence, and gave Temple a firm basis on which to argue for family allowances.

CHAPTER 5

TEMPLE THE CHRISTIAN PHILOSOPHER

It was in the York period that Temple delivered his Gifford lectures *Nature, Man and God* (1932–4). Though written in odd hours and half-hours of free time they are certainly of a very high order and demonstrate Temple's capacity to formulate convictions subconsciously ('All my decisive thinking goes on behind the scenes,' he said[1]), so that they were ready for paper in a well-ordered form. The time has come to pause and present a coherent account of Temple's Christian philosophy, of which *Nature, Man and God* is the most mature expression. For his primary approach to social ethics, that of principles, is integral to his Christian philosophy, as is most evident in *Christus Veritas* (especially Chapter XI). There is a sufficient unity across the period 1908–1934 to make a coherent summary account possible. Any such account has also to note the shifts in that period. In terms of the social ethics, the most notable shift is after 1924. *Nature, Man and God* reflects a much more serious wrestling with the problem of sin and evil, while still aiming to be 'a coherent articulation of an experience which has found some measure of co-ordination through adherence to certain principles.'[2] An account at this point will also enable us to appreciate the significance of the development in Temple's theological and social thought in the last ten years of his life (1934–1944). For though it is by no means a repudiation of his efforts up to 1934, it does, under the pressure of political events and the theology of crisis on the Continent, show a radical questioning of the possibility of synthesis, and result in a much more untidy juxtaposition of several different approaches to social ethics.

From 1908 to 1934 Temple was developing a Christian philosophy. Trained in the heyday of British Hegelianism, he naturally conceived the philosophic task as metaphysical: philosophy is 'a determined attempt to think clearly and comprehensively about the problems of life and existence.'[3] In his three major works, *Mens Creatrix* (1917), *Christus Veritas* (1924), and *Nature, Man and God*, he was engaged in the search for a coherent account of the universe. Like Caird he believed the world had a spiritual and not a materialistic interpretation, and he stressed the category of personality. The world's principle of unity had to be not a purely intellectual one, such as logical coherence, but one which embraced imagination and conscience too; aesthetics, morality and religion itself – indeed every facet of experience – had to be included in the search, which was to be conducted according to Caird's dialectical method. The result is ideally a single system, a concrete universal.

In *Mens Creatrix* Temple conceives himself as working from the world, through the sciences, art, morality and religion, showing how they converge yet do not meet in an all-inclusive system of truth. Then the Christian hypothesis is adopted, and he seeks to show how its central fact, the Incarnation, supplies the missing unity. Thus the first movement purports to be philosophical, from the circumference to the centre, as Temple put it, the second theological, from the centre to the circumference. Most of *Mens Creatrix* is concerned with the first movement. Temple maintains that philosophy can conceive in general the kind of fact that alone would constitute the point of ultimate convergence. 'It is the historic Incarnation of God in a human life of Perfect Love, issuing in a society bound together by the power of that Love.' A basic assumption here is that the universe is a rational whole, and that the human mind can in principle grasp it. 'Philosophy assumes the competence of reason ... to grasp the world as a whole.'[4] It was only in the last few years of his life that Temple moved away from the idea that the universe made sense.

Christus Veritas also works from the circumference to the centre and then out again, but this is only for the purposes of exposition. The book is confessedly written with the Christian revelation in full view from the outset. 'I am trying to set out a whole view of the world and life as it appears to one mind at least from an avowedly Christian standpoint.' His express purpose is to counter the prevailing philosophy which, whilst spiritual and theistic, precluded God from doing anything in particular, and therefore left no room for a specific Incarnation. 'I believe that a very slight touch to the intellectual balance may make the scales incline the other way ... What is needed is the exposition of the Christian idea of God, life and the world, or, in other words, a Christocentric metaphysics.'[5] The core of the book is concerned with the Person of Christ, and the rest surveys such central topics as the Holy Spirit and the Church, God and man in the light of the Incarnation, eternity and history, the Atonement and the Trinity. It is within this context that Temple gives an exposition of the four social principles which formed the basis for COPEC's thinking.

Nature, Man and God was the culmination of this search for coherence. Here is Temple's mature Christian philosophy. It is more philosophical than Christus Veritas, yet unmistakably the product of a person committed to Christ. We shall use Temple's writings from 1908 to 1934, and pre-eminently Nature, Man and God, to give a sketch of the hallmarks of that philosophy, especially as it relates to his social ethics. As we shall see, if one motif binds all the others together it is that of the sacramental.

1. Making sense of life

Temple believes it is the Christian faith, and centrally the Incarnation, which is the master key to making sense of the universe. Three points are very important here:

(a) It is only a Christian philosophy that can make sense of the universe. Temple goes out of his way to stress the theoretical inadequacy of any intellectual map of the world which ignores religion. 'Scientific philosophy', as he calls it, can offer no complete intellectual satisfaction; indeed, it can generate scepticism. The philosopher must put his tools at the service of religion, and for Temple that means Christianity. This is the way of 'Theological Philosophy'.[6]

(b) A Christian philosophy rests on faith. Christianity cannot offer theoretical certainty. The basis of assurance is always faith. Reason can recognise its own incapacity to construct a satisfying scientific philosophy. Now if the Incarnation is posited, then reason will welcome it as the completion of its own work. For reason will recognise that a philosophy of the Incarnation renders the universe intelligible as no other metaphysics can.[7]

(c) A Christian philosophy provides practical solutions to life's problems. Since a Christian philosophy is integral to a living religion, it is related much more closely to life than is a scientific philosophy. It can bring the assurance of God's love experienced in fellowship with Him, and it can offer practical help for living. Just as scientific philosophy cannot provide complete intellectual satisfaction, so philosophical ethics cannot provide the solutions to life's problems. A philosophy of the Incarnation, however, assures us that solutions are to be found in devoted religious practice, that is, in vocation. As Jack F. Padgett puts it, 'Though the principles of the Christian faith are not completely vindicated, all problems yield to its insights; and this justifies employing the Christian faith and following it wherever it leads.'[8]

2. The Christian faith and natural theology

Something further needs to be said here about Temple's handling of the relation between the Christian faith and natural theology (that is, rational enquiry into the nature and validity of religion without appeal to the authority of revelation). For there is a difficulty here. According to Temple, the difference between the two does not lie in the spheres of life they cover, but in their approach to the same spheres. Philosophy's approach is critical, whereas faith entails commitment. The Christian philosopher needs to employ both approaches.[9] Critics of Temple have generally agreed that he has an inconsistent view on this matter. Thus Emil Brunner considered Temple's conception of natural theology (i) approached Christian philosophy, i.e. started from the Christian faith, which then regulated the course of thought; (ii) was intended as thought resting solely on logical argument and facts open to anyone; (iii) seemed to be striving towards a synthesis of Christian faith with reason.[10]

J. F. Padgett, O. C. Thomas, and W. G. Peck all describe Temple as constructing a Christian philosophy. Padgett's is the most thorough-going study, and he means by the term that Temple 'begins his quest for a comprehension of reality from the perspective of the Christian faith.' So too Thomas writes that though Temple professes to engage in natural theology, he does not do so very thoroughly, and his prime concern is with Christian philosophy, i.e. the interpretation of the various realms of experience, including religion, on the basis of Christian theology. Thus Padgett notes that on the journey from the circumference to the centre Temple is prone to equate the God he arrives at philosophically with the God of Christianity. There tends to be an undisclosed ideal assumed which alone can satisfy the mind, and that ideal is equated with traditional Christianity.[11]

Now there is no objection to taking the Christian revelation as one's starting point. For every philosopher is bound to build around some key-category or organising principle. The crux is whether that organising principle is subjected to rigorous enquiry in the light of experience. Here Temple fails to satisfy. Thomas points out that Temple does not seriously consider any other religion than Christianity. As Brunner remarks, Temple's conception of religion is determined *a priori* by the Christian faith, as are his concepts of sin, love and personality. So sure is Temple of his faith that the dialectical method is not really allowed to function. Padgett writes, 'While *arguing* cogently for the dialectical method in which fact and theory emerge jointly in the process of interpreting the data of experience and in which conclusions are constantly checked by the facts, Temple actually *employs* ... an analytical method in which he starts with a specific conception of reality and proceeds to interpret the data of experience by reference to it without checking his assumptions against the facts.' To that extent he falls short of being a Christian philosopher and is instead a Christian apologist.[12]

3.   *Mind and matter*

(a)*Matter as historically prior to mind* Temple accepts the common-sense view, which is endorsed by modern philosophy inspired by science, that the universe existed long before there were any minds to apprehend it. Matter is historically prior to mind. Indeed it is basic to everything else that emerges in the world-process. Within this process there eventually arises mind. The distinguishing feature of mind is its capacity for generating free ideas. It can also freely turn its attention to them. Thus the mind has a basic freedom over against nature. Moreover it has the freedom to achieve a relative mastery over time; for it can hold in a unity an event extending over time, such as the recitation of a poem or the performance of a symphony; it can also reflect upon the past and plan for the future.[13]

(b)*The four levels of reality* Sometimes Temple refers to four levels or grades of reality, thereby showing in more detail his understanding of human freedom and the relation of mind and matter. Matter represents the lowest realm, the inorganic, where objects lack self-motion and are simply acted upon from without. The second level is life, that is, organic life. Here we find the capacity for self-motion: the organism directs itself as a whole towards the outside world in order to satisfy its needs. No longer do we have just external causation; the organism is determined by attraction to what will satisfy it. The third level, mind, is an extension of this process. Mind enhances self-direction; for it enables the organism to envisage various means towards the desired end and to choose between them. When it first emerged, mind was originally preoccupied with the need of the organism to survive. Gradually, however, it came to develop a life of its own and generate free ideas, not of immediate adjustment to its own environment, but of possible goals to be attained. The fourth level, the highest, is that of spirit. Here we find the unique element in personality: the organism is now directed to a future object which appears to be good. Spirit provides direction for us to fulfil our obligations, and these at their highest promote a fellowship of shared love. Thus the basic significance of the emergence of mind and spirit is that they change the whole character of the process; for they do not merely respond to outside stimuli or merely adjust to the environment, but initiate activity with ends in view.[14]

(c) *The sacramental relation of the levels of reality* These various levels are neither separate nor successive in life. There is a marked continuity across them, and the higher always presuppose the presence of the lower. However, the levels must be distinguished in thought. The emergence of the higher is not predictable on the basis of a knowledge of the lower, nor can the higher be explained simply by reference to the lower. In fact, the higher controls the lower. The organism, for instance, uses the inorganic for its own adjustment; spirit directs the lower levels for the sake of a good it has envisaged. Indeed, it is only when the higher indwells the lower that the lower reveals its full potentialities. The lower, then, exists to embody or symbolise what is more than itself. In this sense the universe is sacramental.[15]

(d) *The case for theism: purposive mind as an explanatory principle* Temple thus adopts a realist starting-point in matter. In this respect he is departing from the philosophical idealism of his own training and standing much nearer to materialism. Marx, he readily agrees, was right to start out from the material process. However, though Marx insisted he was a dialectical and not a mechanical materialist, yet, according to Temple, he made mental activity purely reactive to the material order. Mind therefore still lacks the capacity for free ideas.[16] This is a crucial difference between Temple and Marx and it has wide-ranging significance.

Since the philosopher's task is a metaphysical one, he needs to find a principle of explanation which will do justice to the occurrence of both matter and mind in the world process. Because personal existence is the highest level yet attained, it is reasonable to look here for a clue. We require a principle which itself requires no further explanation. The only satisfactory principle known to us is that of purpose. 'That a plank should lie across a stream may call for much explanation if no human beings have ever placed it there; but if men laid it across to form a bridge, so that they could cross over dry-shod, no further explanation is needed.' We are thus led to a theistic explanation of the world-process. 'To adopt the hypothesis that the process of nature in all its range is to be accounted for by the intelligent purpose of Mind is Theism.' Thus if Temple distanced himself initially from idealism, yet now he offers a spiritual interpretation of the universe, indeed one which, as he says, gives him most of the positive content of Caird and Bosanquet. The breach with Marx is now wide. Temple's response to Marx is to try to outpoint him in his use of dialectic. 'If Materialism once becomes Dialectical, it is doomed as Materialism; its own dialectic will transform it into Theism.' For 'it is the occurrence of Mind at all as an episode in the objective world-process which supplies to our Realism its dialectical impulse and leads to a theistic interpretation of it.'[17]

Temple's argument has so far yielded the immanence of mind in the world-process. But this is only part of the explanation of the world-process. Temple again turns to personal existence for clues. The person can never be reduced to, or equated with, his conduct; he transcends his conduct by reference to an ideal which guides his present actions towards its realisation in the future. Whatever therefore is to account for the world-process must account for this phenomenon too; the obvious candidate is a transcendent personal God. Here Temple differs with his contemporary A. N.

Whitehead. He accepts his starting point and basic approach, but complains that Whitehead contents himself with the category of organism as his principle of explanation. But if we are to explain the complex totality of God and the world, we must introduce the category of personality. Temple notes that Whitehead himself slips into speaking of God having patience. What is required to warrant such language is not just an impersonal principle of logical coherence, but personality as the key category. Furthermore, since personality manifests itself supremely in fellowship and love, God is not just purposive mind, but a mind whose actual purpose is love. The creation of persons and value possibilities is thereby explained.[18]

4. Temple's theory of knowledge

Temple is correspondingly a realist in his theory of knowledge. He tries to synthesise classical and modern views in a 'critical realism'.[19] His arch foe is Descartes. For centuries before Descartes it was not disputed that broadly speaking we have knowledge of real objects. The fatal mistake of Descartes was to suppose that mind deals, not directly with real objects, but with its own ideas and sense data, which then have to be related by inference to external objects. For all their acumen in wrestling with a theory of knowledge, neither David Hume nor Immanuel Kant of the eighteenth century were able to supply the corrective.[20] Temple believes modern science-based philosophy confirms the common-sense view: 'I must regard as completely fallacious all theories of Perception which start with a so-called *sensum* as the object of immediate apprehension ... The initial and permanent fact is the organism in interaction with the environment ... What it apprehends is the real world.'[21] The irreducible basis of all thought is the subject-object relationship. Two further points are striking here. First, in stressing the subject-object relationship Temple was departing again from the British Hegelians, who gave emphatic priority to the apprehending subject. In Temple's view, so far as our experience is concerned, apprehension takes place within the world, not the world within apprehension. Secondly Temple recognises the problem of misinterpretation but declines to dwell on it. His was a characteristically believing mind.

Temperamentally he was the very opposite of a sceptic.[22] The proposed synthesis concedes too much to the pre–Cartesian thesis. 'Descartes encourages doubting in order to build a reasonable basis for believing; Temple urges believing in order to provide a reasonable basis for not having to doubt.'[23] His antipathy to Descartes ran very deep. Descartes' subjectivism was held to be partly responsible for the subsequent excessive stress on the individual in western society and for the fragmentation of the unified mediaeval understanding of the world into a set of disconnected disciplines, all asserting their autonomy.[24]

5.   *Fact and value*

(a) *The theory* In our actual experience of process, according to Temple, mind apprehends not only facts about the world, but also values. Fact and value are given together. Temple claims on the one hand that value is objectively real, on the other that it is subjectively actualised. The organism becomes aware passively that certain objects satisfy its needs; actively it can select certain objects to satisfy them. Either way value is actualised when the mind apprehends the value of these objects. 'The value only fulfils its essential nature ... in the moment when it is appreciated. It exists as value for Mind; Mind finds it and appreciates it; but Mind does not invent or create it in the act of appreciation.' Thus though there is a subjective factor here, value is not simply relative to the individual. Indeed 'the self is capable of complete satisfaction only in proportion as it is left out of the field of its own attention. Value exists for subjects; but the subject finds the value only when completely absorbed in the object.' Temple gives priority to the objectivity of truth, beauty and goodness. He appeals to our experience. Truth appears as something august, making a claim on our allegiance. Beauty is in the object, not in the appreciating mind. As for goodness, we experience a sense of uncompromising obligation. There is a right thing to do and it is our duty to find it out. Yet what is objective is only actualised when it is subjectively appreciated. Furthermore Temple stresses that goodness particularly is not merely appreciated but actively created. The moral goodness of mankind is an original contribution to the scheme of things.[25]

(b) *The case for theism: mind determined by Good* Just as matter and mind together require explanation, so do fact and value together. Again we must consult our experience of human personality for the clue. Once again the lower cannot explain the higher. 'If we begin with mindless and valueless fact we cannot give any place in our scheme to Mind or Value without breaking up the unity of the scheme itself.' It is in mind and value that we find the vital clue. The ground of value is the discovery by mind of what is akin to itself. 'If the object is apprehended as good – whether noble, beautiful or true, according to its own nature – that means that Mind finds there are expression ... of itself as it is or as it would wish to be.' Mind thus finds a kinship with the world; mind and the world fit together. The only way in which we can frame a conception of the world adequate to this experience of fact and value as given together is to suppose that the process is pervaded by mind.[26]

From this mind, or God immanent in the world, Temple again infers a transcendent personal God. If truth compels our allegiance, then the recognition of that which is akin is also a recognition of something remote, to be served rather than possessed. If beauty evokes reverence, this is only reasonable on the supposition that we are in communion with a master-mind. 'There is more in Beauty than Beauty alone. There is communication from, and communication with, personal Spirit.' If we fail in our moral duty, this is not only an injury to a neighbour and a degradation of self, it is a flouting of what justly claims our reverence. This datum clearly points to theism as its only justification. For no law, apart from a lawgiver, is a proper object of reverence. It is a mere brute fact, and every living thing, still more every person exercising intelligent choice, is its superior. The reverence of persons can be appropriately given only to that which is itself at least personal. The universe is therefore grounded in mind determined by the Good; it is sacramental, existing to reveal the goodness of God, who transcends and pervades it.[27]

6. *Personality*

In this sacramental universe persons, since they are in the image of God, can most fully express the divine nature. A person is a psycho-physical organism. Body and mind are not two separate entities, nor are they parallel to one another. They are organically one; mind is the principle of control, the body the medium through which it carries out its purposes. Similarly there are no separate faculties in the person. Consciousness is not an entity within the organism, but is itself that organism as related to its environment. Will is similarly the whole person as co-ordinated for moral action.[28]

Mind can detach itself from the flux of the world process, through its capacity for free ideas, its memory of the past and anticipation of the future. It can create forms of unity. Thus in science it can advance hypotheses which grasp the flux. In art it can hold together successive events in time. Most of all mind can envisage a future goal and direct the present towards its realisation. The full unity of the self lies therefore in the future, when the whole person would ideally reach a complete integration.[29] What is involved here is indicated by the different dimensions of personality which Temple presents.

(a) First, there is *individuality*. Persons are not reducible to their behaviour or environment. Stark determinism is stark nonsense. The individual has a basic formal freedom, which is the foundation of legal and moral responsibility. Character presupposes an awareness of one's identity through time, and is the result at any moment of the individual's freedom in constant interaction with the world. In other words for Temple character is the personality as a whole organised in the present in terms of past influences and future aspirations. Temple distinguishes between formal freedom and true freedom. The latter envisages a person acting as a unified self directed freely towards a chosen goal. The importance to Temple of an overall purpose in the unification of the self cannot be overestimated. 'True spiritual freedom would be the state of a man who, knowing an ideal which completely satisfied all aspects of his nature, always in fact conformed to it and could perfectly trust himself so to do.' Temple grounds freedom ultimately in the fact that God is the loving Father of every person and desires the love of his children. Each person is thereby sacred.[30]

(b) Secondly, personality is at the same time inherently *social*. The self cannot of itself attain to unity. It can only do so in the reciprocal relationships of society. Each person's 'whole being is a condensation of society. He *is* his fellow-men's experience focussed in a new centre.' But a person is not to be concerned with others just for the sake of the self's attainment of unity. God has created persons supremely for love and fellowship with Him and each other. Persons therefore need a purpose common to the interests and welfare of all mankind. Only so can the individual person be satisfied and all persons united in universal fellowship.[31]

(c) Thirdly, this means that the fulfilment of the self is only possible through *service* to others. A person is ultimately one whose unity resides in the purpose he has to promote universal love. 'Love is the supreme goal of personality . . . If we want to find the right thing to do, we must ask what will do most to increase the volume of love. Love alone has absolute moral value.' Now loving others and helping them to realise their good means forgetting self; to realise myself therefore means in fact to sacrifice myself in service to others.[32]

7. The problem of evil

Temple wrestled several times with the problem of evil. In *Christus Veritas* he revealed the Hegelian influence by writing that evil is a constituent element of the absolute good. He tended to argue that when evil is overcome it is thereby justified − a view which the Swedish theologian Gustaf Aulén rightly criticised by saying, 'He accepts this too easily as a rational explanation of evil.' By *Nature, Man and God* however Temple has a much tougher view of evil, and writes in terms reminiscent of his American friend Reinhold Niebuhr, whose influence and importance we shall consider in Chapter 15.[33]

(a) *The human predicament* The capacity of the human mind for free ideas is both its glory and its predicament. The will is a real power of choice. 'Nothing forces it to choose one way or the other; it follows its own "apparent good". It is not undetermined. It is determined by its apparent good, and itself determines . . . what shall be to it apparent good. Hence it has − or rather is − the freedom which is perfect bondage. It is free, for the origin of its actions is itself; it is bound, for from itself there is no escape.' Men are not wholly evil, but they do persistently follow an apparent good which is not the real good. Why is this? What theologians have called original sin is for Temple no mysterious doctrine but an evident and vitally important fact. Every human being has in one respect or another a bias or tendency to evil. Each man cares more about what seems to be good for him than about goods which he does not expect personally to enjoy. 'So he becomes not only the subject of his own value judgements, which he can never cease to be, but also the centre and criterion of his own system of values, which he is quite unfit to be.' There is no inherent and absolute necessity about this, but it is so probable as to be certain for all practical purposes. It must be held to fall within the divine purpose, though since it is our fault, God cannot be said directly to will it. It is not that finitude or selfhood is evil in itself; but finitude does by its limitations hinder the mind from apprehending the true nature of apparent good, and it is therefore a practical certainty that finite selves, if left to themselves, will be wicked.[34]

Temple explores the social ramifications of evil. The individual members of society are not mutually exclusive atoms of consciousness. We are in part reciprocally determining beings. We make each other what we are. Therefore the existence of one self-centred soul would spread an evil infection. Others would become self-centred, either by imitation or in self-defence. Self-centredness would thereupon be mutually reinforced. 'Actual human society is to a large extent, though never completely, a network of competing selfishnesses, all kept in check by each one's selfish fear of the others.' Temple stresses that although this might be called an evolutionary account of the origin of moral evil, it is not ascribing the centre of the trouble to appetites or passions which are a legacy from our animal past. 'The centre of trouble is the personality as a whole, which is self-centred and can only be wholesome and healthy if it is God-centred. This whole personality in action is the will; and it is the will which is perverted. Our primary need is not to control our passions by our purpose, but to direct our purpose itself to the right end. It is the form taken by our knowledge of good and evil that perverts our nature. We know good and evil, but we know them amiss. We take them into our lives, but we mistake them. The corruption is at the centre of our rational and purposive life ... Reason itself as it exists in us is vitiated. We wrongly estimate the ends of life, and give preference to those which should be subordinate, because they have a stronger appeal to our actual, empirical selves. That is why the very virtues of one generation lead to the miseries of the next; for they are contaminated with the evil principle, and it is truly said that "our righteousnesses are filthy rags". We totally misconceive alike the philosophic and the practical problem of evil if we picture it as the winning of control over lawless and therefore evil passions by a righteous but insufficiently powerful reason or spirit. It is the spirit which is evil, it is reason which is perverted; it is aspiration itself which is corrupt.'[35]

(b) *The way of deliverance* What then is the way of deliverance from this predicament? For a start, the image of God in man is not totally effaced; our lives are never wholly self-centred. We live as it were with two foci, God and self. Now life cannot be fully integrated about the self as centre; it can only be fully integrated when it becomes God-centred. For God is the real centre of the real world. There is a constant lure of every soul to find itself at home with God. Moral progress is therefore possible; with all deference to Karl Barth, to deny this is wanton. So too Temple describes as fanatical Barth's denial that revelation can, and in the long run must, on pain of being seen as superstition, vindicate its claim by satisfying reason and conscience.

The lure works in various ways. First, even immoral principles themselves prompt an outward prudential morality. A self-centred person may well find it prudent to support what public spirit and even the highest claims of absolute morality require. And certainly virtuous conduct induced by fear is better than vicious conduct. Not only is it beneficial rather than harmful to society, but also its own excellence can make its appeal to the conscience of the person acting. 'It is quite possible for character to improve under the pressure of disciplinary sanctions, and for self-regard to be partly undermined by appeal to self-regarding motives.' Respect for the law rests to quite an appreciable extent on the need of every citizen for the law's protection. So through the action of self-regarding motives men may be led to an appreciation of justice. Yet the self-regarding principle is a precarious support of moral progress, and can become a barrier to further advance.

Temple also notes more positive forms of deliverance from evil, which nonetheless are imperfect. Thus in response to truth, beauty and goodness the self can be drawn out of its self-centredness; yet the reponse may cover only a part of life, and in any case is not always pure. There is also genuine and disinterested love; but so often this is found in combination with hatred of others, as for example in patriotism. Furthermore there has been a growth of humanitarianism, and a widening of the sense of obligation. Yet here too the self remains at the centre of this expanding circle. 'The colossal structures of enlightened egoism to which that way of progress leads will never effect the deliverance of the self from self-centredness.' And self-centredness is incompatible with final well-being. For the self is still prior to God or equal with God. Here Barth and his followers are right in stressing that only by revelation and surrender to its spiritual power can man be saved, and that there is an impassable distinction between Creator and creature, Redeemer and redeemed. 'What is quite certain is that the self cannot by any effort of its own lift itself off its own self as centre and resystematise itself about God as its centre. Such radical conversion must be the act of God . . . It cannot be a process only of enlightenment. Nothing can suffice but a redemptive act. Something impinging upon the self from without must deliver it from the freedom which is perfect bondage to the bondage which is its only perfect freedom.'[36]

How is this to be done? Certainly man is in no position to deserve grace, or to co-operate actively with God in his own salvation. Nor can God forcibly remake character; for to compel or remake character in this way would be to leave the will outside divine control. Man's freedom must not be infringed. 'How can the self find it good to submit willingly to removal from its self-centredness and welcome reconstruction about God as centre? There is in fact one power known to men, and only one, which can effect this . . . for the self as a whole . . . When a man acts to please one whom he loves, doing or bearing what apart from that love he would not choose to do or bear, his action is wholly determined by the other's pleasure, yet in no action is he so utterly free – that is, so utterly determined by his apparent good. And when love is not yet present, there is one power, and only one, that can evoke it; that is the power of love expressed in sacrifice, of love (that is to say) doing and bearing what apart from love would not be willingly borne or done. The one hope, then, of bringing human selves into right relationship with God is that God should declare His love in an act, or acts, of sheer self-sacrifice, thereby winning the freely offered love of the finite selves which He has created.'[37]

8. God's action in Christ

(a) *The Incarnation* In Temple the Incarnation is absolutely central. It arises both as the culmination of a sacramental universe, and as the decisive act of God which begins His declaration of loving purpose to redeem the world. If the universe in its whole extent is sacramental, it can only become this perfectly, so far as our world and human history are concerned, 'because within it and determining its course is the Incarnation, which is the perfect sacrament intensively – the perfect expression in a moment of what is also perfectly expressed in everlasting Time, the Will of God.' God, we recall, is not merely immanent in nature; He is a transcendent Person, perfect in power and love. Now every grade of reality finds its fulfilment when it is possessed by a higher grade. Humanity itself needs to be indwelt by the highest, God's Spirit. The Spirit must be revealed to man in a form which he can understand and to which he can freely respond. He must therefore reveal Himself in the form of a person whose apparent good is always the supreme good. 'In Jesus Christ we shall find the one adequate presentation of God ... But in Jesus Christ we shall find also the one adequate presentation of Man ... Man as he is in his truest nature, which is only made actual when man becomes the means to the self-expression of God.'[38]

This philosophical teaching dovetails with Temple's theological understanding of St. John's Gospel. Here he sees a fusion of the historical and the spiritual which is 'in the completest possible degree sacramental.' Central is the Word. St. John 'is intensely and profoundly sacramental; he sees the spiritual in the material, the divine nature in the human nature, which it uses as its vehicle. The central declaration "the Word became flesh" is the affirmation of this sacramental principle.' As Temple was fond of saying, Christianity is the most materialist of all the world's great religions.[39] 'The root of Temple's view of the relation between the Christian faith and the social order is in this sacramental view of the relation of spirit to matter.'[40]

(b) *Incarnation and Atonement* The Incarnation shows precisely that sacrificial love of God which the predicament of man requires. In His ministry Jesus Christ exemplifies God's love and calls men to a life of love. On the Cross and in the Resurrection He demonstrates God's conquest of sin and death. Through the Cross man learns what sin costs God and knows that his sins are forgiven. Man's sin is made the occasion of the triumph of goodness. Here supremely we see how the value of past events can be transmuted from evil to good, from tragedy to triumph. The Atonement is also the mode of God's being as well. In St. John's Gospel, more fundamental even than the statement 'The Word became flesh' are the words 'God so loved the world that He gave His only begotten Son, that everyone that believeth on Him may not perish, but have eternal Life.' In the Cross the perfect goodness and absolute power of God are shown to be one. 'He reigns from the Tree. Because, and only because, His goodness is so perfect as to include self-sacrifice, His power is known to be supreme and all-controlling.' The Atonement thus completes the Incarnation. 'Our hearts and wills are drawn to God, so that we take His Purpose as our own; as we do so, we vindicate the claim made for Christ that His Personality is representative and inclusive ... When we call His Personality representative we mean that in it we see what all men shall become ... so that in His purpose the issue of our lives is included.'[41]

9.   The Church

If the Incarnation is a divine act of special revelation, the Church consists of men and women brought together by the will of God in response to that divine act. The dynamic of this society is the Holy Spirit; the Church is the fellowship of the Spirit. It is the Body of Christ, His personality which continues the principle of the Incarnation by gathering into itself all men and nations. Salvation involves 'inner and outer unity – the inner unity of complete personality and the outer unity of a perfected fellowship as wide as humanity. For ideally the Church is the community where men and women are set free from self-centredness.'

True, the ideal Church does not exist. The Church is involved in the evil of the world. It 'appears under the guise of a compromising institution.' Nonetheless the Church is sacramental in and to the world. It is an outward and visible sign of the Church universal in heaven and on earth, and its function is the spiritual permeation of the material processes of life. The Church is in the world yet not of it; it is neither wholly world-denying, nor wholly world-accepting, but world-changing. It has the sacramental, prophetic vocation to participate in 'the dominant issue of history, which is the prevailing and increasing supremacy of love in all its forms over self-centredness in all its forms – a supremacy both won and sustained by love's own method of self-sacrifice.'[42]

10. *Worship*

Worship is the distinctive and specially characteristic activity of the Church. It includes all life, and the moments spent in worship as more narrowly understood are the focusing points of the worshipper's whole life. It is a potent way of enabling man to have God at the centre of his life, not self. Worship too is sacramental; man only reveals what it is in him to be when God indwells him. There is a perpetual struggle between self and God. 'The influence of the world still operates; and there is no possibility of increasing our self-dedication until it becomes perfect, unless we deliberately and repeatedly turn our minds towards that Love of God, that God of Love, to whom we would be dedicated. This is the place of Worship in Christian discipline.'[43]

The dominical sacraments are set within a sacramental universe. 'The Eucharist is the heart of Christian worship.' The reason is clear in the following passage. 'Full self-giving is precisely that of which we are least capable. The fundamental problem of the spiritual life is to accomplish the transformation from self-centredness to love. Only by self-surrender is love to be reached, and only by love is self-surrender possible. We are enclosed in a vicious circle. "Who shall deliver me from the body of this death? I thank my God through Jesus Christ our Lord." What I cannot do in and for myself, Christ has done for me and will do in me. He offers His life – the life of perfect love, expressed in the uttermost self-sacrifice – that I may receive it as my own; and in its power I become able to give myself more completely to God.' The implication is that we also give ourselves more completely in love to our fellow-men. The Eucharist has social implications as a fellowship meal; for it is a pattern of how men ought to live. Furthermore, the elements of bread and wine are symbols of the food and drink of our daily life. We bring familiar forms of economic wealth, the product of man's labour upon God's gifts, and offer them as symbols of our earthly life. The Eucharist also has a future orientation; it is a foretaste of the realised Kingdom of God. What is begun here may be perfected hereafter.[44] This brings us to the last hallmark of Temple's Christian philosophy.

11.   *The goal of history*

The goal of the whole process is the realisation of the Commonwealth of Value, as Temple calls it. This is partially realised sacramentally in the material processes of history, but can only find perfection in eternity. The concept presupposes the belief that God brings about true human freedom by causing the true good to appear as good, and it insists on the distinct individuality of every finite mind. By God's grace each individual is to make an appropriate and different contribution to the actualisation of value and so to the entire scheme of good. Temple sees the affinity between this view and Plato's concept of justice. 'For the contribution to the scheme of things which is due from each finite consciousness will be forthcoming only if each finds and fulfils its own place in that scheme.' Temple also follows Plato in postulating eternity for the completion of the Commonwealth of Value. We must imagine God as the King or Head of the Commonwealth, with whom each person has a primary fellowship, and through whom he has a derivative relation with all other souls. 'Such a commonwealth must bind into unity all spirits of all periods of time . . . It involves everlasting life . . . but this life is something more than everlasting. It must, at least progressively even if never completely, partake of the nature of eternity, wherein all successiveness is united in a single apprehension. Only so could the whole value of all the social relationships comprised in it be actualised.' This would include the redemptive transmutation of evil into good. But that is possible only on the basis that the self ceases to think of self at all, and on the basis of forgiveness – where the forgiven man rejoices not in his own forgiven state but in the divine love to which he owes it.

Temple's portrait of the Commonwealth of Value is a conscious attempt to find a synthesis which resembles the mediaeval period in stressing community and order and the modern period in accepting liberty for individuals and associations. 'It is impossible to stress too strongly the individualism of the spiritual world; each is himself alone, and each, because an object of divine love, has infinite value. But it is equally impossible to stress too strongly the communism of that world, if for once we may use the word "communism" with what ought to be its meaning; for each individual becomes his own true self only so far as he fastens his attention not on his own fulfilment but on God and on God's work in creation.' Eternal life then 'is the life of love – not primarily of being loved, but loving, admiring and (in love and admiration) forgetting self. Such a life is not only an entering into, but the actual building of, that fellowship of mutually enriching selves which we have called the Commonwealth of Value ... Its Christian name is the Communion of Saints; its perfection is in eternity, but to bring its divided and warring members into that Harmony and Peace wherein alone it is actual is the purpose which gives meaning to History.'[45]

CHAPTER 6

TEMPLE'S LAST YEARS

It is to the divided and warring world of 1939–44 that we now return. If the First World War had failed to shake the optimistic incarnational theology of the Anglican Church, the domestic and international chaos of the 1920s and 1930s had destroyed the dreams of COPEC and forced theological reappraisal. It was impossible to ignore the new theology of crisis on the Continent, and especially the towering figure of Karl Barth.

One of Temple's greatest achievements was his recognition of the inadequacy of his Christian philosophy. In late 1937 he wrote in his Chairman's Introduction to the report *Doctrine in the Church of England* that the dominant theology from Westcott and the *Lux Mundi* school right up to the 1920s had been a theology of the Incarnation rather than of Redemption. 'The distinction is, of course, not absolute or clean-cut, but the tip of the balance makes a vast difference not only in presentation but in direction of attention and estimate of relative values. A theology of the Incarnation tends to be a Christocentric metaphysic. And in all ages there is need for the fresh elaboration of such a scheme of thought or map of life as seen in the light of the revelation in Christ. A theology of Redemption (though, of course, Redemption has its place in the former) tends to sound a prophetic note; it is more ready to admit that much in this evil world is irrational and strictly unintelligible; and it looks to the coming of the Kingdom as a necessary preliminary to the full comprehension of much that now is. If the security of the nineteenth century, already shattered in Europe, finally crumbles away in our country, we shall be pressed more and more towards a theology of Redemption. In this we shall be coming closer to the New Testament. We have been learning again how impotent man is to save himself, how deep and pervasive is that corruption which theologians call Original Sin. Man needs above all to be saved from himself. This must be the work of Divine Grace.'[1]

Temple developed this thinking much more in an article in *Theology* called 'Theology To-day' (November 1939), which called for the digging of deeper foundations. The relevant features are these. First, Temple recognises the difference in outlook of the world in which he grew up from that in which the younger theologians have formed their habits of thought. The late Victorian and Edwardian age had at least sincerely professed Christianity in the sense 'that it was troubled at any suggestion that it ignored Christian standards of conduct.' Now Christian standards are challenged as radically as Christian doctrine, and men feel there are no ascertainable principles on which Christianity rests. The Christian view of life is either relegated to the background or openly repudiated by Communism or Fascism. Temple sees that the younger generation cannot start from the same point in their theology, and are rightly quite unimpressed by being offered a Christian map of the world. Perhaps even in 1924 it was over-optimistic to believe that a 'very slight touch to the intellectual balance' might 'make the scales incline' towards a metaphysics of the Incarnation. Certainly it was no use in 1939 saying to people, 'You will find that all your experience fits together in a harmonious system if you will only look at it in the illumination of the Gospel'. 'The world of to-day is one of which no Christian map can be made. It must be changed by Christ into something very unlike itself before a Christian map of it is possible ... Our task with this world is not to explain it but to convert it. Its need can be met, not by the discovery of its own immanent principle in signal manifestation through Jesus Christ, but only by the shattering impact upon its self-sufficiency and arrogance of the Son of God crucified, risen and ascended ... In order to fashion true fellowship in such a world as this, and out of such men and women as we are, He must first break up sham fellowships with which we have been deluding ourselves.'

Temple rightly claims that *Mens Creatrix* and *Christus Veritas* did formally allow for this line. He had never said that evil was justified before it was overcome. Nevertheless the emphasis now seemed all wrong. 'Facile generalisations are an affront. We must start from the fearful tension between the doctrine of the love of God and the actual facts of daily experience. When we have eliminated war, it will be time to discuss whether its monstrous evil can then be seen as a "constituent element of the absolute Good" (*Christus Veritas* p. 254). Till then we had better get on with the job of eliminating it by the power of the Gospel, which we must present, not as the clue to a universal synthesis, but as the source of world-transformation.' In a similar way Temple gently reminds the younger theologians that the older ones had not been blind to a doctrine of Redemption. They had sought to persuade their contemporaries, who wanted Christian ethics without Christian doctrine and in complacent ease held a belief in automatic progress, that they needed a Saviour.[2] Certainly Temple himself never believed in automatic progress or equated social progress with the Kingdom of God.

By 1942 Temple could write to Dorothy Emmet, 'What we must completely get away from is the notion that the world as it now exists is a rational whole; we must think of its unity not by the analogy of a picture, of which all the parts exist at once, but by the analogy of a drama where, if it is good enough, the full meaning of the first scene only becomes apparent with the final curtain; and we are in the middle of this. Consequently the world as we see it is strictly unintelligible. We can only have faith that it will become intelligible when the divine purpose, which is the explanation of it, is accomplished. Theologically, this is a greater emphasis on eschatology. Another way to put it is that the Logos is not to be conceived as a static principle of rational unity, but as an active force of moral judgement which calls upon us to be its fellow-workers and agents . . . All this is really there in the Gifford lectures, but I don't think the total presentation in that book or in *Christus Veritas* sufficiently gives this impression of a dynamic process and leaves too much that of a static system.'[3]

The extent of Temple's change of mind is very difficult to estimate. His own account of his past thought is probably too self-critical. His thought after 1939 could not be properly developed in the short time left to him and it remained fragmentary and ambiguous. We can at least notice how Temple expressed himself up to his premature death in 1944. Commentators have generally warned against lazy-minded antitheses, such as 'from idealism to realism', and have found a shift of emphasis within the framework of Temple's position, rather than radical changes to the framework itself. J. F. Padgett thinks that certain Christian concepts received increasing emphasis in Temple's thought and in some instances the concepts became dominant in his presentation of the Christian message. The emphasis on Redemption is a case in point. Padgett conveys the continuity with the Giffords, but surely at the same time the framework itself is at breaking point.

At the end of his article 'Theology To-day' Temple asks 'What is the relation between that Order of Redemption which the Christian enters by faith and the Order of Creation to which he belongs as a man? . . . Is there a Natural Order which is from God, as Catholic tradition holds? Or is there only Natural Disorder, the fruit of sin, from which Christ delivers us, as continental Protestantism has held?'[4] We can certainly say that the direct influence of continental Protestantism on Temple is minimal. There is not the slightest evidence that Temple revised his estimate of Karl Barth over revelation and reason. He did speak once or twice as if principles derived all their validity from the Christian faith;[5] but this probably reflects his belief that the ultimate choice is between Christian faith and scepticism, a belief sharpened in an era of crisis; and he always looked forward to the resumption of the constructive metaphysical task which crisis had rendered impossible.[6]

The importance for Temple of free rational enquiry is also evident from the discussions he arranged with the younger generation of theologians between 1940 and 1944. He became alarmed that Anglo-Catholic enthusiasts for the revival of dogmatic theology and Thomas Aquinas' philosophy were apparently repudiating liberalism as a method of free enquiry and falling into obscurantism.[7]

Yet the importance of the Catholic tradition, and especially its teaching on natural order or natural law, grew on Temple. In his article of 1939 he states what are the tasks he envisages for theology in the light of his reflections. Not surprisingly there is the accent on the proclamation of the Gospel. But significantly Temple starts by saying that there is the task of 'thinking out afresh what are the standards of life to which society must aim at conforming if it is to be in any sense a Christian society.' He feels that in the face of the Communist and Fascist challenge, which tells a man plainly what to think and do, the Church has been leaving men with nothing but principles so general as to offer no actual guidance. Temple particularly stresses the need for an ethic of collective action; for half the decisions that modern men have to take are on behalf of some collective unit. He then goes on: 'In all this field, effective action is possible only if Christians (a) are ready to co-operate with non-Christians who share their aim, (b) are able to present what they believe on Christian grounds to be right as commendable also on general grounds of reason. Here is a field for the utmost co-operative effort in thought and action. The two great Papal Encyclicals *Rerum Novarum* [1891] and *Quadragesimo Anno* [1931], and such writings as those of Maritain, set us an example from the Roman Catholic side. Those of us who, in comparison, are handicapped by inability to accept the Thomist scheme as an assured starting-point, though having nothing which is nearly so complete and thorough to put in its place, must do our best, even if for the time it makes poor showing beside the achievements of our colleagues. Perhaps one main task is to become clear precisely where and why we dissent from the Thomist basis, and see whether the whole structure may not be susceptible of modification in the light of our different or additional principles. But whether in that way or in some other, we must labour for the rebirth of Christendom.'[8]

The Malvern Conference of January 1941 was the great opportunity for the Christendom Group to show how Christendom was to be reborn. The objects of the Conference are significant. They were 'to consider from the Anglican point of view what are the fundamental facts which are directly relevant to the ordering of the new society that is quite evidently emerging, and how Christian thought can be shaped to play a leading part in the reconstruction after the war is over.' Not only is the focus upon the Christian perspective; there is even a narrowing of Christian representation compared with COPEC. Temple was to write later in *The Spectator* that the Conference had been concerned with two major convictions, (i) that there is a divinely appointed order or hierarchy of human activities and functions; (ii) that human sin has led to the desertion of this order and to the establishment of an order at variance with it, which perpetuates and intensifies the sin from which it sprang. Thus the question of natural order was a central one, but it was to be set very firmly within a theological framework. Temple wrote that theology 'determined the presuppositions which were to govern the more political and economic discussion.' He was not looking for anything particularly new. The Conference, he said, was held 'for the ascertainment and registration of the amount of agreement reached among a number of people who had given thought, perhaps for many years, to the themes discussed.' It was to provide a firm, clear Christian basis on which Christians could play an effective part in post-war reconstruction. It turned out to be exceedingly difficult to fulfil either the theological or the practical aim. The format was a surfeit of papers crammed into three days, each followed by cursory discussion. Temple performed his parlour trick, but even he had to admit it was very exacting to pen the common mind of the Conference. Theologically it was too late to register agreement. Barth and the theology of crisis demanded a response. The young Donald MacKinnon inveighed against the smooth syntheses of the older generation. He discoursed on creation, sin and redemption and the problematical nature of the Church as he searched for foundations. This was, of course, precisely the task to which Temple had committed himself by 1939. But there was no time for serious digging. At the more practical level the tendency of the Christendom Group to deduce social and economic order from dogma caused disquiet. W. G. Peck, for example, was later to be censured by R. H. Preston, a trained economist and theologian, for failing to take the empirical discipline of economics seriously.[9]

At the Malvern Conference Temple remarked that neither St. Thomas nor the leading neo-Thomist Jacques Maritain had an adequate appreciation of the power of sin. By contrast Reinhold Niebuhr's 'whole mind is possessed by the sense of that aboriginal sin of man which consists in putting himself at the centre where God alone ought to be ...'[10] The thought of Niebuhr is another major source of Temple's thinking in his last ten years. By 1939 he was acknowledging a change in his social thought which corresponds to, indeed is interwoven with, his basic theological shift. He wrote, 'I think that it is an open question whether an actual preference by one of the interests of the other over its own is ethically right; but, even if the question is open, it is purely academic; when we reach the stage of justice in the relations between Capital and Labour or between one nation and another, we shall have moved a very long way. We had better aim at this before we preach corporate self-sacrifice. I used to preach it once; I thereby gained much applause, which I very much enjoyed; but I have long been convinced that such talk is only "uplift"; it does not affect anything that actually happens. It is a superhuman thing when an individual is lifted above his self-centredness; but the egotism of any corporation except a genuine "fellowship of the Spirit", is something far more intense than that of an individual, because it enlists in its service alike the idealism and selfishness of its members. To establish justice here is an achievement far beyond our present attainment, perhaps beyond our resources.'[11] So the intractable human condition forced Temple not merely to retreat theologically from the confident expectation of syntheses but also to retreat from ethical idealism. Temple's handling of the theme of love and justice and the challenge of Reinhold Niebuhr are discussed in Chapter 15.

This change is well illustrated in *Citizen and Churchman* (1941). In many ways it is a continuation and development of *Christianity and the State* (1928), but it also reflects a deepening concern with the distinction between Church and State, love and justice. A year later, in *Christianity and Social Order* we find the long-standing social principles stiffened by a fine popular exposition of original sin and strong warnings against utopianism.[12] *Christianity and Social Order* was Temple's personal sequel to the Malvern Conference. It was his only book on method in Christian social ethics. Yet which approach was he to select? Or could he make a coherent theory out of natural law, love and justice and his own way of principles? We find that he still gives pride of place to the principles. The approaches through natural law and through love and justice do appear, especially in Chapter 6, but they are only cursorily related to each other and to the way of principles. Probably this reflects the fact that the book had to be written at speed, and Temple fell back on the thought that was most familiar to him. Perhaps too he felt this approach would make most appeal to his British audience and give them the greatest spur to tackle the issues of post-war reconstruction.

Temple first vindicates the right of the Church to intervene in the social order: the supposition of completely separate spheres of religion and politics, economics, and so on, is a modern aberration. He sketches the limits of the Church's competence: 'The Church must announce Christian principles and point out where the existing social order at any time is in conflict with them. It must then pass on to Christian citizens, acting in their civic capacity, the task of reshaping the existing social order in closer conformity to the principles. For at this point technical knowledge may be required and judgements of practical expediency are always required.'[13] He starts out from what he now calls Primary Christian Social Principles – which are really summary Christian doctrine: God and His purpose; Man, his dignity, tragedy, and destiny. From these Temple infers the derivative social principles of freedom (or respect for personality), social fellowship and service – the first three of the four propounded in 1923. The fourth is dropped, in line with his perception of 1939: self-sacrifice can and must be freely practised by individuals, but cannot be forced on others. Temple uses these social principles to make critiques of contemporary British society, notably to expose the curse of long-term unemployment. In the seventh chapter Temple sketches 'the task before us'. Here he sets out six broad objectives which Christians should urge upon the government. For example, 'Every child should find itself a member of a family housed with decency and dignity'; or, 'Every citizen should have a voice in the conduct of the business or industry which is carried on by means of his labour and the satisfaction of knowing his labour is directed to the well-being of the community.' These objectives are in fact instances of middle axioms. In Temple's view this is as far as the Church can go, and he hopes that every Christian will endorse the substance of what he has said so far. He then goes on to outline a programme, with a *caveat* that he is offering suggestions for criticism rather than for adoption, and he rounds off the chapter by saying, 'Let no one quote this as my conception of the political programme which Christians ought to support. There neither is nor can be any such programme.' He deliberately calls this chapter an Appendix, and not Chapter 8, to underline the distinction in status. Here Temple puts forward ideas covering greater state control of banking, land taxation, a planning authority representative of all sides of industry, holidays with pay, and so forth. It was upon the Appendix that most of the criticism fell.[14]

Temple's responsibilities and stature grew apace in his last few years. When Lang retired in 1942, Churchill had no option but to call Temple to Canterbury. Characteristically Churchill remarked that Temple was the half-crown article in a penny bazaar.[15] He was enthroned on St. George's Day 1942. The brief period to October 1944 was phenomenally busy. Temple himself used to remark, 'What wears one out is not what one does but what one doesn't do.' Yet the strain, even for one whose spirituality radiated a profound stillness and peace, was immense. In his social ethics he deepened his Christian perspective on war and power politics along Niebuhrian lines, and some of his finest speeches came in 1943–4. His interest in natural law led him to plan a personal approach to the Vatican, hoping that Anglican and Roman Catholic theologians might undertake a joint study of natural law. Iremonger also tells us of a joint committee of the Anglican and Free Church 'Religion and Life Movement' and the Roman Catholic 'Sword of the Spirit', which was set up in Temple's last years to unite Christians in common social action on the basis of natural law and moral theology.[16] Temple also offered a penetrating critique of St. Thomas Aquinas (he had read his *Summa* right through) to the Aquinas Society in 1943, and he continued to listen encouragingly to the Christendom Group, although he was keen that the movement which had led to the Malvern Conference should not pass entirely into the hands of Anglo-Catholics.[17] His own way of principles, with its stress on the development of persons in community, shaped his reflections on economics and education. He worked closely with R. A. Butler on the Education Act of 1944, and used to the full the more eirenic atmosphere in ecumenical relations to find as much agreement as possible with Nonconformists.[18] For him the reunion of the Christian Church and the reintegration of every aspect of life under the Kingship of God were the dominant and inseparable aims.

In the last year of his life Temple wrote 'What Christians Stand for in the Secular World'.[19] He himself considered it the piece by which he most wanted to be judged, and it gives us the clearest indication of the degree of movement in Temple's social thought from 1937. There is plenty of continuity with the pre-1937 era: the accent on the purpose of God, the importance yet insufficiency of the sciences, the social nature of personality. Yet the emphases have changed. It is for instance the distinction between the tasks of Church and society with which Temple starts out. Similarly he distinguishes between justice, human love and Christian charity.

Behind this is the recognition that the Church lives in a largely alien world, one which does not already make sense, but needs making into sense. Humanism, Fascism and Communism sponsor estimates of man which are at variance with Christianity. The world is moreover a place of egoisms and competing centres of power. Physical nature is exploited; natural forms of human association have broken down. New dogmas and assumptions about the nature of reality have taken the place of the old; new rituals give shape to men's emotional life. The aims of contemporary society may to a large extent remain Christian, but men's souls are moulded by alien influences.

The crisis of the day is thus a cultural rather than a narrowly moral one. It is not enough (and here we surely see Demant's influence) for Christians to be insisting on ideals and intensifying the will to pursue them. 'Christians must free their minds from illusions, and become aware of the impotence of moral advice and instruction when it is divorced from the social structures which by their perpetual suggestion form the soul.' Christianity is not in essence a system of morals. To be a Christian is to share in a new movement of life, and to co-operate with new regenerating forces that have entered into history. The Church must therefore maintain its own spiritual life, its worship, fellowship and beliefs, or it will have no standing ground from which to address the world. It must not retreat to the catacombs but challenge its rivals with its own interpretation of life. True, we must not be too preoccupied with politics; yet political decisions have to be made. Christians must 'restore hope to the world through a true understanding of the relation of the Kingdom of God to history, as a transcendent reality that is continually seeking, and partially achieving, embodiment in the activities and conflicts of the temporal order. Without this faith men can only seek escape from life in modes of thought which, pushed to their logical conclusion, deprive politics, and even the ethical struggle, of real significance, or succumb to a complete secularisation of life in which all principles disintegrate in pure relativity, and opportunism is the only wisdom.' Temple uncharacteristically speaks not so much of principles as of decisions: for God, for neighbour, for man as rooted in nature, for history, for the Gospel and the Church. 'There is scarcely any more urgent task for the Church than that this whole complex of problems should be thought out afresh, and it is obviously a task which can be successfully undertaken only in the closest relation with the experience of those who are exposed to the daily pressures of the economic and political struggle.'

Temple lies buried in the cloister garth of Canterbury Cathedral. At the foot of the horizontal slab are inscribed the words of S. S. Wesley's anthem, which Temple chose for his enthronement at Manchester, 'Thou shalt keep him in perfect peace whose mind is stayed on Thee.' It was the spirituality of William Temple which above all impressed his contemporaries, and still makes such a powerful impression on a later generation. Estimates of his social ethics vary. When Temple died his arch-critic Hensley Henson reflected in his diary on 'the Archbishop's good fortune on being called away precisely at the juncture when popular hopes were fresh and full, before the chill of reaction had chastened enthusiasm, and the exasperation of disillusionment had replaced the exultation of success.'[20] A few days later Reinhold Niebuhr wrote of Temple that he 'was able to relate the ultimate insights of religion about the human situation to the immediate necessities of political justice and the proximate possibilities of a just social order more vitally and creatively than any other modern Christian leader.'[21] Our primary task will be an extensive evaluation of all three of Temple's approaches to social ethics. In Part II a study of Temple's thought and action over industry, unemployment and economics will lead us into a critical consideration of the approaches through natural law and through principles. In Part III we shall look in detail at his handling of international affairs and consider the approach through love and justice. This detailed analysis and assessment of Temple himself in the context of his day will, I hope, bring a deeper appreciation of Temple himself and a greater enthusiasm to take up the urgent task with which he challenged us. The proposals set out in Part IV for a Christian social ethics for today are one attempt to respond to that challenge.

PART II

TEMPLE'S APPROACH TO NATIONAL AFFAIRS

Introduction

Today industrial relations, unemployment and economics bulk large in public debate. In industry, conditions of work and levels of wages are permanent areas of conflict; but behind them lies the question of control – the 'right of management to manage' and the right of the labour force to share in decisions. The alarming rise in unemployment has generated diverse analyses about its causes and many proposals for its cure. The unemployed meanwhile find themselves having to cope with public hostility in addition to their burdens. On the positive side there is a growing volume of scientific research on the effects of unemployment on its victims, and a wide range of schemes afoot which try to meet the needs of the unemployed. The conflicts in industry and over unemployment often reflect deep divisions in our understanding of economic theory and activity. Is Keynesian economics dead? people ask. Is monetarism the way to economic recovery? Is the capitalist system resilient, or is it destined to collapse?

Christians seem permanently divided in these disputes. They disagree not only over technical matters and the consequences of different lines of action, but also over the whole bearing of Christianity on these areas. Some treat economics as an autonomous sphere and Christianity as a religion which is concerned only or primarily with personal relations. Others insist Christianity offers criteria by which economic and political life can be judged.

The next three chapters look at Temple's response to these three problem areas. Certainly we cannot read solutions to our present difficulties out of the past. Yet there are striking continuities, and in any case there is value in gaining distance from the present and seeing what someone in a previous generation had to say, and how he thought the Christian faith provided resources for facing these problems. Chapters 10 and 11 study the two approaches Temple used from a Christian perspective – natural law and principles – in our search for a framework for Christian social ethics today. After the search is complete in Part IV we shall note in Appendix III some questions about these problems, suggested by the framework.

75

CHAPTER 7

INDUSTRY

1. *Temple's early years*

William Temple's upbringing was the perfect background for the assimilation of the outlook of the Christian Social Union. It is easy to show from his early pronouncements two of its characteristics: a strong sense of the way evil becomes embedded in institutions, thus implicating us all, and the conviction that the character, words and methods of the incarnate Christ must act as the criteria for exposing that evil and suggesting a remedy. In particular we see a concern for the defence and development of personality in institutions and for the corresponding pursuit of justice and not merely charity.

In 1907 Temple, as a young don, was involved with the Christian Social Union in mounting a Sweated Industries Exhibition at Oxford. This brought home to him the conditions and wages of many in the matchbox and other trades. In the handbook he points to the system as diseased and to Christianity as a criterion. 'It is the system which is foul and rotten. Producer, capitalist, consumer – all are entangled in the meshes of its net . . . If we listen, there is . . . the desolate cry of the Son of Man: "I am hungry and ye give me no meat".'[1]

Both these points are amplified in a sermon delivered four years later when Temple was Headmaster at Repton. Women are driven to prostitution in order to supplement low wages at work, and because the goods so made lower prices on the open market, and thus increase the purchasing power of our own money, we all become implicated in their degradation. This arises simply because men are as good as we are and no better; social conditions are the product of our selfish un-Christlike character. Temple also reminds his privileged pupils that most of their contemporaries are already at work. The problem here is that as a rule the best paid work gives them no real training, so that for want of a useful trade they drift as adults into the casual labour market, picking up jobs as best they can, and always first to be out of work in times of depression.[2]

In the Bishop Paddock Lectures, delivered in New York in the early part of 1915, Temple deals in a more extended way with the defects of British industrial organisation. He claims to know what is the root of labour unrest in England through his concern with the Workers' Educational Association, though he admits that his contact is with picked men. The root is a sense that the whole organisation of life is a standing insult to the personality of the poor man. Thus the well-to-do man can secure medical attention, but the poor man often depends on voluntary institutions. 'It is quite compatible with gratitude to those whose generosity maintains these institutions to feel that for such service he should not be dependent upon anybody's charity at all ...' The denial of personality is felt above all in the organisation of industry. The regulations of an industrial firm invade a man's home, determining when he shall get up or go to bed, and whether he shall have any leisure for the pursuit of any interest of his own. Men feel that they are the tools of other men, 'hands' not persons. Control of an industry may well be in the hands of a Board of Directors which meets only a few times a year in London, and never sees the people whose lives and destinies they control. The shareholders who want their dividends make no enquiries as a rule about conditions of work. If the Board of Directors mismanages its business, a whole village may go hungry. If the Board takes on a large contract when it already has a full supply of work, the village works overtime. In all this working men have no voice. They have no opportunity of making their views understood except by the threat of a strike. 'Whatever else that is, it is not liberty, and in the judgement of the people themselves it is not justice ... The economic organisation of life comes far closer to the individual citizen than the political organisation, and the development of justice remains incomplete until it has secured liberty of an economic as well as a political kind.' The central problem is thus the denial of personality; the formula for describing the justice to be practised in the state is 'the recognition of personality'. The method of Christ requires that we demand opportunities for the development of free personality; and if indeed we are 'members one of another' then a Christian investor, for example, should find out the conditions under which his dividends are going to be earned.[3]

2.   The years of high idealism: 1916–1920

The First World War, so far from destroying Temple's reforming zeal, raised it to new heights. His thought shared in the euphoric desire to create a country fit for heroes and largely coincided with the Archbishops' Fifth Committee on Christianity and Industrial Problems. His editorials in the weekly *Challenge*, his speeches in Convocation and his thought in *Mens Creatrix* (1917) and *Fellowship with God* (1920) reveal development both in content and in method.

In the name of justice Temple presses for the living wage. Not only should labour get a fair share of the proceeds of industry; the reward of labour should be the first charge on it. Everyone who was willing to do a full day's work ought to be assured a living wage. A minimum wage was not only the clear claim of justice, but was also a sound economy; for it was a disastrous waste of capital to let people's energies degenerate for want of the necessary resources.[4] Temple also pressed for better conditions of work. Supporting a government report he demanded reconstruction over long hours, overtime and the shift system.[5]

The central issue for Temple is undoubtedly the control of industry. He vacillates, however, about forms of control. In a single editorial he recommends first the permanent right of labour to be fully *consulted* and later labour's full place as a partner in the *management* of industry.[6] He is conscious of greater co-operation between capital and labour during the war. Typically he calls on the Church to support all efforts to promote closer fellowship between employers and employees in their service to the whole community.[7] But he fears it could founder on conflicting class outlooks. Temple predictably follows Thomas Arnold and the Christian Socialists in attacking the individualism of *laissez-faire* capitalism. When people in the past attacked industrial legislation in the name of freedom, they meant freedom from external control. That is indeed indispensable, but it is not sufficient in itself. 'Liberty so understood is simply anarchism tempered by so much of government as may make it tolerable.' *Laissez-faire* is attractive to the respectable and leisured classes; what is more, it is they who control legislation, and they naturally legislate against tendencies in others rather than against their own. So this kind of freedom may be complete in principle yet negligible in result, for instance in freedom of contract in an industrial system.[8] Now whereas the social philosophy of the share-holding classes has been based on the doctrine that every man should first seek his own interest, morality merely coming in as a check on the process, the labouring classes have never been individualistic in this sense. 'Their whole experience drives in upon them the fundamental law ... that if one member suffers, all suffer.' The interest of the individual and the interest of the community to which he belongs in the long run always coincide; hence the solidarity of working men in strikes, fantastic though this may seem to the middle-class point of view.[9]

Temple also returns to the question of charity. The industrial system, he asserts, constitutes a standing insult to the poor man. Why should he be dependent on the good-will of others? 'To give or to receive charity is excellent when equality is first assured; but to be dependent upon anything in the nature of charity for the reasonable necessities of civilised life is an outrage.' Where charity is a working off of superfluity to satisfy the impulse of compassion or is merely a response to an abstract sense of duty, recipients are denied true freedom.[10] Elsewhere Temple writes that however benevolently autocracies and bureaucracies may govern industry, they cannot give the necessary basis of freedom and justice. Labour should therefore fully share in the management of industry.[11]

It is clear that Temple here deserts his philosophical habit of making a synthesis out of opposing outlooks; he is definitely on the side of labour. His uncritical enthusiasm arises partly because he shared the guilt feelings of the Christian Social Union about the role of the Church towards the working class during the Industrial Revolution. He also tended to meet only those working men who shared his own ideals. The heady early days of the Workers' Educational Association only reinforced his confidence in the power of idealism. Temple also seems at this time to have had conceptual tools which were as blunt as Westcott's. Competing selfishness is contrasted with love, individualism with fellowship. The penalty of the opaque moral antithesis is that it obscures all but moral factors in a situation and leads by a process of deduction to unqualified endorsement of one position. The opposite position (or rather a caricature of it) is correspondingly repudiated. 'The Labour point of view is fundamentally Christian,' he writes. The labour movement is an effort to organise society on the basis of freedom and fellowship. If labour keeps true to this ideal, 'the material will come right'; that is 'the message of Easter.'[12] Announcing in Convocation in 1918 that he had just joined the Labour Party, he claimed it was Christian to help to secure comparative equality of circumstance to citizens and substitute the service of the community for private gain as the chief motive in industrial enterprise.[13]

Through his reflections on the management of industry Temple did move towards a somewhat more discriminating method. In an editorial of 1917 he wanted the Church to go beyond airy principles towards something more specific, yet to stop short of a detailed programme. Reflecting on the Whitley Report, which urged the establishment of joint committees of employers and working people for the management of conditions in industry, he believed it embodied the recognition of the personality of the worker, and thought the Church could support the idea of joint control of industry, whilst leaving it to others to devise particular programmes.[14] Though this is in essence a traditional Anglican view, supported for instance by Westcott and Pinchard, and though it still moves on a predominantly moral plane, at least it does offer some defence against straight deductions, in that it leaves concrete decisions to those with practical experience of the circumstances.

In fact in the Temple of this period we find juxtapositions of sober realism and high flown idealism. We can take as an example the article 'The Moral Foundation of Peace', written in 1920 at the height of post-war idealism. Temple wonders how the greater co-operation in industry generated by the war can be developed further. On the one hand he recommends moral opportunism. Our duty, he said, is 'the very difficult one of maintaining an ideal while adopting in the most realistic manner the steps which are best calculated to lead to its attainment.' On the other hand he appeals to labour to accept voluntarily a principle which capital is in no position to practise, the brotherhood of man and the duty of forgiveness. He calls on all to refrain from allocating blame. 'Judge not' is a Christian maxim of supreme importance in industrial politics. Those who have the right and the power to punish should choose instead to promote the common interest. 'For the moral foundation of peace in a perfectly ordered world is justice. But our world is disordered. And when evil has come in, it can only be expelled through suffering voluntarily accepted by the innocent; in our world the moral foundation of peace is self-sacrifice.'[15] The tussle between realism and idealism in Temple was a long one. First the word 'ideals' was to give place to 'principles', and eventually self-sacrifice was to be deleted from the list of social principles.

3. The strife of the 1920s

The national post-war euphoria was soon replaced by disillusionment in the face of economic difficulties. Temple's idealism was subjected to severe test in the 1920s, and nowhere more so than in the crises of the coal industry. Unrest broke out soon after the end of the war. The miners pressed not only for wage increases but also for complete public ownership and workers' control of the industry. Because of the great shortage of coal the government was obliged to counter a strike threat in February 1919 by setting up a commission representative of both sides under Mr. Justice Sankey. It recommended both a seven-hour day and a wage rise. By a narrow margin it also proposed the nationalisation of the industry, and Sankey himself became the miners' hero and adorned their banners. The government had committed itself in advance to carry out Sankey's recommendations 'in the spirit and in the letter'; but Lloyd George exploited the disagreement to take no action over nationalisation, thus irritating the miners.[16]

The settlement of the miners' strike of 1920 provided a scheme whereby above a basic rate wages would be linked to the output of the industry taken as a whole. Temple instantly saw in this 'national pool' a concrete instance of his principle of fellowship. Miners of more profitable pits were declining to fare better than those less fortunately placed. 'That is plainly a Christian course of action and the miners . . . deserve full credit for a genuine idealism.' So far Temple is running true to form. Yet he does recognise that the owners have a case: they are right to be wary of giving up an incentive known to be effective for a method calling for moral qualities whose existence is doubtful. He himself is sceptical about the depth of genuine fellowship among labour: it is largely spurious, resting in part on a common antagonism to a system and a social class. Sudden success in abolishing capitalism would result in the disintegration of the movement through internal pugnacity. Labour's fitful idealism can only succeed in Temple's view if it is grounded in Christianity: only faith in God can sustain personal character in the face of the demands of a new social order, and only belief in the presence of the Kingdom of God can provide true fellowship through a common devotion to an enterprise where all can succeed.[17] Unfortunately Temple simply glosses over the intractable sociological problem that even in the heyday of Victorian religiosity the working class were largely absent from the churches, and the experience of two decades of the twentieth century, including the National Mission of Repentance and Hope, held out no prospect of a reversal of working-class practice.

The government, however, were faced with the increasingly unprofitable state of the coal industry, partly because some of Germany's reparation payments were made in coal, and in 1921 they returned it to private enterprise. The miners had been hoping for the creation of a National Wages Board, but the new owners played divide-and-rule by insisting on only district agreements, and demanded wage reductions of up to 49%. The miners struck again, but lacking the full-blooded support of the transport workers and the railwaymen they had to settle for district wage agreements, even though a National Wages Board was set up. However, the climax of the crisis was delayed, largely because of the weakness of other coal producers, such as France and Germany. There was a temporary improvement in the prospects for the industry which gave the miners some substantial wage increases on the national minimum addition to the basic rate.[18]

It was during this lull that Temple was preparing as chairman for the Conference on Christian Politics, Economics and Citizenship (COPEC). In 1923, having distinguished ideals and principles, as we saw, and delineated four social principles, he proceeded to apply them to industry. In the name of freedom and fellowship he once again demanded that labour be seen not as a commodity, but as human beings; that workers should have a voice in determining conditions of work as a right; that there be partnership in the control of industry. This thinking remained essentially unchanged right up to Temple's death. Once again it is over the principle of self-sacrifice that Temple is most unsure of himself. On the one hand, he writes, sacrifice is at the very heart of the Christian religion. 'Real progress comes by self-sacrifice. In a society that had never become corrupted, fellowship might rest on justice; but once corruption has set in, it can only be based on self-sacrifice . . . The Cross is the means of salvation.' Yet he also recognises that it may be right for labour forcibly to resist aggression by capital, and he thinks that real progress comes from men's sacrificial constancy in the hardship of a strike. Temple's uncertainty is reflected in his remark: 'We have scarcely dared to apply the principle to social and international questions even in thought.'[19]

Three years later Temple was required to apply his principles to the great strikes of 1926. The financial position of the coal industry deteriorated rapidly after 1924. In July 1925 the Prime Minister, Stanley Baldwin, averted a strike threat at the last minute by setting up a Royal Commission under Sir Herbert Samuel, and offered a subsidy to maintain existing wages for nine months.[20] Temple approved: Baldwin had been right to delay taking this step as it was a serious precedent to bolster one industry in difficulties by a tax on others; yet he was also right to avert a general strike. Temple can see both sides have a good case. The owners appreciate that reduction in world demand requires reduced prices and therefore reduced wages. Yet the miners have very low wages already. In any case, any reduction would also be at the expense of miners in other countries, since their wages would also be forced down. Temple backs centralisation of the industry for the sake of greater efficiency and economy.[21] Yet he does not give any evidence of calculation, and one suspects he simply saw an affinity between centralisation and his social principles, and therefore assumed its effectiveness. Or perhaps he accepted the majority view of the Sankey Commission, and the miners' charge of inefficient management, and thought that it was somehow possible to maintain the levels of both wages and employment.

The Samuel Commission, reporting in March 1926, tried to steer a middle course between nationalisation and the owners' point of view. It basically proposed no increase in the working day, but a reduction in the sum paid above the basic rate, though not of the subsistence rates to the lowest paid. As for the subsidy, it must never be repeated. The slogan resounded from the miners, 'Not a penny off the pay, not a minute on the day.' The owners pressed now district agreements, now a longer working day.[22] The

General Strike lasted 3–12 May; the miners stayed out until the autumn.

Temple's first extended comment is in *The Pilgrim* of July 1926. His judgements are entirely determined by whether an action was likely to conciliate or not. No doubt this reflects the operation of his principle of fellowship and his dictum that industry is co-operation in the public service. His estimate of labour is that they were motivated primarily by loyalty to their own folk; there was no bitterness or revolutionary ferment. The T.U.C. had not been planning for a strike, nor was it committed to calling a strike simply if the miners were dissatisfied. However, a general strike could not be justified in a democratic country; for it was bound to cause widespread suffering to innocent people and to have a tendency to civil war and revolution. The government had therefore been quite right to refuse to negotiate with those who called it. The owners had shown deplorable insensitivity: they had given the miners less than two days to accept or reject their terms, and they had demanded freedom from interference by the government when they had received £23 m. in subsidies from it. 'For people who supply a public necessity to say that the public must go without while they settle their own quarrel is constructive treason.' The miners' position however was in Temple's view equally impossible. Industry could not go on with the existing wages. 'Reductions there must be, and re-organisation there must be, so we come to the one hope of settlement – the Report, the whole Report, and nothing but the Report.'

Temple also hailed as an 'immense influence' the publication by the Archbishop of Canterbury, Randall Davidson, of an Appeal from the Churches during the strike. Temple liked the document's distinction between principles (the spirit of fellowship and co-operation for the common good) and cautious practical suggestions (return to the *status quo* before the strike, involving simultaneous cancellation of the General Strike, government renewal of temporary financial assistance, and withdrawal by the owners of new wage scales). He believed the appeal in no way undermined the position of the government by putting these three proposed actions on a par.[23]

The controversy surrounding the Appeal was as nothing compared with the furore Temple stirred up in the July of 1926, as the miners' strike dragged on. By chance he was out of the country during the General Strike, seeking a cure for his persistent affliction, gout. Shortly after his return he joined a group which came to call itself 'The Conference of Members of the Christian Churches which is seeking to mediate in the coal dispute'. It consisted of Anglicans (including ten bishops) and members of seven other denominations. On 19 July, after consultations with both sides, representatives of the Conference saw Baldwin in a vain attempt to break the deadlock. One upshot was a rumpus in the correspondence columns of *The Times* which began even before the Conference's own statement there on 24 July and abated only after Temple's letter, printed on 21 August. It was a familiar division. On the one side were those who separated religion and economics, claiming of economics that it was a wholly autonomous sphere, and of Christianity that it offers a purely personal morality. Hensley Henson is a good example, and I shall return to him in Chapter 11 and especially in Appendix I. On the other side were Temple and those in the tradition of Christian social teaching running from Thomas Arnold and F. D. Maurice. They insisted that economics was not immune from moral critique, and that Christianity, with its insistence on the sociality as well as the individuality of persons, supplied the tools to make that critique.

The Conference's letter stresses the 'spiritual and moral aspects' of the dispute – the privation of miners, their families and others in other industries, and the impairing of mutual trust, forbearance and goodwill. The only basis for lasting peace is 'that the worker, in return for efficient service, may receive adequate remuneration and enjoy humane conditions of labour.' The spirit of 'a fight to the finish', sometimes thoughtlessly uttered, is dubbed anti-Christian; arbitration is proposed as a practical expression of the New Testament ethic. Temple writes in August: 'As Christians, and most of us Christians charged with official responsibility, we saw two parties doing great injury to the community, by a continued conflict which was bound to be ended by negotiation sooner or later; our religion and our office required of us that we should do anything which lay in our power to bring them, in the literal sense, to reason ... We felt a responsibility for trying to secure that the settlement should be not only economically sound in itself, but reached with the minimum of bitterness or resentment and the maximum of goodwill.'

It is quite evident from both letters that, whatever the merits of the group's action, the intention was to respect the authority, expertise and position of the parties involved. They took no action until there was a deadlock, and they were careful to meet representatives of the coalowners' Association and the executive of the Miners' Federation to hear their views. The only proposal made by the group itself was a return to the report of the Samuel Commission. During the meeting with the miners the group detected the withdrawal of the miners' slogan, and thought this justified an approach to the government with proposals which had the support of the miners' executive. These included: an immediate resumption of work on conditions obtaining on 30 April, including hours and wages; financial assistance pending a national settlement within four months; and further detailed work by the Commission on the re-organisation scheme and the reference to wages. If disagreement persisted, a joint board, consisting of representatives of both parties, should appoint an independent chairman, whose award would be accepted by both parties.

In the event Baldwin interpreted 'financial assistance' as a subsidy, rejected it, and published the group's terms even before the deputation saw him. The owners declined to alter their position. By October Temple was mournfully castigating the blindness of the government to economic and psychological consequences. From an economic point of view, he claimed, the question was whether the grant of a subsidy would shorten the strike by a period sufficient to balance the cost of the subsidy. But beyond that there were psychological or 'human' considerations which were equally important, and indeed part of the economic situation itself. It was worth a good deal to the country to secure a settlement that caused no bitter resentment. The government, moreover, had forced through a bill which raised the working day to eight hours. This reversed the award of the Sankey Report and was contrary to the views of the Samuel Commission. It might have gone through as part of a comprehensive measure of re-organisation, but by itself it was odious.[24]

By November the miners were forced back without the

negotiated settlement. In a mood of disillusionment Temple described the end of the strike as utterly unsatisfactory, and a humiliating episode in our history. It was a chapter of waste, folly and obstinacy. The owners had been inflammatory, the government supine; miners and owners had 'behaved like sulky children in an ill-managed nursery.' He feared that the Miners' Federation would be a purely fighting machine.[25] Two years later Temple suggested an Industrial Parliament with legislative powers, but subject to the veto of the national Parliament. His dictum here is that as soon as any group has real power, it should be treated as responsible. One should throw on conflicting voluntary associations the legal responsibility for maintaining their own peace.[26]

The whole episode of 1926 certainly throws up questions about Temple's approach through social principles, as well as the propriety of a group of prominent Christians entering the arena of political and economic conflict. Unresolved problems of COPEC reappear here and they will be considered in the context of a discussion of Temple's way of principles in Chapter 11.

4. *The closing years*

Temple's thought on industry changed very little in substance or approach in the remaining years of his life. However, an interesting new departure is to be found in a letter Temple and nine others wrote to *The Times* in 1933. A group of business and professional men had been meeting at the Economics Department of Leeds University to study the inter-related problems of industry, agriculture and finance. A special concern was price levels, on which the group had made recommendations to the government. It was felt that with a larger background they would carry sufficient weight to influence public opinion. Approval had therefore been given to establish a Yorkshire Institute of Industrial Affairs, with three objects: to form an intelligent body of public opinion on the needs of industry and land in relation to finance and national welfare; to investigate the problems of industry and land in the light of modern thought on industry and finance; to develop constructive proposals for the co-ordination of industrial, agricultural and financial affairs. The Institute would be strictly non-political, and its driving power would derive from the knowledge, expertise and interest of its members, together with the active policy pursued by groups under its aegis.[27] This is a significant move towards a corporate inter-disciplinary approach to social problems which reflects a more empirical outlook than Temple had shown hitherto. We shall find a similar instance in the field of unemployment. However, many of his other remarks in this period are more personal ventures which run counter to the rationale of the Institute.

The advent of the Second World War drove Temple to reflect much more on control of industry at the level of high finance. Within that context and his advocacy of a 'vast extension of public control of private enterprise', he continued to press for labour's share of control, but he has rather different ideas about the form this would take. He notes that labour has historically been very reluctant to accept a share in the control of industry for the direction of its policy, and he is doubtful whether it would generally accept places on Boards of Directors, or make very good use of them if it did. 'There is need on any showing for a new enterprise of planning in Industry and this must obviously be undertaken by the State. It may be that Labour will best exercise its control, at any rate at first, through the organ of Government responsible for this.' Temple follows this up with a note which is his strongest comment on the Trade Unions since 1927. They were constituted to deal with the chief problems of the nineteenth century and are structurally and psychologically ill-adapted for the chief opportunities of the present. They see their main task as the defence of hours, wages and conditions for those in work, whereas really it is that of security of employment. As a natural consequence they produce few leaders strong enough to carry out the prerequisite of union reform. The vested interests of labour are just as difficult to overcome as those of the capitalist. 'The source of the trouble is not wealth; it is sin – which is the perquisite of no class ...'[28] It looks as if Temple believed his fear had been partly realised that labour would become a belligerent defensive force, whilst he himself had moved on in the 'thirties to see unemployment as the central issue, and through that in the 'forties to consider the wider context of industry. At this point his disillusionment with labour may well have reinforced his preoccupation with public control through the state.

Not that this deterred Temple from advocating improved wages and conditions. He declares that expert opinion believes the five-day week would increase rather than diminish output. But as usual it is the human rather than the economic aspect which carries most weight with Temple. The larger the city, the more a man's half-day holiday is eroded by travel. His need for rest would be better met by two consecutive days off. Temple also favours holidays with pay. This principle is important to him in three ways: 'It recognises the status of the worker in the industry and is a repudiation of the notion that he is an external factor hired for the hours when his labour is needed and no more; secondly, it recognises that the process of recreation is essential to the quality of his work and therefore to the welfare of the industry; thirdly, it gives better opportunity for that freedom of enjoyment which is necessary to fulness of personal and of family life.'[29] Naturally this requires stability of wages to be effective, and Temple proposes an equalisation fund out of surplus profits for the maintenance of wages in bad times, even if hours of work are reduced.[30] Within the factory Temple shows increasing concern about mass-production, on the grounds that it respects neither individuality nor community. Individuals sense frustration and futility because they lack any personal allegiance to a community to which they truly belong and which values them as persons. In the factory a mass or crowd is not a community, because the individuality of each man is irrelevant. 'In much modern industry each workman is no more than a part of the machine which has not yet been invented; when it is invented, he can go. And outside the works, physically weary and nervously jaded by monotony, he still finds no real community. In the modern big town human beings are jostling atoms, and each must fend for himself.'[31] This concern is also expressed by reference, not to the first two of Temple's four social principles, but to the third, in the form of vocation. It is, he says, a great evil that work is so monotonous and engages so few human faculties. It is hard for a man to find in it any real vocation. True, God's vocation may be to self-sacrifice. But only a perfect saint could perform such tasks 'as unto God' because it was his contribution to human welfare. It is sheer mockery to expect an ordinary man to do so. He cannot therefore worship in any full sense. 'For worship is the offer of our whole being and life – therefore very prominently our work – to God.'[32]

Lastly, Temple perceptively notes the rising position of management in the running of industry and wonders whether they can mediate between capital and labour; for though they are technically employees of directors, representing the shareholders, they do have a natural interest more in the efficiency of processes of production in service to the community than in profit. True, management could become a bureaucracy, and thus be the enemy of responsible citizenship, which is the essence of true democracy. But the dangers can be avoided if managers are not only trained in the workings of the machinery, but even more importantly given the kind of education which will enable them to understand the men themselves. Temple looked for a planned economy, combining control and enterprise, where management would be responsible to the state as much as to directors, and the state would nominate members to the boards of directors, thus giving the consumer a voice through the state.[33]

Temple's comments during the Second World War are clearly personal meditations on his social principles and it is striking how specific are his recommendations. Some, though not all, are in the Appendix to *Christianity and Social Order* and are therefore qualified as being merely suggestions for criticism. But if they were really to deserve to carry weight in public debate, they needed to appeal to careful interdisciplinary investigation, perhaps by the Yorkshire Institute. Yet no such appeal is made. Some critics complained that a false authority was being given: Temple's words would have an unwarranted influence simply because he was an archbishop. Certainly there are problems here about how the Church can most responsibly move beyond principles in the direction of more specific proposals, and in what circumstances, if any, a prominent Christian such as an archbishop should venture as far as Temple. We shall look further into these problems at the end of Chapter 11.

CHAPTER 8

UNEMPLOYMENT

'Unemployment is the testing point of our contemporary civilisation.'[1] We have already seen Temple's censure of the trade unions in 1940 for failing to recognise unemployment as the central issue and to act vigorously. Temple himself showed considerable vigour, especially from the financial crisis of 1931 onwards. Before that his thought lacks any distinction. On the whole Temple has no clear idea about the causes or cure of unemployment, except that the whole issue is very complex. He is valuable chiefly for his recognition of the effects of unemployment in human terms. Unemployment is a 'desperate evil causing widespread misery and degradation of character.' Even when one is in work one suffers from the nightmare of insecurity, and there is no encouragement to practise prudence and thrift. This fear for the morrow is a new form of poverty, rooting man in his own self as effectively as any riches. 'The "poverty" which is spiritually desirable is that which provides a sufficiency for the needs of a real human life, but not enough to mark a man off from his fellow-citizens, and so make difficult the widest fellowship.'[2] Temple thinks the state should provide against unemployment; everyone who is willing to do a full day's work ought to be assured a living wage. There should be an extension of out-of-work insurance.[3] The dictum 'If a man will not work neither shall he eat' is valid as a moral principle, but it should not be the basis for legislation, for a Christian sociology, he says, will lay great stress on the right to property. 'It will desire that every citizen should possess enough property to support bare life even though he does no stroke of work for it; for so his work and service will be more nearly free and personality will have a fuller scope.'[4]

The crisis of 1931 sharpened churchmen's concern over unemployment. Temple responded with an article published in 1932, which is his most connected piece of writing on unemployment and economics.[5] He is more realistic than usual, recognising that circumstances impose a choice between evils. He was deeply dismayed at the necessity of reducing unemployment benefit and social (particularly educational) services. However, financial insecurity was so great that this was the lesser evil, even for the poorest classes themselves. He acknowledged this with the greatest reluctance, for in the nineteenth century 'every possible reform or advance was resisted precisely on the ground that it would spell ruin to those whom it was intended to benefit.' Unemployment was objectionable not so much because it was a burden on industry or a condition deserving sympathy, but because it was demoralizing and a real affront to men's personalities; for it created the sense that they were not wanted. As for a cure (and here Temple is very general), the problem of unemployment was chiefly a selling problem. The view that production would create new purchasing power to make it profitable no longer applied. The market was overstocked; the problem was excessive abundance. It was now no longer profitable for a producer to produce. Because of mechanisation, demand could not keep pace with production. 'The aim of the new school of economic thought' (Temple mentions no names but is probably thinking of J. A. Hobson rather than Keynes[6]) 'is to create demand by distribution of such purchasing power as will set all the nation's productive plant working.' Hitherto we had been preoccupied with making production profitable; the new approach of making produce marketable seemed 'more consonant with Christian principles', because it began not with goods but with people. The whole problem would need international solution, not by a super-state but by mutual agreement; for 'we are members one of another'.

Temple's most notable achievement was his enquiry into the human effects of unemployment. 'I am inclined to think that the enquiry did represent what would have been a new departure in method for him – though the immediate threat of war prevented this from being at all widely employed – viz. the creation of small groups of men to think out the relations of this, that, or the other social problem.'[7] W. H. Oakeshott is here writing of the investigation which culminated in the production of *Men Without Work* in 1938. We have already seen how in 1933 Temple supported the creation of the Yorkshire Institute of Industrial Affairs. In the same year he invited a group of people to consult with him about unemployment. The following January the group issued a manifesto to test and elicit public support; it set out the claims of the unemployed as persons and insisted that only a tiny minority of the unemployed were work-shy.[8] The group also formed a committee, which became convinced of the need for a far more thorough investigation of the work that could be done by voluntary societies for the unemployed, and saw that this would involve an enquiry into the effects of unemployment and the real needs of the unemployed. In 1936 the Pilgrim Trust agreed to finance such an enquiry, and gave responsibility to certain members of the committee, whilst nominating one or two additional members itself. The reconstituted committee included the Bishop of Chichester (Dr. G. K. A. Bell), Sir Walter Moberly, Dr. J. H. Oldham, and Temple as Chairman. They were backed by a team of investigators. Oakeshott himself was given four terms absence from Winchester College to take part.[9]

The significance of this venture for Temple can be gauged by what he himself said in the Introduction to *Men Without Work* and in House of Lords debates, and also by his comments on unemployment in the last ten years of his life. Even if there was a new departure in method, in no sense was there a volte-face. His social principles stand, as does his conviction that there can be no divorce of the economic from the moral and religious sphere. What is new is that he really acts on the insight he had long recognised in theory – that the right thing to do is the right thing in the circumstances – and sets about having the circumstances expertly investigated.

Temple's delight with *Men Without Work* is expressed in these words: 'It is a genuinely human document, which being readable as well as scientific, may well win the attention of a large public.'[10] The document was certainly scientific. The team included specialists: an expert in political and economic planning, an economist, and a psychologist who had already taken part in a survey of unemployment on the Continent. It was evident at the outset that they must begin with an exact account of the unemployed themselves. They had to know types of local unemployment and the needs which these create. 'It is impossible to consider the effectiveness of any of the voluntary enterprises without first understanding the situation with which they are faced and the peculiar problems, physical, psychological and moral, to which unemployment gives rise.' The document itself shows the scientific thoroughness of the investigation. It proposes to study 'Who are the unemployed? What kind of men are those who are out of work, and why has the disaster of unemployment overtaken these and not others?' It explains why long unemployment was selected as the focus of study, and why the six areas (Deptford, Leicester, the Rhondda, Crook, Liverpool and Blackburn) were chosen. It gives the rationale for the sampling, and shows how and why selection and chance are both operative. It publishes the case record card and a large number of statistical tables. It carefully distinguishes between and within the physical, psychological and moral problem, and looks specially in turn at the wage problem, and at the particular predicament of the older men, the younger men, and unemployed women. The last part relates these findings to the contemporary Social Service Movement, estimating its effectiveness with close attention to local characteristics.[11]

The document is 'human', not simply in the sense that it deals with voluntary bodies whose emphasis is on a personal approach to the unemployed. The report itself also 'represents a new approach to the problems created by unemployment, and one which I am persuaded gets much closer to the real difficulties than a purely economic approach could have done.' For, says Temple, the report exposes an intolerable human situation. 'Because the issues raised are largely personal, they are easily understood. We can deal with them from a personal as well as an administrative point of view ...'[12]

The very method of investigation brought this personal dimension to the fore. Out of 1,086 persons in the complete sample, 880 were visited in their homes. The case record card had space for the interviewer to record more personal details: the atmosphere of the family, the man's attitudes, his relations with the local social institutions. In this way it was possible to form a picture of the effects of unemployment on the ordinary man. The influence of subjective factors was recognised, but it was believed that these personal aspects, even if they could not be measured or stated in terms of figures, were important if a real analysis of the needs was to be made.[13]

The report must have confirmed Temple in his belief that unemployment is complex in its causes and ramifications and that the psychological and moral effects are of paramount importance. As early as March 1934 Temple urged fellow-Christians who paid income tax to let the government know that, if taxation could be reduced, the restoration of the cuts in allowances for the unemployed should take precedence over any other concessions, including remission of income tax. Since people were no longer obliged to spend all their time and energy securing subsistence, the long-term aim should be a redistribution of working hours, so that unemployment did not fall unfairly on one section of the community. Till then we should make sure that two and a half million people were not prevented by malnutrition and depression from engaging in creative activities; National Insurance was never intended to provide subsistence for victims of an industrial slump. However, Neville Chamberlain, the Chancellor of the Exchequer, was not impressed by this 'interference'.[14]

The influence upon Temple of the Committee's work is evident in two directions in 1935: 'I don't think I ever appreciated, until I looked into this question of unemployment in England, how deeply penetrating are our Lord's words that it is more blessed to give than to receive. So long as the work undertaken consists of doing things for the unemployed it is quite unredemptive and leads to no restoration of character. The only experiments, now I am glad to say very numerous in England and rapidly spreading, which show that effect on character, are those which invite the unemployed to give what they can for the community ... The unemployed have no money to give, but they have themselves to give.'[15] Temple here cites the case of a co-operative scheme which had benefited the whole community. In the report itself there is a fairly full account and assessment of the Wigan Subsistence Production Society and the Lincoln People's Service Club. The former made a frontal attack on poverty by producing goods and aimed to restore fellowship in work; the latter tried to restore people to their function in the community by arranging jobs for them which the community needed. Iremonger records that 1500 occupational centres were started in the period between January 1938 and September 1939.[16]

Temple makes the same point more pungently in *Christianity and Social Order*. The worst evil is that the unemployed feel they have fallen out of the common life. Worse than physical need is the fact that they are not wanted. That has the power to corrupt anyone not already far advanced in saintliness. He has no opportunity for service and is turned in upon himself, to be a contented loafer or an embittered self-seeker. The only answer to moral isolation is for a man to do something needed by the community. 'For it is part of the principle of personality that we should live for one another.' The only long-term answer to futility and frustration is that we find a social order which provides employment steadily and generally. Christian sympathy demands this. Clearly Temple is appealing here to the social principles of fellowship and service, and his position is reminiscent of his strictures on charity and his emphasis on freedom and responsibility. In the Appendix to *Christianity and Social Order* Temple tentatively advocates that the 'State should maintain a certain number of works beneficial to the community, from which private enterprise should be excluded, which it would expand or contract according to the general demand for labour at the time. Such works would include prevention of coast-erosion, afforestation, new roads and the like.' Training centres should be established on a large scale. We may infer that, however great the contribution of voluntary bodies, Temple thought state provision was essential, should unemployment come anywhere near the pre-war level.[17]

The second effect of the report was to persuade Temple to call for financial support in the form of family allowances. This, he said, was the only proposal strongly advocated in *Men Without Work*. In 1939 he spoke in a House of Lords debate on population problems. He deplored the prevailing system whereby a man with a large family could receive more money on the dole than at work. Only family allowances, short of a profound modification of the entire economic system, could have the effect both of encouraging the birth of future citizens and of discouraging their parents from choosing to be unemployed.[18]

Three years later, less than a month after his introduction into the Lords as Archbishop of Canterbury, Temple took his reasoning further in a debate on family allowances. If people were in effect encouraged to be unemployed, that would be as unacceptable as its opposite, the principle of less eligibility in the Poor Law Act of 1834. He argued that by family allowances relief could be given to the worst types of poverty – 'and none of us, I imagine, would wish to say that the people should be held in any way guilty for what they are suffering.' He believed payment should be made to the mother, principally as a recognition of her self-sacrificing care for the family. He raised the question of cost but disclaimed special competence to discuss it. Nonetheless, he was sure it would be all a matter of internal adjustment, the wiser distribution of wealth; and in the circulation of resources all would be spent on necessities, on those goods which create the largest amount of employment in their production. It would therefore be investment rather than expenditure. Therefore we could certainly afford it. Once again, however, the principle of justice was more important to Temple than economics. Not only parents but the state too is rightly concerned with the care of children; it should therefore take its share of the burden. Temple knows that some people fear the erosion of parental responsibility and family affection. But Temple asserts that family allowances will actually strengthen family life, for they will relieve intolerable strains and anxieties. 'There is an appeal for sympathy, but it is more than an appeal for sympathy. It is, I think, a real appeal to justice on which the case for Family Allowances must rest.'[19]

Men Without Work was not concerned with the wider causes of unemployment. Temple cannot resist making suggestions, but there is no detailed analysis. There is no more connected exploration than the article of April 1932, but Temple suspected a link between unemployment and economics on an international scale. Indeed his concentration on the economic system in his closing years was to earn him a measure of notoriety.

CHAPTER 9

ECONOMICS

1. *Basic convictions and diagnoses*

Temple was convinced for the whole of his working life that economics cannot be divorced from ethics and religion. His Malvern Conference of January 1941 was a conscious effort 'to cancel the divorce between theology and economics which was silently decreed in the latter part of the fifteenth century ...' One conviction of the Conference, as we saw earlier, was that there is a divinely appointed order or hierarchy of human activities and functions. Economics is a means, which must be pursued with the effect (and motive as far as possible) of realising the end – religion, art, science, life itself.[1] Christian principles suggest that the well-being of men and women is more important than maximum economic wealth. Economic methods and structures must be tested on economic grounds for their efficiency, as must any improvement of them proposed on humanitarian grounds. But we must also ask: 'Does this economic method or structure either help or hinder the development of persons in community?' Human sin has created an order which makes the economic life supreme, and once created it perpetuates and intensifies the sin of self-interest from which it sprang. It disintegrates society: men are used for efficient output irrespective of social ties and traditional roots. 'And if we plan only for prosperity and comfort we may create a society which is comfortable, contented and spiritually dead.'[2] Governments should not become preoccupied with economic considerations. Temple agrees that capitalism 'has certainly given to the mass of the people a higher standard of life – a larger enjoyment of material goods – than any previous system. Moreover, it seems nearly certain that no other system would have developed so rapidly or so far the new powers conferred by modern science.' However, according to natural law or natural order the economic process is not an end in itself; and even if a system delivers the goods, it may still be condemned on moral grounds because it intensifies divisions and hostilities and is a source of wrong personal relationships.[3]

Temple naturally refers to the classical exponents of the free market economy, especially Adam Smith. Its so-called laws, he said, are neither divine decrees nor axioms. They are generalisations from experience, and therefore hypotheses. Approving of John Ruskin's attack on *laissez-faire* in *Unto this Last*, Temple says that theorists assumed self-interest as the only relevant motive. 'They not only set forth the laws which (in the main) the commercial world of their day was following; but they made conformity with these expressions of greed into a system of ethics.' True, some economic principles stand firm: the impossibility of permanently carrying on any business at a loss, or of distributing goods which have not been produced; but they are few. True, there is plenty of selfishness in the world. 'The economists were not so very far wrong . . . in their reading of the facts. Their disastrous error was the assumption that those facts were unalterable.'[4] Among modern political economists Temple accepts Marshall's dictum that the two greatest influences moulding character are religion and the economic structure of society. For Temple the task of the Church is to lay down what Christian morality requires, without discussing the exact political or economic adjustments by which it is to be secured. It must rebuke any confusion of means with ends, and try to restore activities to the natural order which is God's purpose for them.[5]

A purely or predominantly competitive system, says Temple, cannot be regarded as neutral. Competition pervades the whole of our life; it is simply organised selfishness. 'A great deal has been said in praise of competition, and most of it is rubbish. It is said, for example, that you must not interfere with natural processes; you must let the cream come to the top. But the scum comes to the top quite as much as the cream.'[6] Actually, the chief means by which the species succeeds, even in the competitive struggle, is by being co-operative; and in history we see that selfish purposes do fail. Temple was not wholly opposed to competition. He could see that appeal to the self-regarding motive could yield results. It is good if a man has to stand on his own feet in a world of fierce competition. But it is bad if he has to fight for his own interests to avoid submersion. Historically the trend since the Renaissance has led to headlong individualism and a widespread belief in the moral, social and political value of unfettered competition. The result has been economic anarchy, and wage slavery for the majority. In reaction, value has been seen in the whole society alone, as in Communism and Fascism. 'If we are to preserve and develop freedom it must be by maintaining a true balance between the two elements [individual and community] in the divine purpose . . .'[7]

By 1940 Temple had developed a general interpretation of the economic system. It owed much to the diagnoses of Major C. H. Douglas and the Christendom Group, though Temple was much more wary than they were over Douglas's ideas on social credit. Deeply suspicious of the profit-motive, he believed industry and economics largely rested upon it. Contrasting this with the service-motive, he asserted that finance controlled production. This was an inversion of the natural order, in which finance properly serves production and production exists for consumption. Not that there is anything wrong about profits as such: 'It has always been recognised that both the producer and the trader are entitled to a profit as their own means of livelihood, which they have earned by their service to the community. Further, there can be no profit except so far as the needs of consumers are being met. But it is possible nonetheless for these two to get into the wrong order, so that the consumer is treated, not as the person whose interest is the true end of the whole process, but only as an indispensable condition of success in an essentially profit-seeking enterprise.'[8]

But if there is no profit unless consumer needs are met, how can the system go awry? 'Science has enabled us to produce wealth in wholly unexampled abundance, but our organisation of life is based on the expectation of expanding the markets to absorb expanding production; and the markets do not any longer expand in that degree. So it happens that the ease with which we produce becomes a reason for not producing at all, because the markets are glutted, though human need is not satisfied. Under existing conditions we can only solve the paradox of poverty in the midst of plenty by abolishing the plenty!' Food is destroyed while men are hungry, because they do not have the means to make their need constitute a market. Worse than that, the economic system 'contains the seeds of war, because it relies so largely on the profit-motive, with which love of power is closely bound up.' Few businesses profit by war, and most industrialists desire peace. But they also desire what tends to destroy peace, so the system leads to international rivalry, jealousy and conflict, if not open war.[9]

Though production exists for consumption, this does not mean, says Temple, that producers exist for consumers. It is people who produce, and they should not be thrown out of work or denied the opportunity to realise their personality in fellowship in the process of production. What is wanted is the whole view, and that, Temple acknowledges, is very difficult to consider.[10]

Such is Temple's critique of the free market economy. Insofar as that economy is an ideology, Temple is right to expose it as defective in the light of human psychology and ethics. Where Temple is weak is in his supposition that the laws of economics are generalisations from experience. Economic theories are basically models constructed by human imagination as tools of exploration. Temple apparently did not appreciate this.

2. *Remedies*

In his reflections about economic remedies Temple had much to say about the domestic role of the state in relation to the economy. Already in the First World War Temple had noted without demur the increased role of the state. In 1943 he wrote: 'It is quite true that every kind of planning involves the diminution of some liberties; but the chief enemy of freedom to-day is not an intelligent plan but the irresistible pressure of blind forces. We must gain control of those forces, and that involves planning ... We must plan for freedom, for the exercise of responsible citizenship in real community.'[11] Temple rejected Sir Richard Acland's proposal of universal communal ownership. That would create an immense bureaucracy, 'and human egoism would find its outlet in laying hold of the levers of the bureaucratic machine.'[12] Communism and State Socialism are rejected, for they 'ignore the fact that a man is still a human being in his activity as a producer and not only as a consumer; he ought to have free play for his personality, as far as may be, in the act of production – and this is the root-truth of individualistic capitalism. Our task must be to do justice as far as possible to the truth of capitalism, as well as to the truth of socialism.' Temple welcomes the proposals of the recent Uthwatt Report, aimed at combining the advantages of public ownership and ultimate control with private initiative, and says that its proposals should not be whittled down by concessions to vested interests. We could not expect men to be guided by motives of service, but we could so organise life that self-interest prompted those actions which were of the greatest social service. The right of ownership was one of administration, not of exclusive use; public interest should be secured against private depredations. This particularly applied to primary requisites of life – but that did not necessarily mean national ownership.[13]

This brings us to the most specific of all Temple's suggestions. They must be read both in the light of his broad principles and also in the light of his disclaimers: 'I offer these proposals not as dogmas but as matter for discussion and as indications of a spirit rather than as a definite policy. It may be that there are other and better ways of attaining our object.' 'I do not ask you to believe anything I say about credit; but I do ask you to think about it.' 'I think it most improbable that every Christian should endorse what I now go on to say.' Temple felt the necessity to be more specific than he had been in the body of *Christianity and Social Order*, and both Keynes and Tawney supported the inclusion of the Appendix.[14]

First, there is the matter of land. Temple goes back to the Law of Moses, where the purchase of land in perpetuity is forbidden, since the land belongs to God and is granted to His people for their use. This is in accordance with the principle of maximum personal freedom but no exploitation (in this case the formation of large estates at others' expense). Applying the principle to England, he says landowners hold not absolute dominion but the use of the land subject to public interest. The critical question is whether the owner discharges a social function. In Temple's view the rural landlord does, and 'as family tradition in this field is a valuable social asset I should personally urge the total exemption of all agricultural land from death duties.' He believes the present system leaves the private landlord in possession but makes it impossible for him to discharge his social responsibility. Land nationalisation, whatever some socialists might say, is no answer for Temple. It is the urban ground landlords whom Temple would like to see eliminated, because they perform little social function. He would not support mere confiscation but would cripple them with drastic death duties, and forbid the sale of urban land except to the public authority. He would also prevent a landlord deriving private profit from the additional value land may acquire through the enterprise of others or through communal activity. He passes on the suggestion of a general valuation of all land, which would place a ceiling on the sale price or the rent as a percentage unless the landlord had increased the value by his own action. Tax should in any case be levied on land, not buildings. It was absurd that tax should be decreased for a landlord who had neglected his property, and increased if he improved it.[15]

Temple is even more severe with the ordinary shareholder; his social function does not exist. Temple favours the application to shares of the ancient Law of Jubilee, whereby once every fifty years the original equal distribution of land in Israel was to be restored. 'It can be done in any one of three ways or by a combination of these: shares may take the form of debentures and be repayable at a certain date; or invested capital after bearing interest for a number of years may lose a proportion of its value each year until it is extinguished; or the inheritance of it may be curtailed by drastic death duties.' The basic purpose was that 'no-one by investing capital alone can become possessed of a permanent and saleable right to levy a tax upon the enterprise in which he invests his money together with a voice in the control of it. Thus the grip of profit-seeking capital upon indusry will be loosened.'[16] The type of enterprise, the degree of risk, delay in returns upon outlay, and similar factors, must be taken into account in determining the maximum profits, the period during which the capital sum remains intact, the rate of interest, and the rate of decrease after that period. Interest should be related to the service rendered, not to the relative strength and weakness of the parties to the transaction.

Social justice, Temple claims, requires that limitation of liability should carry with it limitation of profits. The early Christian Socialists advocated this, and the world would have been saved much evil had their warnings been heeded. Surplus profits should be allocated to: an equalisation fund for the maintenance of wages in bad times, even though hours of work be reduced; a similar fund for the maintenance of interest to shareholders at a specified minimum; a sinking fund for the repayment of invested capital; a fund for the extension of fixed capital; and a public service fund, to be administered as a rule by representatives of the workers (including management) and of the national, state or local authority.[17]

Turning to the banks, Temple acknowledged with gratitude the stability of the banking system and the ability and integrity with which it was administered. Nonetheless he believed that it was unjustifiable in modern conditions for the banks, even the Bank of England, to meet national needs by creating credit which earned interest for themselves. The state must resume the right to control the issue and cancellation of every kind of money. It was a false principle for a body within the community to control what was vital to the welfare of the community. Any monopoly in a universal necessity like credit should be taken under public control. In May 1940 Temple favoured nationalisation of the Bank of England and the Joint Stock Banks; later in *Christianity and Social Order* he preferred public utility corporations to state ownership and operation. As a corollary, Temple viewed with profound mistrust a proposal for a World Bank designed to control the credit of the world. It would be an enormous instance of irresponsible power, which was always an evil. For it would plainly be a long time before there was anything like a World Government, to which it could be responsible. In any case the scheme for a World Bank seemed to assume absolute fluidity of labour, which would be inhuman.[18]

Temple's thinking is an attempt to apply to modern conditions the doctrine of the prohibition of usury, found in the Old Testament, Aristotle, and persistently in Christian history. The principle behind it, says Temple, is that money is a medium of exchange; those who handle it should be remunerated for their integrity and honesty in dealing with it, but should not be able to manipulate it to create new values which do not correspond to any useful services to the community. Speculation in foreign currency was Temple's prime example. Theological moralists would also have been 'very shy' of systems of mortgaging, he said in 1943, even if this was the only way in which quite necessary security was obtainable. Just a week later Temple explained in reply to the Director of the Banking Information Service that his anxiety about mortgaging lay in the risk of exploitation of the weaker by the stronger, and the danger of property being mortgaged for personal purposes when public interest would be jeopardised. He also acknowledged difficulty in the application of the doctrine, but suggested an important distinction was between loans for objects that involved some risk, and loans where the principal was secure; in the latter case there was no proper partnership in the enterprise, and there should be a limitation upon the return.[19]

The other doctrine to which Temple appeals is that of the just price. The principle, stated in past ages 'as part of a complete theology', was that 'the price of an article should be fixed on moral grounds with due regard to cost of material and labour and to reasonable profit; the vendor is not entitled merely to ask the utmost that the purchaser will pay. Above all, he must on no account charge more because the buyer's need is great.' In the Middle Ages 'reasonable profit' was estimated with regard to 'the current habit of society and the kind of position that society was expecting you to maintain.' Calculation was easier because society had a fairly rigid structure. Whatever the gains of a later shift to a society on a contractual basis, the nineteenth century acceptance of the law of supply and demand was totally at variance with the doctrine of the just price. Temple favoured a recovery of that doctrine in the interests of human fellowship and the richness of human personality.[20]

Temple seems here to have deserted the corporate approach of the Yorkshire Institute and the Pilgrim Trust enquiry, and indulged again in personal reflections, whereby both diagnosis and remedy are arrived at primarily by moral considerations. He received much criticism for his views, and we shall look at the best in Chapter 11. First, however, we shall follow up Temple's references to natural order and natural law. What was Temple's own estimate of this approach? What critiques have been made of it since his day? In what form, if any, is natural order or natural law a valuable approach for us today in our search for an adequate Christian social ethic?

CHAPTER 10

NATURAL LAW

Natural law has been condemned as profound theological error, and stigmatized as an empty formula. It has a long history going back to pre-Christian times, and even an eminent supporter has ruefully confessed that it was a notion laden with ambiguity even in the days when it was considered self-evident.[1] Any definition of natural law can therefore only be expressed in broad terms, but we shall not be far out if we say that it articulates the conviction that human life has a fundamental structure, which has been implanted by God as Creator, and which is apprehensible to human reason both as something given and as an obligation upon us. There is therefore a proper ordering of human life (hence the interchangeable phrase 'natural order'), to which human thought and human laws should attend and conform. Conflict has raged in theological circles over the legitimacy of natural law in the light of revelation. Natural law has also been severely criticized for its imprecision – and also when it has received more precise articulation, as for example by St. Thomas Aquinas.

We could then simply dismiss Temple's use of natural law in economics, and his hopes for joint Roman-Anglican study of natural law and for the rebirth of Christendom. It is better however to take up his own suggestion of a critique and modification of natural law. Not only did Temple and his Christendom Group friends engage with natural law as part of an important search for deeper foundations in the face of world crisis; at the same time many Catholics on the Continent found in natural law a practical defence of the person against totalitarianism. Heinrich Rommen, for example, was a German layman trained in the law who resisted Hitler with traditional Thomist natural law. He conveys both its solidity and its scope in his book *The Natural Law* (English version 1947): a theory of knowledge, an understanding of persons, state and law, as well as more specific normative content. Meanwhile the French Catholic philosopher Jacques Maritain, in such books as *True Humanism* (1938), *Scholasticism and Politics* (1940), and *The Rights of Man* (1944), was developing Thomist thought in order to respond more adequately to the pressures and insights of the modern world.

The period from 1945 onwards demonstrates the persistence of at least natural law assumptions. In the Nuremberg trials the prosecution could prevail against the Nazi war criminals' plea of 'not guilty' only on the assumption that there are norms binding upon men as men which transcend the laws of the state. In many countries, including the Federal Republic of Germany, the constitution acknowledges the dignity of the person prior to the state and its laws. In the theological world Protestants, with varying degrees of reserve about natural law, are now much more hospitable at least to ideas of natural morality, that is, morality based on reason. They concede that abuse – even of natural law – is no final bar to use. In Britain Ian T. Ramsey and John Macquarrie have sketched a rehabilitation or reformulation of natural law. Most importantly Roman Catholic theologians, inspired by the Second Vatican Council (1962–65), have undertaken a thorough reappraisal of natural law. The recurrent phrase 'the new humanism' symbolises a radical recasting which nonetheless stands in a definite continuity with the traditional natural law. A good example of a Catholic rehabilitation of natural law, which pays close attention to human needs as a basis for ethics, is by the Jesuit philosopher Gerard J. Hughes in *Authority in Morals*.

Although therefore it is true that natural law is of minor importance in Temple's thought compared with his principles, it cannot be readily written off and may yet have an important place in a radically revised form in any truly ecumenical social ethics. As a first step we can look more precisely at Temple's positive evaluation of natural law. For clarity's sake we should note that Temple makes no explicit distinction between 'natural order' and 'natural law'. Yet his preference is for 'natural order'; 'natural law' appears only in conjunction with 'natural order'. This presumably reflects his concern for social structures, and perhaps an awareness of some of the problems inherent in 'natural law'. We shall consider first not only his explicit remarks on natural law but also its affinities with his Christian philosophy, which helped to make it congenial. Here the conclusion will be that at a general level Temple was right in his commendations, but beneath the surface natural law appears a dubious ally. The dubiousness, it must be stressed, lies not so much in the thought of Aquinas himself as in some of its development by his successors, which had become traditional in the Roman Catholic Church. This will lead to the second step: the criticisms of natural law, starting with Temple's own, and the reappraisal.

1. By 1939 Temple was asking two crucial questions: Is there a natural order? If so, what is its relation to the order of redemption? The figure of Karl Barth loomed over Temple and the Christendom Group. When Donald MacKinnon described himself as a Barthian-scholastic he knew the difficulties of holding the two terms together. By 1942 Barth was writing that the divine grace brought the refutation, conquest and destruction of all human answers to the ethical problem.[2] In *Nature, Man and God* Temple had, as we saw, welcomed Barth's insistence on the impassable distinction of Creator and creature, Redeemer and redeemed; but it was wanton to deny moral progress, and fanatical to reject the idea that revelation must in the long run satisfy reason and conscience. He told the Aquinas Society in 1943 that the Bible is indeed the record of a vertical thrust of the Word of God into the horizontal process of history, but it 'is none the less itself the prophetic record and interpretation of that process regarded as the arena where a divine purpose is being fulfilled and divine judgements are manifest in the operation of causal laws.'[3] He comes down firmly on the side of natural theology. No synthesis was possible here between Catholicism and continental Protestantism, and Temple was certainly not prepared to abandon at a stroke all confidence in reason, and so his whole Christian philosophy!

Temple was quite right, and the theological history of the last fifty years confirms his good sense. First and foremost the Catholic Church of the Vatican II era has endorsed a positive attitude to human reason. Moreover, John Macquarrie has appealed to the Christian conviction that the image of God is not totally extinguished by the fall; indeed, if it were, our very consciousness of sin would be impossible. No doubt, he writes, the Christian finds his idea of authentic humanity enlarged, corrected and perhaps even revolutionised by the concrete humanity of Christ; yet unless he had some such idea it is hard to see how Christ could ever become Christ for him.[4] Among Protestants this same point is made by the Scottish theologian N. H. G. Robinson. He conducts a very thorough investigation of neo-Protestantism before concluding that we cannot dispense with the idea of a natural morality. Men are moral beings apart from revelation; the Bible itself (e.g. St. Paul in Romans 2.14ff.) agrees. The doctrine of the image of God implies that man always stands in the presence of his Creator, and the symptom of this is the elusive challenge of his moral consciousness. Even though the Christian is in some sense a new creature, he is basically a man transformed or renewed, and that presupposes an understanding of his existence as a creature independent of that renewal. Redemption is not just a second instalment of creation. True, goodness is entirely dependent on God, but we should think in terms of a general knowledge of goodness apart from and prior to God's remedial revelation.[5] Temple, Macquarrie and Robinson all agree that natural morality can form a bridge between Christian and non-Christian, enabling them to make moral contact with each other, to communicate and co-operate. This conviction that it is possible, if at times hard, to find common ground on the basis of rational discussion, is of vital importance, both in a pluralistic world where hard-line ideologists deny it, and in a Church tempted to fall back on unreflective appeals to the authority of Scripture.

What then is the relation of natural morality to the order of redemption, of reason to revelation? As we have seen, Temple's own philosophy was ambiguous. The Malvern Conference failed to find an answer. Though it said much about natural order, it seemed really to be deducing a Christian sociology from Christian dogmas. In fact traditional Thomism sharply distinguished nature and supernature. Natural order belonged to the lower of two tiers which, though both were oriented towards God, stood in a relationship of external juxtaposition. No-one responding to Karl Barth's demand for a Christocentric ethics could rest content with such a scheme, least of all when they knew that Barth believed a similar juxtaposition in the Lutherans' doctrine of two kingdoms (the religious and the political) was a major source of their inability to stand up to Hitler. Thomism was indeed an ally in the defence of natural morality, but a poor one in the quest for an adequate relation of natural morality to the order of redemption. At this point Thomism needed to undergo radical modification. Temple's own Christian philosophy, though ambiguous and too inclined to syntheses, at least avoided a two-tiered scheme, and in its strong sacramentalism offered a better prospect for the resolution of a difficult problem. Indeed, as we shall see, his own criticisms of natural law open up the difficulties which his more general commendations gloss over.

2. Temple and the natural law tradition also agreed in general terms on how our natural knowledge is acquired. Though their theories of knowledge differ in articulation, they both are realists, holding that the mind deals primarily not with sense data but with actual objects in the world. They also agree that we apprehend value objectively present in the world, however much we may subjectively qualify, shape or supplement it. Fact and value are given together.

Once again Temple was basically right. In his search for a new synthesis of the mediaeval and the modern eras his 'believing mind' may indeed have betrayed him into an unfair treatment of Descartes and too many concessions to the pre-Cartesian world. However, Temple is justified in appealing to a science-based philosophy for his main points, and his analyses of our experience of beauty and goodness ring true. It is a pity that Temple did not respond in print to the emotivist account of ethics given in A. J. Ayer's *Language, Truth and Logic* (1936), which reduces ethical statements to expressions of the emotions. However we can draw on Keith Ward's astute defence of objectivity in morals in his *Ethics and Christianity* (1970). Against emotivists (and the later prescriptivists, like R. M. Hare), he argues on the basis of our moral experience that we do hold there is a moral truth to be found which claims our whole being, and that this moral truth is not reducible to empirical facts, but points to a metaphysical understanding of reality. Such an objectivist reading is vital not just for Christian ethics, but for ethics in general; and the emotivist and prescriptivist cannot do justice to the moral facts.[6]

Once again, however, natural law was a dubious ally. The problem lies in what the values are and how readily they are apprehended. Thomism follows Aristotle in distinguishing in an object between particulars and the essence. Particulars are grasped by the senses; the intellect then abstracts from sense data to grasp the essence. It is the unchanging essence which is of central importance to Thomism, and it embraces both what an object really *is* and what it *ought* to become.[7] This predisposes Thomists to think in terms of unchanging moral absolutes, and to suppose that human reason can with certainty abstract from particulars and read off the absolutes from nature. There is of course a superficial attractiveness about such moral certainties. Perhaps Temple felt this at a time when he longed for a Christian ethic strong enough to stand up to Fascism and Communism. He himself certainly sounded scholastic when he declared that to consider the natural order was to consider 'the various departments of life in the light of the essential function of each.'[8] Yet the Thomist scheme at this point too was far less able to meet the challenges of the twentieth century than Temple's Christian philosophy; and each of Temple's own criticisms of natural law will only underline the need for a drastic reappraisal of Thomism.

3. Temple and Thomist natural law agreed also on the primacy of persons. Addressing the Aquinas Society in 1943 Temple commended St. Thomas's perception, taken over from St. Augustine, that the troubles of the world stemmed from the confusion of means and ends. For Temple the true ends of life are 'religion, art, science, and above all, happy human relationships.' The only real progress 'is in the development of personality in fellowship.'[9]

Temple, Rommen and Maritain also broadly agree in their understanding of persons. Just as Temple expresses in his first three social principles the importance of individuality, fellowship and service, so Rommen stresses the dignity of the individual, his inherent sociality, and his need always to consult the common good.[10] There is a particular affinity between Temple and Maritain, for both were keen to take account of the accent on individuality in the modern world, whilst rebutting individualism. Maritain, like Temple, asserts that man, being in the image of God, has a dignity anterior to society. If however in this sense he is a 'whole', he is an 'open whole', in that he has a capacity for love and a need of material, cultural and moral goods which can only be fulfilled in society. In this sense he is a part of the whole political community and exists with a view to the common good. Yet the common good must never be abstracted from the 'wholes', but flow back to them and aid their development. Maritain thus characterises a society of free men as both 'personalist' and 'communal'.[11]

It is this basic understanding of persons which lies behind Temple's remarks about the economic process or the prohibition of usury or the just price. Money is a means, persons are an end. Exploitation is a sign of the confusion of ends and means. The same is true of any form of property. Temple approves of St. Thomas's defence and limitation of the rights of property, 'a most wholesome doctrine much needed in our day, avoiding as it does the unsocial outlook of the individualist and the socialist's check upon initiative.' All that is needed is adjustment of St. Thomas to modern conditions.[12]

It is very important to notice that agreement on the meaning of persons also promoted agreement on the state and the law. Rommen offers a positive justification for the state. It is not just a dyke against anarchy. It arises naturally from the needs of the person and has the positive function of promoting the common good, or, as Maritain puts it, the freedom and friendship of persons. This very justification of the state entails also its limits: the eternal destiny of persons gives them natural rights in relation to the state. The Catholic doctrine of subsidiarity, publicised especially by Pope Pius XI in *Quadragesimo Anno* (1931), asserts the importance of the natural groupings of people and forbids the state to arrogate their functions to itself. The first duty of the state is to recognise these rights and groupings, and then to protect and promote them.[13] Furthermore, legislation is not primarily an act of coercive will; it is a rational matter, to be framed with a view to the common good.[14] Temple's own views can easily be read in *Christianity and the State* (1928), *Christian Democracy* (1937), and *Citizen and Churchman* (1941). He too grounds the state not in the sin of man but in his social nature. He agrees with Aristotle that though the state emerged to preserve life, it continues in order to promote the good life. It trains people for citizenship. Its limitations are also rooted in the nature of persons. The state exists for man, not man for the state; a person has an eternal destiny, whereas the state does not. He strongly supports lesser groupings against an omnicompetent state, and asserts the ultimate authority of God over the state.[15] Similarly the authority of any law is not the state which enacts it but its own justice, rooted in the righteousness of God. It is only for the maintenance of such laws that coercion is entrusted to the state. In international relations Temple implies the existence of an unwritten law (*ius gentium*) as a criterion; and when he speaks of subjecting force to the law which should be the expression of the highest welfare of mankind at large, and must be continually revised to that end, he plainly means something like natural law acting as a critical norm of international law.[16]

These broad concepts of person, state and law are extremely valuable. In the first place some basic understanding of persons is indispensable for social ethics. As V. A. Demant so rightly pointed out in the 1930s, it is fatal to embrace an ethical idealism which is detached from the basic presuppositions people have about themselves and their place in the world. Reinhold Niebuhr in the same period attacked idealistic apostles of love who ignored the realities of men and their communities. The co-ordinates of personality offered by Temple and natural law are not sufficient in themselves, but they are necessary. They are certainly an effective defence against extreme versions of individualism and collectivism. The concepts of person, state and law were durable weapons in the resistance to the Nazis. They are equally important against the darker side of Communism, since they stress the dignity of each individual person, the importance of natural groupings independent of the state, and the basic rationality of politics. To use J. L. Lucas's terminology, natural law enshrines 'principles of constitutional criticism' against doctrines of unlimited sovereignty and the elevation of mere legality into an abstract principle.[17]

The disadvantage of Thomist natural law as an ally in this area lay not so much in the theory as in the practical record of the Roman Catholic Church. The history of the hundred years before Temple's overtures reveals that several popes pursued a retrograde policy of aggressive authoritarianism. For the loss of the Papal States to the growing republic of Italy Pope Pius IX (1846–1878) compensated with a strong emphasis on papal authority in the sphere of the Church's life, and especially its dogma. Under his successor Leo XIII (1878–1902) this broadened into a determined attempt to regain for the Church the cultural guardianship of the world. His encyclical *Rerum Novarum* on the condition of the working classes (1891), which Temple praises, should be read critically in the light of this policy. Though sympathetic to the oppressed working man, Leo plainly detested continental socialism and feared democracy. To ward off these ideological demons he maintained that only the Church, the true interpreter of the natural law, could safeguard human dignity. Moreover, to counter diversity of opinion within the Church and bolster his 'grand design', as he called it, Leo decreed that only Thomism was to be taught in Catholic seminaries. *Rerum Novarum* itself did encourage some progressive schemes of Catholic social action, but these were later asphyxiated by clerical authoritarianism. This bid for papal direction of social affairs was continued, for example, by Pius XI (1922–1939) in his enthusiasm for the refurbishing of the guilds of the Middle Ages, in the concordats of Church and state, and in his support of Franco in Spain.[18]

Temple largely suppressed these problems when he wrote about natural law – an index no doubt of his ecumenical generosity, his instinct for the greatest possible agreement with others, and his preference for the world of ideas to the passions and policies of historical men. In *Christianity and Social Order* he writes in praise of natural law for holding together the ideal and the practical. Negatively he is ruling out two positions: utopianism ('either we start from a purely ideal conception, and then we bleat fatuously about love') and pure pragmatism ('or else we start from the world as it is with the hope of remedying an abuse here and there, and then we have no general direction or criterion of progress'). Natural law insists rightly on the primacy of persons. But it is also true, says Temple, that 'a *conditio sine qua non* is more indispensable to an undertaking than its goal.' The economic is more indispensable than the cultural; if men starve they can neither write poetry nor enjoy it. In a similar way freedom is finer than order; but order is more indispensable. Because natural law insists that we see the activities of men in concrete societies in the light of their proper social function, Temple believes it offers a wise *via media* between the conservative temperament which tends to dwell on what is indispensable, and the radical which dwells on the higher ends of life. It enables men to grasp the vital importance of safeguarding what is indispensable while reaching out towards higher ends.[19] All this surely tells us a good deal about Temple's wrestling with the problem of the ideal and the practical (visible especially in his switch from ideals to principles in 1923) and something about Aquinas' handling of the same problem. However, if we go by the practice of the Roman Church, Temple is generous to a fault. What was required on their side was a sharp break with the past and a radically new atmosphere. This is exactly what happened in the Second Vatican Council.

We turn now to criticisms of natural law. John Courtney Murray once remarked that critics of natural law are for ever burying the wrong corpse. To avoid wrong corpses we shall confine ourselves to three criticisms which at least are valid against influential tendencies within the tradition up to Vatican II. In each case Roman Catholic theologians loyal to the spirit of Vatican II are making an impressive radical reappraisal of their tradition. We shall note one area of weakness in Vatican II theology which has a particular relevance for the future of social ethics.

1. Temple criticises the Thomist scheme of static essences and changing particulars, in that it cannot do justice to the understanding of the world which science has brought us. Our experience is of process; our thinking is historical in method. The scholastic approach is mathematical, and its very precision and indifference to time are defects. We cannot set aside the facts of experience simply because they do not fit in with this ideal. We must not sharply separate being and becoming. Our task is not to escape into a timeless realm of static truth, beauty and goodness, but to live fully within the historical process in which we and those realities have actual being.[20] Plainly Temple's plea, consistent with the dialectical method, is for a much more experiential approach to knowledge.

The doctrine of essences, says Temple, is particularly ill-equipped to cope with such a kind as mankind. 'To me it often seems as if St. Thomas is speaking of the human genus without due recognition of the fact that one characteristic of this genus, differentiating it from all others, is the high degree of individuality discoverable in the specimens – a degree so high as to make the particularity of each as fully constitutive of his essence as the generic quality.' With this defect Temple associates two more. First, Thomism gives priority to knowledge as distinct from love; the inadequate appreciation of individuality leads to an insufficient emphasis on actual personal relations. Secondly, Thomism accepts the view that revelation is given primarily in propositions, whereas for Temple the primary medium of revelation is events. What is revealed is God Himself in action; the Holy Spirit, without overriding individual qualities of the recipient, enables him to appreciate that action. Propositions may be described as 'truths of revelation', but it is the event which is the primary revelation.[21]

Temple's criticisms have been a commonplace in the last half-century. John Macquarrie, for example, in effect develops them by remarking that man does not fit in with nature as if with an immutable order. He can envisage ever new possibilities of using the material of the universe to create new objects and extend his capacities. Furthermore this change is not something external to man. It affects the very models of his self-understanding. In short, the most obvious fact about the world and man is their dynamic character.[22] We should also note how linguistic analysis, in making us more sensitive to category confusions in language, has exposed the unwitting assimilation of the language of natural law to the mathematical or biological, and so opened up the question of what kind of language it actually is.

Some critics of natural law have also appealed, like Temple, to the way God reveals Himself to us. They have stressed the predominantly existential character of Christian decision-making. Central to the Gospel, so the argument runs, is the action of God revealing Himself in passionate loving concern to each individual. He confronts men and women personally in the Person of Jesus Christ. It is their task to recognise the signs of the times. God calls them to decision in and through their particular situation. The Gospel shows us how this man Pilate, how these particular Jewish leaders respond to the challenge of Jesus. The thrust of the Gospel is quite different from natural law with its universals and its casuistry. Indeed it is precisely those who consult their rule-book who miss the significance of Jesus. They cannot fit Jesus into their legal categories and therefore they reject Him. Surely then natural law has far more in common with Jewish legalism than with an authentic response to the Gospel.

Many recent Roman Catholic theologians have responded in an extremely positive way to this kind of criticism. They point with relief to one vital feature of the Second Vatican Council. The era of enforced Thomism is over. 'Contemporary Catholic theology', writes Charles Curran, 'recognises the need for a pluralism of philosophical approaches in the Christian's quest for a better understanding of man and his reality. There is no longer "one Catholic philosophy".' Theologians acknowledge the potent and misleading influence of the Platonic and Aristotelian doctrine of essences, and of the Stoic call to the rational man to fit in with a rational universe. Charles Curran particularly points to the jurist Ulpian (died A.D. 228), who tended to read off absolutes of natural law from the physical and biological processes men share with the animals in abstraction from the whole person. Here we encounter a two-tier account of the person: a self-contained bottom layer of animality related only externally to the top layer of rationality.[23]

Timothy E. O'Connell summarises constructive Catholic response in the phrase 'the central openness of ourselves and our world'. Reality is basically changing, evolving, historical. It is to be seen more in terms of relations than essences. This is supremely true of persons: relationships are fundamental to their very constitution. The personalism of the Vatican II era is indebted to the explorations of Maritain, but reflects many other strands of thought too. There is a stronger emphasis on individuality. Bernard Lonergan and Karl Rahner have employed a transcendental method in philosophy which lays greater stress on the knowing and deciding structure of the free human subject than on moral value as an intrinsic property of external objects or acts. The Protestant H. Richard Niebuhr's concept of the responsible self has also been influential. A common feature is an understanding of the person which overcomes the dualism and abstraction of the past to see him or her as an integrated whole living in a community of persons. Typically Richard McCormick appeals to the depth sciences to declare that the meaning of human sexuality cannot be grasped by purely physical considerations; rather sexual acts are an engagement of the whole person.[24]

This outlook gives to modern Catholic theology a dynamism lacking in traditional Thomism. Human nature is not so much a finished fact as a project or experiment; it therefore follows that natural law is open to change. Natural law has been described as 'a dynamically inviting possibility, a concrete project'.[25] This has two major implications. First, ethics must start from the data of experience. It is in and through our experience that moral truths are mediated. Natural law itself points to our experience of unconditional obligation.[26] Secondly, many writers underline the importance of creativity in moral decision-making. Böckle and Curran both remind us that Aquinas favoured a 'living according to reason' in which men participate in God's providence by themselves defining and imposing norms. Natural law then involves not so much the application of external laws as the deliberation of human reason. John Finnis shows that for Aquinas the source of natural law lies in the experienced dynamisms of our nature, and then in the intelligible principles which outline the aspects of human flourishing, that is, the values basic to all human beings with the nature they have. These values are to be pursued by a process of practical reasonableness, which is the basic good of being able in freedom to bring one's intelligence to bear effectively on the problems of choosing one's actions and life-style and shaping one's own character. By this process, which is never complete, one participates in the basic values and looks for development as a person and for a meaningfulness of one's existence. McCormick takes natural law to be the imperative implied in our very being, and he sees a correlation between this and the gift and challenge of the new life in Christ witnessed to in the New Testament. He castigates the minimalising moralism of those who are preoccupied with avoiding external acts in breach of a legally conceived code. 'The adventuresome pursuit of Christ is gone, and in its place we find a stoic correctness unfamiliar with the notions of growth, dedication, heroism.' O'Connell too insists that the discovery of human nature must be an experiential process grounded in love; otherwise the moral enterprise is reduced to a series of hoops through which the Christian is commanded to jump. 'It is to reduce the dignity of moral living to an empty and dehumanising game. And that is the insidious implication of a legalistic moral theory.' We are rather called creatively to find meaning in the world and to shape it.[27]

2. Temple's second criticism concerns the conditioned character of our moral reasoning. The social teaching of St. Thomas, he remarks, was relative to the society in which he lived. The grades of that society were broadly fixed, and had their several rights and responsibilities. But there was no criticism of the social order itself in the light either of its own underlying principles or of some accepted ideal. By contrast the Renaissance and Reformation led

to a new accent on individuality, and so to a change from a society of status to that of contract. Even if this new accent has sometimes received faulty expression (and here Descartes takes another beating!), it is a great gain, and requires that we positively direct social change. We must develop a type of responsible citizenship for which St. Thomas's world made no opportunity. 'There is a danger that devotion to St. Thomas without readiness to supplement his teaching may make us blind to one chief duty of our generation, and make us the allies of the forces of inertia.'[28]

Criticism of the conditioned character of natural law has of course been given a much keener edge in the last fifty years through the further development of sociology and psychology. Sociology discounts the idea that reason can be insulated from social context and freely apprehend moral truths. It is not necessary to embrace a thoroughgoing Marxist perspective in order to appreciate the force of social context in shaping our moral perceptions. Equally there is no need to accept Freud's extreme determinism and critique of religion to believe that non-rational factors in our psyche affect our moral convictions. Moral absolutes in particular can be highly damaging projections of an immature psyche.

Vatican II theology has certainly begun to take up the challenge of the social sciences. We have already seen how McCormick draws on the depth sciences for a deeper understanding of sexuality. Several Roman Catholics have handled the recent history of the Church itself from a sociological perspective. It is now much more clearly recognised that even seemingly timeless Papal Encyclicals stem from a particular historical and sociological context. Our earlier brief sketch of Pius IX and Leo XIII's policies was indebted to Bill McSweeney's *Roman Catholicism: The Search for Relevance*. He shows very well that what is presented in encyclicals as solidly rational thought, transparent to any man of goodwill, in point of fact reflects the historical pressures on the Papacy.

Bound up with this of course is the tendency to absolutise a past social order. The failure to appreciate the conditioned character of our thought leads to the confusion of passing historical patterns with unchanging verities. Temple himself knew that some members of the Christendom Group (like A. J. Penty) abominated the industrial age and thought Christianity could only flourish in a revived mediaeval Christendom. Franz Böckle readily admits that in the name of natural law several questionable views have been treated as permanently valid, such as the rule of supposedly more rational men over women and children or a hierarchical understanding of the partners in marriage. If the response to the social sciences in the Catholic Church is not as yet really extensive, it is true that none of the churches has made much headway in relating the social sciences to the enterprise of theology. Broadly speaking the task is to avoid on the one hand presenting natural law as if it were a watertight form of knowledge merely parallel to the social sciences, and on the other hand collapsing ethics into sociology. Böckle and others are wisely exploring the middle ground between these extremes. We shall look closely at Dietmar Mieth's discussion of this problem and his proposal for a model-ethic in the next chapter.[29]

3. This sociological argument has an even stronger theological counterpart. William Temple declared at the Malvern Conference that neither St. Thomas nor Jacques Maritain had an adequate appreciation of the power of sin. Catholic moral theology, he suggested to the Aquinas Society, perhaps under the impulse to meet the needs of the confessional had concentrated attention on objective acts of sin, and thereby diverted attention from the essential sin: the perversion of will from which those acts flow. This tends in practice to an unconscious Pelagianism by suggesting that if we find the right technique we can put ourselves right with God. Temple thinks there is no trace of this in St. Thomas, but his quasi-mathematical method of exposition is unable to express the tragedy of human nature to which Luther made men once more alive. 'Certainly we need to recover the sense or feeling – not only the intellectual conviction – of utter impotence to respond to the divine will, and of complete dependence for all power to serve God upon the divine grace ... The Thomist tradition as commonly presented does not adequately convey the awful pervasiveness and penetrating potency of sin in all departments of human life, including in its sphere of poisonous influence even our worship and our generosity.' To the Malvern Conference, as we saw in Part I, Temple commended Reinhold Niebuhr as a Christian whose mind was possessed by the sense of that original

sin of man which consists in putting himself in the centre where God alone ought to be. As a consequence of man's sin, all politics is in part power politics, and will remain so until redemption is consummated; and since that consummation is scarcely conceivable within history, it will serve only as the standard of judgement whereby we are all 'concluded under sin'.[30]

Niebuhr himself mounted a sharp attack in 1940 on the two-tier scheme of natural law from the standpoint of his own understanding of grace and sin. He argued that according to Thomistic doctrine the fall robbed man of the capacity for faith, hope and love, but left his nature intact. Fallen man therefore needs sacramental grace for the restoration of these supernatural virtues, but his capacity for natural justice is not seriously impaired. In Niebuhr's view this is doubly wrong. First, it ignores the fact that all statements and definitions of justice are corrupted by even the most rational men through the power of self-interest. Reason is not capable of defining a universally valid standard of justice. Roman Catholicism insinuates religious absolutes into historically contingent moral judgements. It rationalised feudal aristocracy's dominant position in society in the Middle Ages, and is betrayed into a furious self-righteous defence of feudal types of civilisation in contemporary history, for example in Spain in the 1930s. Secondly, Catholic theology also errs in holding that in the fall man lost the structure of ultimate freedom and love. On the contrary, says Niebuhr, man's potentialities for freedom and love are sustained after the fall. Niebuhr himself often speaks of 'common grace': the possibilities of love do not depend on explicit Christian belief and practice, but are maintained by God for all men in the very structure of their existence.[31]

The problem of sin was presented even more sharply by the Lutheran Helmut Thielicke in the 1950s. A basic question is the relation of the world's fallen to its pre-fallen state. Thielicke believes that we can know that certain things ought not to be, but we cannot work back to an original order. We can only know that we are fallen and that God has appointed emergency orders, like the state, to provide an orderly framework as a dyke against anarchy. True, Roman Catholics know of a relative natural law, where absolutes are modified to take account of sin; but under the pressure to maintain clear and certain moral guidance they practise a deductive casuistry, as if there were no serious difficulty in determining the necessary modifications. In fact decisions are beset with uncertainty, and that is grounded in the sinful structure of the world itself. Thielicke's view of creation and the fall is matched by his eschatology (or way of conceiving the decisive coming of the Kingdom of God). Fundamental to the Gospel is the tension between this age and the age to come. We live in the interim between the first and second coming of Christ, members simultaneously of both ages. Such a dramatic situation is not amenable to a natural law which presupposes immutable timeless norms from which clear-cut rational answers to moral questions can be inferred. History on the contrary is characterised by ambiguity, and we walk by faith and not by sight.[32]

It is on this issue of sin that Catholics have been least successful in their response to criticism. Certainly they are justified in rejecting Thielicke's claim that we are totally unable to work back to an order 'before' the fall. Curran says rightly that this would completely take away the basic goodness and positive meaning of creation. If (to take an example from Thielicke himself) torture is never morally admissible, that necessarily implies a positive view of the dignity of the human person as created by God. The problem for Catholicism lies rather in the pervasive optimism of Vatican II itself. The Protestant, Robert McAfee Brown, responding to the document *Gaudium et Spes* (The Church in the Modern World), says that in the laudable desire to affirm the world it may affirm it too uncritically. It tends to assume that the Gospel crowns the life of natural man, rather than being as well a challenge to, and judgement upon, that life. It 'minimises the degree to which the Gospel is also a scandal and a stumbling-block, by which men can be offended as well as uplifted ... Similarly ... there needs to be more recognition of the pervasiveness of sin in men and human institutions, so that the hopes raised by the tone of the document will not be unnecessarily dimmed by the hard realities of the world ... If this be Protestant pessimism, it is at least a pessimism we have learned from Scripture and tradition as well as from the daily newspaper.'[33]

Among Catholics Charles Curran has given particularly thorough attention to this problem. He welcomes Vatican II's strong emphasis on Scripture, but like Brown he fears that

Gaudium et Spes is excessively optimistic, even naive, in its view of the world. It tries too hard to integrate the natural into the Christian perspective. *Populorum Progressio* of Paul VI seems to imply, Curran thinks, that the complete development of individuals and communities is feasible. John XXIII's *Pacem in Terris* (1963) equally reads as if perfect peace is a possibility here on earth. The document is strong on ideals, but weak on a realistic assessment of obstacles. Curran himself pleads for a greater recognition of the persistent reality of sin and of the finiteness and limitations of the creaturely, which will always be present despite the basic goodness of creation. He also agrees that sin has been reduced too often to external actions in disobedience of God's law. Rather we should follow Genesis and see it in intensely personal and relational terms: the refusal of creatures to accept their relationship of loving dependence on God. That refusal also disrupts man's relationship with his fellow-creatures and with the world. Like many Catholic theologians Curran sees sin as a fundamental option against God; such a view stands in continuity with a Thomistic standpoint, that sin is an orientation of the person away from God towards the self as one's true end. Rejecting all dichotomous views of nature and supernature, Curran believes creation is constantly affected by the drag of sin and the pull of grace. The disrupting influence of sin colours all human reality. Here too he can point to a neglected strand in the tradition, which, in contrast to the two-tier scheme, spoke of man being wounded by sin even in his nature. Very interestingly Curran is bold enough to link these insights with Luther's insight that man is *simul justus et peccator*: at once justified and yet a sinner.[34]

Furthermore Curran acknowledges that a false view of sin can blind us to its social dimensions: gross inequities of our world, the exploitation of the poor by the rich, the failure of people to accept their responsibilities for the world. Curran interestingly criticises Catholic tradition right into the Vatican II era for calling too easily for co-operation in the interests of the common good. Because of the classical inheritance it has seen the world in terms of hierarchical order and harmony. In the economic order the different elements are to work for the common good in due co-ordination and subordination. Pius XI's support in the 1930s for the corporate society followed this model. As late as 1963 John

XXIII was insisting that natural law proclaims an order for society whose principles are absolute and unchangeable. What response, asks Curran, should Catholics make to the Marxist analysis of history in terms of conflict? Certainly conflict should not be elevated to an ideology or ultimate explanation of reality; but the Church should attach far more importance to it. There is a corresponding need to develop a theology of power. Papal Encyclicals have tended to suggest that reason alone is sufficient to bring social change and a proper social order. However, the existing order is never the product of pure reason but also of power struggles. At the root here is the question of eschatology. *Gaudium et Spes*, with its emphasis on Christ as the perfect man, thinks too much of the Kingdom as already realised. Rather we need an eschatology in process of realisation, where we continually make a negative critique of the *status quo*, and feel the tension between the imperfections of the present and the final fulness to which we are called in Christ.[35]

It may be helpful at this stage to summarise the requirements of a radically revised form of natural law, which can be carried forward in our search for an adequate Christian social ethic.

(i) It acknowledges there is a natural morality, valid independently of the Christian revelation.

(ii) It upholds the rationality of moral discourse and the possibility of common ground and co-operation between people of different beliefs.

(iii) It endorses the objectivity of morality.

(iv) It defends the primacy of persons: man is a relational being, the dimensions of whose personality include the dignity of the individual, his sociality, and his need to serve the common good.

(v) As a reflex of (iv) it fosters a view of the state as the servant of the common good; politics and law are rational activities to that end.

(vi) In the light of science and experience it sees the world and man as fundamentally dynamic, changing and historical; it recognises the conditioned character of our moral reasoning, and the need to pursue moral truth in and through human experience and in relation to other disciplines, in order creatively to take decisions and shape our future.

(vii) It sees a correlation between the above and insights of the Bible, for example, the relational character of personality, the centrality of love, and the adventurousness of the moral life as a response to the gift and challenge of the new life in Christ.

(viii) It will have an eschatology which reflects a deep sense of the ambiguities of history, and will deal with the themes of finitude, sin, conflict and power. It will articulate the fundamental motif of the dramatic tension between this age and the age to come, between the Kingdom of God as already realised and the Kingdom as yet to come.

The first seven of these points fit extremely well with Temple's Christian philosophy and the social principles which spring from it. In the next chapter we shall explore some of them further as we evaluate his way of principles. Over the last point, however, neither Vatican II nor Temple's Christian philosophy can be said to be adequate. Curiously they share an optimism bordering sometimes on naiveté, and a belief in a synthesis or integration of the natural and the Christian. Yet by the time he wrote *Nature, Man and God* Temple was already developing a strong sense of the human predicament, and in his last ten years he comes to recognise the need for a new framework which will start out from the fearful tension between the doctrine of the love of God and the facts of daily experience. In Part III we shall see the basis for such a fundamental understanding, and in Part IV give it expression in our proposed framework for Christian social ethics.

CHAPTER 11

PRINCIPLES

Christianity and Social Order of 1942 was a tract for the times, designed to give Christians the tools and the inspiration for the task of post-war reconstruction. Behind it lies a wealth of thought. Though topical, it is also a summary of Temple's longstanding approach to social ethics. We have already seen in Part I that it is in continuity, despite modifications, with his 1923 article 'Principles or Ideals?' Moreover the principles are integral to his Christian philosophy. It is the ethical dimensions of that philosophy which must now be presented, so that we can make a critical evaluation of Temple's way of moving from principles to practice.

Are there unchanging moral absolutes? We saw in the last chapter the problems of working with static essences and absolute moral rules, and favoured a revised natural law laying more stress on the dynamic character of our world and the mediation of moral truth through our experience. This accords well with Temple. In Chapter 5 we could observe the centrality of purpose in his philosophy. He once remarked that constancy of purpose is shown, not by rigidly following rules, but by perpetually adjusting conduct to circumstances. Human beings need purposes; but they must also be sensitive to circumstances. Purposes are therefore best served not by absolute rules but by principles. 'I do not myself believe that there is any rule of conduct, strictly so called, that is of absolute obligation ... But though there is no universal rule of action, there are universal principles to be applied in action.'[1] Let us explore these two sentences in order.

Temple was opposed to a biblical fundamentalism which would take texts as exceptionless rules of conduct. For instance, 'Thou shalt not kill' cannot so function. It *is* exceptionless, if it is construed as 'Thou shalt do no murder'; but then it is a tautology. Temple also sharply rejects Kant's argument that certain acts are intrinsically evil because they are self-contradictory, for example, that lying is always wrong, because if everyone lied it would be self-defeating. Temple thinks this ignores the fact that circumstances are relevant to moral choices, and Kant's logical rejection of lying 'parts company with common sense and the common conscience.' Similarly the rules about paying debts and keeping promises and telling the truth cannot be exceptionless; some 'elasticity' is rightly recognised as desirable.[2]

Temple is quite explicit about the utilitarian component of his thinking. He repeatedly declares that the right thing to do is the thing that is the best in the circumstances. He applies this not only to individuals but also to political and economic systems. Nowhere does he deduce a system directly from Christianity. For instance, his social principles predispose him to support democracy because it is best suited to educate people in responsible citizenship; but he recognises that whether democracy should be introduced or not in a particular country depends on circumstances.[3]

Temple defines a man's act as the whole difference that he makes to a situation. In many cases, he acknowledges, the ramifications are immense, for we are unsure about our scale of values. There is therefore an irreducible element of uncertainty in moral choices. So far from being disconcerted by this, Temple relishes the experimental nature of the moral life: it is inherently an adventure.[4]

All this, however, in no way implies that Temple's position is structureless. He offers 'universal principles to be applied in action.' These are at various levels. First, he offers two formal principles: (i) though people in different parts of the world may disagree over what things are right or wrong, the difference between right and wrong remains, and is not purely a matter of circumstance or convention; (ii) an absolute obligation rests upon us to do what is right, that is, we are absolutely obliged to be conscientious. There is therefore an absoluteness in morals, but it attaches not to rules or acts, but to the person's conscience. This helps us to see why Temple lays such a heavy stress on character.[5]

Now to will the good of other people is to love them. A further universal principle is Kant's second formulation of the categorical imperative, 'Treat humanity in yourself and others always as an end and never only as a means.' There is no harm in using people as a means to our ends, as when anyone performs a service for us. But we should never treat him as a means only and not also as an end in himself. Temple believes Communism and Fascism deny this principle, whereas the Bible endorses it in the form 'Thou shalt love thy neighbour as thyself.' This, says Temple, is the supreme principle of morality, the only absolute moral law.[6]

Temple does not leave the matter at this very high level. He follows Plato in declaring that the true end of human life is righteousness. Here he dissociates himself from the historic school of utilitarianism, which held happiness to be the supreme good. Moral value, he says, resides supremely in the righteous character. 'This is the character which subordinates all other considerations to the claims of the community of persons. But because it is of persons, the highest interest of the community and its members is a personal interest, the fulfilment of their being as Persons; and this is Righteousness.'[7]

It should be noticed at once that though Temple stresses character to such a high degree, he by no means supposes that one can make do with a purely attitudinal morality. To love is not simply to have a loving attitude, it is also to do the loving thing. At this point the structure of love is unfolded in the dimensions of personality. This is obvious from *Christianity and Social Order* itself. Love is considered only briefly within a late chapter. The heart of the book is concerned with an articulation of the dimensions of personality and how they can supply directions for concrete decisions.

Temple's deployment of these dimensions acts as a strong check upon a preoccupation with calculations of utility. Though the exceptionless rules of conduct are tautologies, they are not merely tautologies. If we really grasp the meaning of personality, says Temple, we can see that to inflict injustice in the form of suffering or death on innocence 'is an outrage on the sanctity of personality, while voluntarily to inflict it is to repudiate that sanctity and the obligations which it imposes.' Similarly, though a certain elasticity is desirable in the application of rules, Temple's immense stress on the sanctity of personality prevents any preoccupation with exceptions. 'It is this recognition of the ultimate value of Persons which clothes with so austere a sanctity those duties that arise out of special personal relationships. . . . A promise creates a personal claim, and to break it for any reason which the man to whom it was made cannot be expected to regard as compelling, is to ignore his claim and so to flout the sanctity of his personality.'[8]

Temple's defence of the individual's rights is always balanced by an emphasis on the needs of the community. Though he underscores the right to liberty and property, and would not have dissented from Jacques Maritain's list of rights in *The Rights of Man* (1944), Temple speaks far more of duties – a term no doubt correlative with rights, but better calculated to underline man's social nature and the need for service to the community. It is striking too how in his critique of Thomism Temple links the emergence of the modern concept of personality not with rights but with responsible citizenship.[9]

Temple's caution against a destructive individualism is compounded by his estimate that the legal system and conventions of Britain are fundamentally good. He may be critical of some departments of life, but at least 'our established order of life recognises the sanctity of Personality in many ways. We have freedom of thought and speech in England, at least in the sense of absence of legal restrictions upon them, such as has seldom been achieved in any nation. We have freedom within the law and equality before the law – except so far as the cost of litigation may interfere with this equality.' Ordinary moral conventions have an immense authority simply because they embody the experience of so many generations. They 'represent an immense inductive process too vast to be adequately traced out ... It is the collective reason of innumerable individuals, who all agree (though it may be unconsciously) in the major premise that it is desirable to maintain social life.' We must neither accept them without question nor reject them by looking for their rational grounds in a crude manner. Particularly in an age when conventions are breaking down we should criticise them by asking what principle is supposed to underlie them, and then decide whether to uphold or defy them. 'We are bound to defy conventional moral judgements when we see that they are wrong; but we are bound to obey them so long as we fail to see that they are right; and our standard must be the principle of those judgements themselves.'[10]

Thus, in spite of the furore provoked by Temple's social comment, he was reformist not revolutionary. His caution is reinforced partly by his views about education. Put very briefly, he took a Platonic line, maintaining that children are not inherently wise, but need discipline and training through intercourse with more mature minds if they are to attain to internal unity and a right relationship with the world. The process does not end at the age of majority. Temple's strong conviction of the basic self-centredness of man forbade any facile view that conscience is a reliable index of what is right. True, it is conscience that a man must obey; but his prior duty is to make sure that what his conscience tells him *is* right.[11]

Temple's ethical stance is clearly similar to the situation ethics of the 1960s, sponsored by men like Joseph Fletcher and John Robinson. Almost simultaneously with his book *Situation Ethics* (1963) Fletcher produced a thoroughly engaging study, *William Temple, Twentieth-Century Christian*. Though this is a portrait and not a critical study, Fletcher incidentally creates the impression that Temple and he are in basic accord in their ethics. Certainly they are one in their rejection of all absolute moral laws except the law of love, and in their resort to utilitarianism. Yet there are several important differences, and in each case the criticisms which fell justly upon Fletcher are not valid against Temple.

The central point is that where Fletcher tries to operate solely with the notion of love and the utilitarian calculus, Temple provides us also with mediating principles. There is a serious instability in situation ethics' base. As Bernard Häring put it, Fletcher's concept of love is structureless. To simplify ethics by taking love as the sole key is to run into moral anarchy; its openness can actually lead equally to sentimentalism or to hard utilitarian calculation. In fact Fletcher does, I believe, have an unexamined understanding of man which is unsatisfactory on close inspection. For man is highly functional, almost a succession of atomic moments; yet, as J. Macquarrie insists, man 'is more than what he does; out of his acts he builds up a unity of a personal self.' Moreover, Fletcher's man seems to exist only in atomic situations. It is as if each situation were unique and limited to the immediate principal actors. 'No social morality was founded or ever will be founded upon a situational ethic,' wrote Paul Ramsey, as he pleaded for an ethic of 'in-principled love'. Fletcher, he complained, fatally obscured the importance of the relational norms of life – continuing moral relationships where loyalty is central, such as marriage or promise-keeping. N. H. G. Robinson emphasised the need for a Christian to 'embrace the ongoing life of the world in its entirety' and to face difficult questions of social policy. This he linked with a call for an eschatological vision, lacking in situation ethics, of God's purpose for humanity: the Christian must not think of isolated acts, but of action between the Incarnation and the Consummation. All these criticisms only serve to endorse the ethical stance of Temple and especially his use of mediating social principles.[12]

In the 1960s Joseph Fletcher provoked an outcry from the Roman Catholic Church. In part he brought it on himself, for though he made some telling points he fell into the trap of caricaturing his opponents, and in any case failed to produce a viable alternative. Many Catholics sturdily charged to the defence of absolute moral norms. Since then there has been a more balanced evaluation, assisted by Fletcher's own modifications. The gap between St. Thomas's conception of men living according to reason and Fletcher's situationism is not so great after all!

However, a much more striking affinity is between some Roman Catholic moral theologians and Temple. Naturally Fletcher's fellow-Americans have responded more than most, but Josef Fuchs provides us with an excellent illustration from the European Continent. He observes that within Catholic thought there is a division between those who are allergic to absolute norms, on the grounds that they cannot take due account of our concrete and dynamic world, and those who continue to support them, fearing the collapse of moral truth into mere relativism. Fuchs sees that both sides agree that the Christian must recognise what is absolutely valid, or what always corresponds objectively to the concrete human (and therefore Christian) reality. The basic question, as Fuchs sees it, is therefore how the absoluteness is to be construed.

Turning first to the Bible in search of absolute norms he pleads that Christ's mission was not to establish a new moral law but rather to redeem sinful men by grace. If we study contemporary biblical exegesis, we find the fundamental imperative is a life of faith and love in obedience to God. And though Scripture speaks of particular attitudes and values, these are still not operative norms of behaviour. The demands of the Sermon on the Mount, whilst undoubtedly of absolute validity, are models of behaviour rather than norms. Moreover St. Paul's specific teaching is often culturally conditioned. Nor can the Church offer timeless norms. For the fact is that genuinely new problems do arise; they are not just old problems in new guise. There can also be a genuine pluralism: men with dissimilar experiences can generate a variety of self-images and projects within the scope of right reason. It is in fact only if norms of conduct *can* include culturally and historically conditioned elements that it is possible for them to be responsive to concrete human reality and so be objective. Mutability, says Fuchs, belongs to man's immutable essence!

To be sure, Fuchs goes on, '*a priori*, some essential elements of man's nature can be identified: body-soul unity, personality, accountability, interpersonality.' By *a priori* Fuchs seems to mean that these elements are indispensable presuppositions of human living itself. Here, then, we do have constants, which can serve as criteria, for example of technological and economic progress. Yet even these inalienable elements of man's nature subsist in variable modes.

Fuchs is clearly trying to find a middle way between absolute unchanging norms on the one hand and a mere relativism on the other. Quite apart from tautologies like 'Thou shalt do no murder' there are, he concedes, norms of conduct where we cannot conceive of any exception (e.g. cruel treatment of a child which is of no benefit to the child), and many norms which suffice for ordinary practical living. But Fuchs is very reluctant to speak of negative rules that are inherently absolute. Rather we are absolutely required to find the right response to concrete human reality by attending to the given constants of human nature and the circumstances. Every action that is objectively – according to right reason – not justified in the concrete human situation is inherently wrong, and therefore absolutely to be avoided. It is objectivity, not relativism, that is the critical question. The problem of relativism can be minimised if we remember that we are not isolated in our moral experience, but can find the right solutions by relating to the moral perceptions of the community and the Christian wisdom of the past.[13] In the more traditional terminology of ethical theory Fuchs appears to be piloting his way between a goal-oriented (teleological) ethic which is preoccupied with the consequences of various actions, and an ethic of duties (deontological) where obligations are to be fulfilled irrespective of circumstances. Charles

Curran also follows this middle way, founding it upon a model of man as a relational being, responsible to God and his fellow men. This he rightly believes is more in tune with modern understanding and with the biblical accent on love, grace and covenant.

There is obviously a strong affinity thus far between Temple and leading Catholic moral theologians to-day. Such an ethical stance can begin to allay Protestant hostility to the whole notion of principles. This hostility is grounded in the distinction of Gospel and Law. The fear is that the Gospel is threatened by an interposed realm of timeless absolutes and deductive casuistry, which tempts man to legalism and self-justification. The Gospel by contrast speaks of the sovereign freedom of God to confront man directly in his concrete situation, and the freedom of the Christian to respond existentially as the Spirit guides him. In fact there are to-day signs of a growing convergence between Catholics and Protestants. Whilst Catholics are moving away from a preoccupation with absolute moral norms to a more experiential and biblical stance, Protestants are accepting more readily the notion of constants or guidelines grounded in God's creation and perceived by human reason. This will become clear if we explore further how principles arise, which ones are indispensable for society, and what contribution the Christian faith can make to their elucidation. I shall first illustrate how Anglicans and Catholics are relating principles to experience and to other disciplines. I shall then consider some recent German Protestant discussion of a Christian attitude to human rights. However, all talk of affinity with Temple will be loose unless we face an ambiguity within Temple's Christian philosophy which we noted in Part I.

In *Christianity and Social Order* (as in his 1923 article on ideals and principles) Temple's social principles read like straight derivatives from Scripture, as if empirical considerations only enter in when the principles are to be applied. It is hard to know whether Temple really was deducing, or whether we just have the impression of deductiveness, occasioned by the condensed nature of a tract, the specifically Christian audience, and Temple's longing for a strong explicitly Christian contribution to social thought and action. Even if he was deducing, the fact is that Temple's Christian philosophy points (if ambiguously) to a rather different origin of principles. For he recommends Caird's dialectical method, which entails the constant oscillation between theory and fact. At any one point in time we have an understanding of reality which has been steadily built up by a reciprocal process: we use our understanding of reality to interpret our concrete experience of living, and we allow our experience to modify that understanding. A great merit of the dialectical method is the clear intent to be thoroughly concrete and avoid abstractions. In Temple's case two factors seem to have made it especially attractive to him. The first was his love of the arts. In science, Temple wrote, the intellect pursues hypotheses, thus framing universals under which particulars are subsumed. Art however has a subtler logic, claims Temple, calling for imagination which grasps the infinite delicacy of the logical structure of the concrete world. The whole object of art is to give perfect individual embodiment to a universal truth or value. The second factor is the Incarnation. Temple holds that each person is a concrete universal, and he correlates this with the Incarnation. For if we can speak of perfect individuality as the perfect synthesis of universal and particular, then the way is open to seeing in one man, born at a particular time and place, the adequate embodiment of universal spirit. It also opens the way to seeing how love is the master key to the universe; for love must express itself in service to individuals.[14]

However, this dialectical method needs two corrections. First, it needs to be freed from its Hegelian matrix. The principal weakness lies in the assumption of a rational universe in which rational human beings can 'reach a systematic apprehension of the facts where each fits into its place.' Hegelianism is notorious for the scant justice it frequently does to the fact of evil. Temple's intellectual pilgrimage can be understood as a gradual emancipation from the spell of Hegelianism. But it was only partial; and only in the last few years could he say that the universe did not make sense. The very Hegelian background short-circuited a dialectic which stringently related fact and theory. There is much truth in Jack F. Padgett's claim, which we saw in Part I, that Temple never properly allowed the dialectical method to function. In Temple's case this was compounded by the fact that he simply accepted 'his own religious experience and the orthodox doctrines of the

Christian faith as offering definitive interpretations of the nature of reality without subjecting these interpretations to critical scrutiny.' Padgett particularly criticises Temple's handling of the concept of personality and the problem of evil, and his downgrading of scientific philosophy, so that theological philosophy can step into the breach and offer a metaphysics of the Incarnation and the practical solution of the problems of ethics. Temple thereby becomes a Christian apologist, employing an analytical method which interprets the data of experience by reference to a specific conception of reality without checking his assumptions against the facts. The price is a loss both of empirical and also of theological adequacy. Padgett would rightly welcome a more thorough use by Temple of the dialectical method.[15] He believes it is in his social ethics that Temple came nearest to letting his ideal conception be modified to cope with the empirical situation. This is probably true, but even here the practice is rather variable, as we shall see.

The Hegelian matrix carries with it a further danger, which Temple warded off. The notion of a rational universe can lead one to think (and T. H. Green is a good example) that God is wholly immanent, and that history moves ever onwards to the goal of its own realisation. This is frankly impossible to square with certain basic Christian convictions: the distinction between the Creator and the created order; the unique and decisive act of God in His Son Jesus Christ; the incompleteness of creation and history until God fully redeems them from sin and death and transforms them. It is not a matter of insinuating Christian assumptions into the dialectical method, but of preventing their exclusion at the outset by Hegelian or any other assumptions. They must be allowed to enter the public arena of debate.

The second correction relates to Temple's loose use of the word 'fact'. Our concrete experience of living is of value as well as fact, be it an encounter with a close relative or another religion, or experience of a football match, the letters of Brother Lawrence, a novel, or whatever. By 'fact' Temple presumably means a given item of reality, whose objectivity we must strive to respect as we subjectively appropriate it (and, of course, interpretation is inescapable in this process). When the reciprocal process is carried out, then sometimes there will be a close fit between understanding and experience; but sometimes there will be a dissonance between them, which requires a modification either in the overall understanding or in the interpretation of the experience.

It is a major contention of this book that Temple is at his best when he really does stringently relate overall understanding and interpreted experience through the dialectical method. This applies to the last ten years of his life. Here we see him perceiving in a new way the harsh realities of daily existence and sensing some dissonance with his understanding of the Christian faith hitherto, which provokes him to re-examine his grasp of the faith and so find deeper resources for handling the crises of the 1930s and 1940s. It is only if this reciprocal process is implemented that Christian social ethics can hope to be empirically and theologically adequate. The following examples from recent Anglican, Roman Catholic and Protestant literature are not beyond criticism, but they do illustrate what it could mean to practise the dialectical method or reciprocal process in earnest.

The empirical grounding of social principles comes out very clearly in Ian T. Ramsey's article 'Towards a Rehabilitation of Natural Law'. Unlike Temple Ramsey devoted much of his philosophical endeavour to dialogue with empirically-minded philosophy. His starting point here is the attempt of the legal philosopher H. L. A. Hart to find a purely empirical basis for natural law. Hart starts from the contingent fact that men want to survive. From this he derives five 'basic rules of law and morals' or 'natural necessities', the truth of which is contingent on human beings and the world they live in retaining their salient characteristics. Thus the fact that men are physically vulnerable points to the need to restrict violence; because men are neither devils nor angels, there is the need for altruism; but because of the darker side of man's nature we also need sanctions. Ramsey interestingly develops Hart's thesis in three moves. First he argues that Hart has introduced a covert 'ought': implicit in the notion of survival is its moral necessity. Secondly Ramsey interprets this 'ought' as a claim which is not restricted to observables and is therefore metaphysical; it transcends while it includes the facts. Morever, in thus being committed to survival we come to understand ourselves as persons who transcend what we factually are and do. Thirdly Ramsey can see no reason why we should restrict the basic rules to five. 'Ideally, or so it seems to me, we would become morally more and more mature as we developed moral principles and built up a framework of such principles as the fruit of our moral thinking and experience.' Our array of moral principles arises from exploring moral obligations on countless occasions in widely different empirical situations, and so provides us with the best map and guide-book to date. When we contemplate a certain course of action, we bring its pattern alongside our pattern of principles which express our moral insights hitherto. Whatever we decide will either confirm, modify or supplement our principles. Moral thinking will thus always be exploratory, though Ramsey, like Temple, thinks it wise to be cautiously conservative towards the principles we already have. Ramsey believes that in spite of world-wide diversity and rapid social change some principles will be so stable as to be virtually sacrosanct as long as human beings remain broadly what they now are. But we should not think of them as copy-book principles. They each point back to an obligation revealed through and around the empirical facts of countless situations, an obligation matched only by a decision in which we realise ourselves characteristically as persons. This, thinks Ramsey, is the core in the truth in the situation ethics and existentialist approaches.

Ramsey significantly goes on to claim that the logical structure of Christian ethics is identical with that of natural law. Christians use a number of key-ideas, such as resurrection, salvation, unconditional love, each of which fits in the whole pattern of Christian discourse and whose meaning is rooted in the sayings and narratives of the New Testament. These key-ideas will be associated with certain principles of behaviour. The Christian has repeatedly to set various possible behaviour patterns alongside this Christian perspective of behaviour patterns and principles to see which is the best match. If from this repeated exercise there arises a code, it will not be 'external', for it will have arisen from principles which themselves originated from behaviour patterns expressive of a commitment. Ramsey is unsure whether the key-ideas of Christian ethics are supplementary to those of natural law, or in partial conflict.[16]

The issues Ramsey confronts have been pursued with characteristic thoroughness among Catholics in West Germany.

Encouraged by the spirit of Vatican II to be open to the world, they have entered into critical dialogue with contemporary thought, notably with members of the Frankfurt school, such as Horkheimer and Adorno. J. B. Metz is a well-known example. Less fashionable, though excitingly adventurous, is the thought of Professor Dietmar Mieth.[17] In 1970 Alfons Auer produced a pioneering book called *Autonome Moral und Christlicher Glaube* (Autonomous Morality and Christian Faith). Mieth and his colleagues at Tübingen have developed Auer's insights, not only over Christian and general morality, but also over ethics and its relation to experience and the empirical disciplines. A major proposal of Mieth is for a model-ethic. In very rough terms this amounts to a principles-ethic. This he places alongside the idea of a norm-ethic or a rules-ethic. The precise relation between the two is not entirely clear, but Mieth is obviously reacting against the heavy emphasis on norms of conduct in Catholic moral theology. A model-ethic is no substitute for a norm-ethic. We need moral norms to relieve us of the burden of constantly creative decision-making. But norms can easily be too abstract, external or casuistical. The two ethics need to complement each other. Let us focus on the model-ethic. Mieth faces an apparent dilemma. On the one had a speculative ethic disconnected from the empirical does not carry conviction. Mieth himself calls in question the old Catholic model of essences and particulars, since it implies an unchanging kernel or superstructure of man immune from empirical considerations. He fears that historically moral theology tended to interpret what were really insights from experience as *a priori* general first principles, which were then applied deductively to concrete issues. The Encyclical *Humanae Vitae* of 1968 dealing with birth control was the culmination and end of this process. On the other hand, if ethics respects the empirical, can it afford to become just an inductive sociology of man? Has it anything authentic to contribute? Mieth believes that there is no need to be impaled on the horns of this dilemma. The crucial question is the scope of reason. In the first place, science is not merely value-free information. Scientific knowledge is not purely objective, because scientists select and interpret. The very choice of a field for research may be socially conditioned and ethically significant. Moreover, science is not the only rational way of interpreting reality. Mieth draws on Gibson Winter, the American sociologist, who distinguished between unreflective everyday practical experience and the several disciplines, which are not so immediately empirical but are forms of mediation of that experience. Thus sociology theorises about the conditioned character of everyday life, whereas ethics evaluates its intentional character.

Mieth's model-ethic is grounded in everyday experience and related to other disciplines. Ethical action is not the application of abstract theory, but is rooted in forms of experience. The ethical model is a construct of experience, our view hitherto of the meaning of existence. It is continually modified critically in experience. Conversely the ethical model should perform an analytical and critical function in relation to that experience. Drawing on the structuralist H. Rombach's ideas about change in social systems, Mieth notes how systems are broken by men's experience of their negative side. Resistance to the *in*human is the experience of meaning which all men share. This reaction against a negative needs to be channelled into the positive liberation of latent possibilities and so further the creation of a more human world. Practice thus results from an interplay of experience and model.

In this search ethics must join with other disciplines. By a process of mutual criticism they must look for what Mieth, following Rombach, calls 'structural correspondences' in the search for an integrated understanding of persons. He is particularly interested in the correspondences of the arts and a model-ethic. Both are subjective and defy objectification. But this does not mean that they run counter to reason: literature, like ethics, is a dimension of rationality. In its handling of such themes as justice in injustice, mercy in guilt, literature can provide illumination for a model-ethic. At the same time it can preserve more effectively than any moral law the mystery of God and man. The very forms of literature can be highly significant for a model-ethic. The sayings of the Sermon on the Mount have the form of 'picture-sayings' which discourage legalistic imitation in favour of the creative shaping of one's practical response. The parables strike home with their concrete action model far more than chains of argument. The scribe wants a definition of the neighbour to guide his casuistry. Jesus breaks this rigid mould with the parable of the Good

Samaritan. The question 'Who was neighbour to him who fell among thieves?' and the injunction 'Go and do likewise' both construe the word 'neighbour' in an active sense: act as a neighbour and you will cease to ask who your neighbour is! Parables touch us directly, convince and change us. Indeed Mieth, like Metz, stresses the importance both of the narrative character of the whole Gospel record of Jesus and of narrative as the form in which man gives shape to his experience. Both are foundational for a model-ethic.

Models suggested from these sources have no finality. But there is no way out. We cannot have a total grasp of history. We have to live with a plurality of perspectives. We are relational beings, set within an open and dynamic history. Yet we do not live in a state of total flux. The tissues of meaning that we construct do not change daily. They can serve as guidelines and have a claim to objectivity. We have for instance come to a stable recognition of the vital importance of the personal and social aspects of sex for any integrated view of it. But if the Christian wishes to convince others of the power of this model to integrate other models of sexuality, then he must bring his humanising claim to the test of historical experience. For the authenticity of an ethic, like the authenticity of the Christian faith itself, can only be guaranteed in experience, and not in spite of experience.

The issue of principles and the relationship of ethics to experience has received close attention in West Germany in a lively debate on basic values (*Grundwerte*).[18] This was sparked off in 1976 by reforms in the law on abortion, marriage, pornography and sexuality. There appeared to be a crisis of morality: did this signify the collapse of all norms, or was it that certain received norms needed to be changed to meet changed social circumstances? This naturally precipitated the question whether there is a core of norms which are indispensable. The debate was all the more emotional for being unclear over the meaning of the term *Grundwerte*. The Catholic bishops issued a declaration which incorporated the whole of natural law into the term: moral values such as freedom, peace and love; principles such as the common good, solidarity and subsidiarity; rights, such as the protection of life and the value of the person; and natural and legal institutions such as marriage, the family, the state and even democracy. The Protestant Martin Honecker, discussing human rights, prefers to confine *Grundwerte* to basic attitudes in distinction from rights, but beyond that would prefer to substitute for *Grundwerte* 'ethical standards or basic norms of ethical conduct.' Even here the possible number is very large and Honecker does not distinguish clearly between attitudes and guidelines for action. He concentrates helpfully on three *Grundwerte* which are clearly social and have in fact been championed by all the political parties in West Germany. They are variously expressed as freedom, justice, solidarity (Honecker), or freedom, equality, participation (Huber and Tödt). They clearly cover basically the same ground as Temple's first three social principles, and confirm the wisdom of his choice.

There are two important aspects of the German discussion which need a special comment. The first is the grounding of *Grundwerte*. Some follow the tradition of natural law or philosophers like Max Scheler and Nikolai Hartmann, and cling on to the idea of *Grundwerte* as unchanging essences. The problem then, as Honecker points out, is that they cannot answer satisfactorily the question how we come to know these eternal timeless values, and how they come, so to speak, from heaven to earth. Honecker writes, 'In place of an objective grounding of values people to-day therefore generally substitute subjective value-experience. The consideration of basic values can then be understood as a question about ethical constants within social and historical change.' Honecker does not mean here that values are irrational or arbitrary; it is rather that we cannot stand outside history, and must apprehend values in and through our experience. Further, he does not necessarily imply that constants are totally unchanging. Presumably our understanding of them can be modified. The point is that they are so basic that it is inconceivable that society could with impunity dispense with them. This fits with Josef Fuchs and Franz Böckle's idea of necessary *a prioris* of human existence. Honecker does not attempt to determine a theory of value but simply takes as his starting point the recognition of the givenness of basic values and their significance for the formation of the social will and political activity.

For a Christian to recognise basic values in this way is tantamount to agreeing that they are not simply derived from and validated by the Christian faith. Similarly the Protestants Wolfgang Huber and Heinz Eduard Tödt in their book

Menschenrechte (Human Rights) do not dispute that human rights and basic values have a validity independent of Christian faith.[19] Historically their long development has often been to the shame of the churches, and even in the teeth of their opposition. Though strongly influenced by Karl Barth, Huber and Tödt reject all deductions of human rights from a 'theology from above'. Nor are Christians called upon to devise a new set of human rights from Christian presuppositions. That would not only fail to do justice to the character of human rights, but also convert the Gospel into Law. Rather, human rights is a topic which requires co-operative effort: the insights of the different disciplines need to be related to one another, and people of varied faiths and convictions must aim at dialogue and consensus. As a consequence Huber and Tödt first look carefully at the concrete situation of human rights to-day, and then investigate their legal character and philosophical basis before they eventually discuss their relation to the Christian faith.

So far this is very similar to the approach of Mieth or Auer or N. H. G. Robinson. However, Huber and Tödt rightly take a step beyond Auer and Mieth, and this is the second important aspect of German discussion, the relation of basic values and human rights to the Christian faith. Whereas Catholics tend to stress the continuity of natural and Christian insight, Huber and Tödt envisage a more radical contribution from the side of Christianity. They do not mean simply motivation, but rather criteria for an approach to human rights. They use a model of 'analogy and difference' to express the relationship of human rights to Christian faith. On the one hand there are correspondences or analogies between Christianity and human rights which have 'orientating significance'. On the other hand Christianity relativises or radicalises talk of human rights. To elucidate their position they use the term 'decode'. Basically they believe that neither human rights nor ethics in general are perfectly intelligible without reference to the Christian faith. Christianity can unlock the puzzles and correct the distortions of general ethics. Let us illustrate this 'decoding' in action by looking at two of the three core elements of human rights they discuss, freedom and equality.

Huber and Tödt note that classically freedom is treated as an inborn quality. It is neither borrowed from society or state nor is it at their disposal. Freedom is rather the capacity of man to dispose of himself (*Selbstverfügung*). This in turn implies that if one lacks such a freedom then one is no longer free. It also readily suggests an individualistic view of man with a freedom isolated from any community. In each of these respects Christianity 'decodes', especially by reference to the doctrine of justification. Agreed, it is a true insight that man is not at the disposal of others. However, freedom understood as an inborn quality leads not to self-realisation or salvation, but to entanglement in slavery to Law, sin and death. True freedom is not our possession or achievement, but is grounded in God's promises and faithfulness to his creation. It is the freedom into which He sets us free in Jesus Christ (Galatians 5.1) as part of the eschatological liberation of the whole created order. Man receives his humanity through the glory of God, which is revealed in the very powerlessness of Jesus on the Cross. By the same token, this freedom can be known even in suffering, when there is the lack of power of disposal over ourselves. Moreover, as Luther states so clearly, if the Christian is set free by God, he is freed in order to serve others in love. If one belongs to Christ, who has set one free, then one bears a responsibility for others (cf. I Corinthians 6.12). This is grounded in the fact that God took man's mortality on Himself and in Jesus Christ became the man for others. Freedom and responsibility, autonomy and sociality therefore go hand in hand. The freedom of faith is a 'communicative freedom'.

Huber and Tödt insist that this understanding of freedom is not to be confined to a religious sphere. If man's humanity is not a product of man but a gift of God, then performance cannot be part of the definition of the person. Performance societies, both capitalist and socialist, run the risk of ignoring this basic criterion of a humane society. The true depth of freedom is lost if rights are made exclusively dependent on performance of duties. Moreover, if the freedom of some is practised at the expense of others, then freedom itself is at risk. The freedom of the market cannot justify itself simply by its undisputed merit of having raised productivity and living standards for vast numbers of people. In fact its beneficiaries are mainly the better off; it can justify itself only when it really benefits all men. A further Christian insight is that the man of faith is free from the compulsion to self-realisation. Readiness to forgo his own claims to freedom for the freedom of others is itself an expression of freedom; the possibility of the renunciation of rights is therefore a basic aspect of a Christian understanding of rights. And freedom from the shackles of self also means readiness to venture even beyond the bounds of cultural ties and let oneself be called in question – and enriched – through communication with others. In the face of current ideological, social and political constraints upon such communication this criterion of freedom only underlines the necessity of international agreement on human rights.

In concentrating first upon the question of freedom Huber and Tödt are characteristically Lutheran. The criteria of equality and participation are almost a reflex of the delineation of freedom. The reference to the equality of all in the Virginia Bill of Rights of 1776 enables us to be critical of the *status quo*, particularly where state power discriminates against individuals or groups by excluding them from basic opportunities and rights. The demand for equality also acts as a corrective against a concept of freedom as the unfettered unfolding of the individual. Christianity decodes equality. It is not just that the Golden Rule is significant for its interpretation. Huber and Tödt focus on the doctrine of man in the image of God, which denotes not an indwelling quality but the relation of man to God. It is as a consequence the measure of those relations in which man stands to his fellow-men. To live according to the image is therefore to show responsibility – for one's fellow-men, for future generations, and for the world in general. Against older, more pessimistic forms of Lutheranism, they assert that although sin perverts these basic relations it does not destroy man's image. Galatians 3.26ff. ('There is neither Jew nor Greek, slave nor free, male nor female, but you are all one in Christ Jesus') takes us a step further, revealing a fundamental equality of the children of God, which is not created by men but a promised equality given in baptism. Analogously man has a claim to equality at the level of human rights, which he has not created. Huber and Tödt are clear that there is a difference between a minimum equality based on law and Christian equality based on love, where people meet in the unity of Jesus Christ. It is not a question of deducing worldly rights from Christianity, nor should the law be overtaxed by maximal Christian or humane demands. Law is primarily to protect the minimal conditions of the common life and thereby keep open the possibility of qualitatively higher relations. Nonetheless Christianity does, for example, forbid a collective national egoism which simply takes for granted inequalities in other parts of the world; it does require a solidarity with the victims of discrimination.

These excursions into Anglican, Catholic and Protestant thought in recent years have been an attempt to understand what it could mean to practise the dialectical method in earnest. We have focussed on principles, discovering how they arise, which ones are indispensable for society, and what contribution the Christian faith can make to their elucidation. We shall need to return to these points in the last chapter. It is now time to focus on Temple's own deployment of his principles in dealing with concrete issues. How faithfully does *he* carry out the dialectical method in his social ethics?

He is certainly at his best in his initiative over long term unemployment. Here Temple was really acting on his insight that the right thing to do is the right thing in the circumstances. The method employed, as we saw, was similar to that of the Yorkshire Institute of Industrial Affairs: the convening of a group with diverse expertise to investigate a social problem in a concrete manner which was both scientific and human. It is the dialectical method in action. The exercise started out in 1934 on the one hand from the facts and the experience of the unemployed themselves and on the other from a set of convictions about persons – the social principles – held by Temple and his colleagues on the basis of their Christian experience. The convictions certainly determined the priorities and thrust of the enquiry; but at the same time they were put to the test by it. The enquiry was thoroughly empirical: it analysed scientifically the causes and categories of unemployment, and it offset any tendency to generalisation and impersonal administrative solutions by the technique of personal interview. It was a triumph. *Men Without Work* was well received nationally and gave great impetus to practical schemes for the unemployed. Temple was confirmed in his convictions and he used the findings as a springboard for arguing for family allowances. It is interesting that the exercise also modified the theory at one point; for as early as 1935 (as we saw in Chapter 8) Temple had a deepened appreciation of Jesus' words that it is more blessed to give than to receive.

Over other issues however Temple is not so successful. We saw that a number of criticisms were made of COPEC in 1924. Though Hensley Henson was rather unfair, he was right when, like Sir Max Muspratt, he thought moral idealism was triumphing over empirical and practical considerations. The Conference did not calculate the costs of its recommendations or estimate whether a reformed industry would retain its wealth-producing properties. Nor did it face up to the fact that Britain was not effectively a Christian nation. The trouble was partly that COPEC was conceived and executed by people who tried to harness national euphoria to their own optimistic conviction that the Christian faith gave the vision and power essential for solving social problems. By 1924 the euphoria had faded and hard questions needed to be faced. The failure to do this reflects a failure of method, which is ultimately theological. The delegates largely supposed that one could start from Christian moral principles and move, without deep analysis of the facts, to middle axioms, i.e. statements intermediate between principles and programmes, recommending the direction in which society should go. Facts became chiefly relevant in the transition from the middle axioms to programmes – which was the task of others. It is this assumption, rooted in a liberal theology, which underlies the composition and format of the Conference. Far too many delegates were clergy; far too few had long practical experience of the areas under discussion. The format precluded even the raising, let alone the probing, of contentious questions. Yet the delegates reflected only one segment of the current theological spectrum, albeit the strongest. What was needed was the break-up of their comfortable consensus in order for Christians to grope after a better theology which would itself entail a closer attention to the empirical.

The strikes of 1926 only exposed more cruelly the gap between COPEC and reality. Most of the criticism which fell upon the members of the Standing Conference was quite misplaced, but at two points, both of them empirical, they can be faulted. First, Temple has a charming confidence in the power of ideas. The industrial counterpart of his principle of fellowship is arbitration; therefore he supposed the miners' strike was bound to be ended by negotiation. This was completely falsified. The miners (whatever the subsequent myths!) lost. G. W. McDonald shows very well how they were defeated by the employers' use of their superior power with the connivance of the government. The publication of the Archbishop of Canterbury's Appeal from the Churches also had far less influence than Temple thought. It took Temple a long time to adjust his idealism to the realities of power, interest and conflict. Secondly the intervention of the Standing Conference, whatever the logic of its arguments, was nevertheless very problematic in the event. As it was stocked mainly with bishops it could certainly carry enough weight to secure an interview with Baldwin, but the price was that the miners believed that the churches as a whole were on their side. They therefore broke off discreet negotiations already in progress with the group led by the Quaker B. S. Rowntree. Temple later admitted to Rowntree a tendency to try to make capital for the Church out of the episode by publicity, when it ought to have been kept entirely private.[20]

In spite of Temple's initiative over unemployment and his self-critical insights of 1937 onwards, the same problems are present at the Malvern Conference and in *Christianity and Social Order* and the subsequent campaign Temple conducted up and down the country to propagate its ideas. At Malvern the deduction of a Christian sociology from dogma eclipsed empirical factors; the discipline of economics was either treated with disdain or handled with incompetence, and there was a mismatch between the ideas of the Christendom Group and what was feasible in an industrialised and half-secularised Britain. In his own writing and speeches Temple certainly made errors in the very empirical matter of banking. The best (and wittiest) comment came from the Editor of *The Financial News*, who reminded readers that there are no simple interpretations in economics, and put his finger on Temple's tendency to obscure hard dilemmas by an excessive preoccupation with moral principles. 'He is not the first who has pricked his fingers in that particularly briary field [the techniques of banking]. Nor when bankers themselves can never agree whether banks make loans or loans make banks, will he be the last. It has been said, not wholly without reason, that the Archbishop seems to have in his mind's eye the picture of a trade-less, capital-less community, where the main pre-occupation is not so much to maximise the product of human endeavour as to prevent the bananas getting into the wrong hands.' When Temple talks of balance, it is really the question of the antithesis of economic costs and social costs. 'The difficulty is that to express the kind of problem with which Dr. Temple is grappling entirely in moral terms is to over-simplify them. Reconciliation of the two sets of considerations, which human welfare and restored fellowship obviously require, . . . has always been the most difficult task which those responsible for the ordering of society's institutions have had to face.' *The Economist* regretted that Temple tended to weaken the force of his general arguments by making economic mistakes, so giving his critics a handle for their rebukes. It also asked Temple to ponder the fact that the mainspring of the free and competitive economy is not the greediness of individuals for profit but their readiness to risk losses.[21]

To record these criticisms is of course by no means to invalidate Temple's social ethics, least of all to endorse the theological assumptions of his critics. In fact, I shall argue in Appendix I that Temple's social ethics is far more adequate than any of his critics! The question is, if Temple is not empirical enough, what corrective can be suggested? We can achieve a partial answer if we use the insights earlier in this chapter to comment briefly on Temple's method, seen clearly in *Christianity and Social Order*. Like COPEC *Christianity and Social Order* implies a procedure which moves from the central doctrines of the Christian faith to a Christian understanding of persons, which is then used to make a critique of the *status quo* and suggest middle axioms. Temple believes all Christians should be able to agree with him up to that point. In the Appendix confidence yields to tentativeness, since programmes involve disputable estimates of probable consequences, experience, and often technical expertise. Let us focus on middle axioms, and especially how they arise.

Middle axioms came into prominence in 1937 at the Oxford Conference on Church, Community and State. In the preparatory volume J. H. Oldham wrote, 'Between purely general statements of the ethical demands of the Gospel and the decisions that have to be made in concrete situations there is need for what may be described as middle axioms.' The middle axiom was not only promoted by Temple (he mentioned it by name at the Malvern

Conference), but also by Reinhold Niebuhr and John C. Bennett across the Atlantic, and by H.-D. Wendland in Germany. The World Council of Churches at first favoured and later abandoned the middle axiom, preferring other methods of relating Christianity to political and economic decisions. Part of the trouble has been the ambiguity of the term. Taken at face value 'middle axioms' suggest logical confusion and a deductive movement from faith to action. As long ago as 1971 Professor Preston tried to dispose of this misunderstanding. In an article in *Crucible* he stressed that 'middle axioms are arrived at by bringing alongside one another the total Christian understanding of life and the analysis of the empirical situation.' More recently, in response to an essay by Professor Duncan Forrester, he has clarified the place of experience in the formation of middle axioms. Forrester criticised the process of reaching middle axioms on the grounds that it seems to presuppose a static unchanging deposit of faith which is then applied to moral issues. Is not *praxis*, he asked, to be regarded as a criterion of Christian truth? Preston's response is an illuminating one. He does not believe any such presupposition is involved in middle axiom thinking. 'Usually, however, such a static view of doctrine goes with a wooden way of "applying" it rather than the flexible way of middle axioms. It is true that doctrine held cerebrally, with no attempt to live by it, is misunderstood as much as it is understood, and that appreciation comes by the reciprocal relation of *praxis* (if we are to use this Marxist term) and formulations of doctrine, each fertilizing the other.'[22] This fits very well with the insights of Ian Ramsey and Dietmar Mieth. Christians' experience of living their faith is indeed foundational alike for principles, middle axioms and practical programmes. Logically it does not matter whether one starts the process from the Christian understanding of life or from the analysis of the empirical situation. However, because of the misunderstanding of middle axioms and the complexity of so many social problems, and because of the persistent tendency of the churches to be far too deductive in ethics and insufficiently empirical, it is best to start out from the empirical. In fact Preston himself normally starts an enquiry into a social problem by asking what is going on in the world before he introduces theological concepts. The same practice is now almost standard among those groups which study social issues under the aegis of the churches' Boards of Social Responsibility and whose recommendations are usually at the level of middle axioms. Certainly it is best to avoid the statement that middle axioms are formed by moving *from* a Christian world-view *to* the empirical.

Temple's intent in the Appendix to *Christianity and Social Order* was to provoke Christians to think for themselves, and there is no harm in that. At bottom it is a sad comment on Christians that Temple felt he needed to produce his suggestions at all. Though he made mistakes and was a little naive in supposing his ideas could be detached from the fact he was an archbishop, there cannot be a total embargo on bishops speaking their mind on social issues simply because they might be mistaken or misunderstood. By the very terms of their consecration there will be occasions when it is right for them to speak out. This is particularly so when there are blatant violations of human personality. Some of these may even fit Paul Ramsey's category of 'at the gateway to Auschwitz'. Even in lesser cases bishops should not necessarily await the pronouncements of committees. One is reminded of the jibe against a cautious archbishop, that if the last trump sounded he would set up a committee to decide whether it really was the last trump or the last trump but one. No one should object to a little panache from bishops! The proviso is that they have a clear head about the relation of Christianity to social order and take pains over the facts of the case. They should also use discretion, as is evident from 1926, about the manner of intervening. Discreet influence behind the scenes may well be more effective and less misleading than public declarations. Over most issues, however, because of their complexity, it will be best to implement the dialectical method by setting up an enquiry which draws on first-hand experience and the perspectives of various disciplines and aims at a report which is thoroughly empirical as well as theological.

When J. F. Padgett said that it was in his social ethics that Temple came nearest to letting his ideal conceptions be modified to cope with the empirical situation, he particularly commended Temple's handling of love and justice. Now love and justice are concepts Temple employs almost exclusively in the international arena. It was here that he really faced up to the intractable facts, and especially the fact of power. In the search for an adequate social ethic we must therefore turn to Temple's treatment of international affairs.

PART III

TEMPLE'S APPROACH TO
INTERNATIONAL AFFAIRS

CHAPTER 12

PACIFISM

Temple was no pacifist. True, he was always prepared to agree with pacifists that 'all war is contrary to the mind and spirit of Christ'. He writes in 1914: 'Members of the Body of Christ are tearing one another, and His body is bleeding as it once bled on Calvary, but this time the wounds are dealt by his friends. It is as though Peter were driving home the nails, and John were piercing the side.' All war is 'devil's work'. Yet Temple does not infer the pacifist answer. Similarly in 1924 the COPEC Conference passed a resolution that 'All war is contrary to the spirit and teaching of Jesus Christ'. But when the Jesuit Fr. Francis Woodlock complained in a letter to *The Times* that this meant all Christians should be conscientious objectors, Temple replied that this was not so: it did not follow, when once the spirit and teaching of Christ had been deserted by some nation or group of nations, that armed resistance was un-Christian. Again, Temple is prepared to say in 1916 that all war is sinful, but not that it is always sinful to engage in war. By 1939 he expresses it this way: Killing is right in some circumstances; yet it is still sinful, for it belongs to an order of things which has departed from the rule of God. Clearly there is no inconsistency here, since Temple in effect distinguishes sins for which a man is personally responsible from sin in which he is implicated through his membership of a sinful order.[1]

Temple was in no doubt both in 1914 and in 1939 that Britain was right to go to war. In 1914 there was 'no honourable way of escape'. War may be a duty, especially if the strong attack the weak. 'As long as we ask what England's duty was and is, only one answer is compatible with elementary morality.' And in 1939: 'But as the fact that we are right now does not obliterate our past sin, so our past sin in no way alters the fact that we are right now'.[2]

Temple's appeal to 'elementary morality' does not mean that his case against pacifism is either simple-minded or secular-minded. It is true that he always had a great respect for the basic moral convictions of ordinary men. He was also glad to go as far as he could in reconciling philosophy and Christianity. But his case here flows from an attempt to be thoroughly theological.

On several occasions Temple commented on specific biblical texts relating to the issue of pacifism. In 1936 he described as delusion the idea that non-resistance was the essential principle of Christian ethics as a whole. Even if the principle was stated decisively in the Sermon on the Mount, the illustrations showed that there was a special and limited reference. 'In the first place the injuries or grievances specified are such as concern only the person whose conduct is in question, not any third party. In face of this it is illegitimate to argue that the command not to resist evil, or the evil man, is rightly interpreted as a command to stand by in idleness while he maltreats another. St. Thomas is perfectly justified in his comment – Patiently to endure injuries done to one's self pertains to perfection; but patiently to endure injuries done to another pertains to imperfection and even to vice.' Secondly, the aim in the illustrations is to turn the relation of demand or claim into a relation of fellowship. Thirdly, what is represented is a spirit: the injuries are such as most irritate a man in whom self-concern is strong, but to a truly converted man are seen to be no real injuries at all. 'Here as always our Lord is not legislating but indicating a spirit by which we should live; it is the spirit of non-resentment which is, so to speak, the reverse side or negative aspect of the spirit of love. Resentment is absolutely condemned, but not, in all possible circumstances, resistance.' In fact the essential principle is rather that we should be perfect, like God; and that means that 'Christian ethics is very definitely a department of Christian theology'.[3]

In the same passage Temple refers to the saying of Christ: 'He that hath no sword, let him sell his garment and buy one.' Whatever these words symbolise, says Temple, it is not non-resistance. In a letter dated 26 April 1944 he writes: 'You seem to assume that Our Lord Himself was a complete pacifist. I am sure that is not true. If it was, how did there come to be two swords in the little company of His disciples right at the end of His Ministry. He Himself said that if He were concerned with an earthly kingdom His servants would be fighting. He seems to me plainly to recognise that it would be right to fight for an earthly kingdom or civilisation, but it cannot be right to fight for spiritual truth itself because that wins its way only so far as it is freely accepted, and to try to uphold it by force is in fact to betray it.'[4] Whatever the value of the exegesis here, the distinction between 'spiritual truth' and 'earthly kingdom' will turn out to be of great importance to Temple.

Equally, Temple cannot interpret the commandment 'Thou shalt not kill' in a pacifist sense. It was not so interpreted in Old Testament times; it was acknowledged that there is justifiable homicide. Temple thinks 'Thou shalt do no murder' a more accurate version, 'that is to say ... killing for personal advantage, or the satisfaction of personal passion.' He goes on: 'There is a great deal in the Gospels that is very terrible, as well as all that is said there about love and peace, and we have no right to take one part without the other.'[5]

Temple has thus rejected the idea that a biblical text can be taken as a straightforward action-rule to be applied without exception, and has suggested that the bearing of Christianity on the issue of war must be determined by the broad consideration of the total witness of the Gospels. In fact, he means something even broader than this.

One of Temple's most forthright pronouncements on pacifism occurs in the York Diocesan Leaflet of November 1935, when he declares that it is heretical in tendency. This does not apply to those pacifists whose decision is based on the view that to engage in modern warfare will almost certainly do more harm than good; for that is a judgement concerning a balance of values, not a judgement of principle. The pacifists he has in mind are those who say it is, as a universal principle, un-Christian to use in support of law whatever degree of force is requisite, even to the taking of life, in restraint of lawless force or violence. This position he sees as dubious in three ways, 'and in many cases I have thought that all these heretical tendencies were combined'. First, it is an essentially Marcionite attitude, as if the Old Testament could be set aside; whereas the Christian view is that the New Testament completes and therein corrects the deficiencies of the Old Testament, but does not supersede it. Secondly, it is Manichaean in tendency, as if matter were evil; whereas the Christian view holds that matter and material forces can be completely subordinated to the spirit, and that spirit normally manifests itself by directing and controlling what is material. Thirdly, he says, it is Pelagian in its assumption of man's capacity, apart from conversion and sanctification, to obey the Counsels of Perfection; whereas according to Christianity man is incapable of living by love unless the grace of God has both converted and sanctified him, so that the law of love is not applicable to nations consisting in large measure of unconverted or (as in the case of most, if not all, of us) very imperfectly converted citizens.

It is clear from the leaflet that friends had been puzzled by Temple's claim in the October leaflet that pacifism is heretical. He is careful to explain that he did not call any individual a heretic – there was no question of personal condemnation. Perhaps because of possible misunderstanding Temple did not persist in using the term 'heretical' or refer to the three ways by title. There is, however, no doubt that his theological criticisms of pacifism are in effect against these three tendencies, sometimes singly, usually in combination, over more than thirty years.

Criticism of the Marcionite tendency is found most clearly in 'A Conditional Justification of War' (1940).[6] Given that the highest ethical axiom is 'Thou shalt love thy neighbour as thyself' the question is not simply: How can we show love to Germans? The question is: How can we show love to Frenchmen, Poles, Czechs, and Germans, all at once? If it can be said that Britain is fighting to overthrow Nazi tyranny and secure for all whom her action may affect a greater measure of freedom, then resistance of Germany by force is a way of loving Germans themselves as well as others. 'In the world which exists, it is not possible to take it as self-evident that the law of love forbids fighting. Some of us even hold that precisely that law commands fighting.' Fighting is not a direct expression of love; it becomes an expression of love only because every alternative is worse. 'What things it is right to do may be very much affected by circumstances.' To prevent a human brute killing a child it may be not only permissible but obligatory to kill him; 'and that obligation is rooted in love'. The rightness of most acts is relative and not absolute; but this does not mean that the rightness is doubtful. 'The general principle is that relative terms are absolute in their appropriate relations. To kill is right, if at all, relatively and not absolutely; that is, it can only be right in special circumstances. But in those circumstances it is absolutely right.' Temple's strong sense that every act is a link in a chain of cause and effect disposes him to doubt if any act is right 'in itself'.

Temple proceeds to dismiss the view that the indiscriminate character of modern warfare always makes it unjustifiable. His principal two comments are, first, that the crux lies in balancing the evil of causing suffering to the innocent against the evils which may be checked as a result; and secondly that, although war does not distribute suffering justly, neither is it totally unjust, since 'no citizen can claim to be totally innocent of his country's wrong-doing'. Here Temple is using the same sort of distinction as was noted earlier in connection with sin. Nor will Temple allow the fact of Britain's guilt to disqualify her from fighting. The mistakes in the Versailles Treaty and the failure fully to operate the Covenant of the League of Nations mean that Britain is in part responsible for Hitler and for the course of events which culminated in the war. However, 'the fact that we failed to do our duty at an earlier date is no reason why we should fail to do it now'. And even if it is true that we have acted belatedly because our own interests are involved, our duty is to act justly.

For Temple the whole question comes down to this: 'Is the Nazi threat to civilisation so serious that the evil of allowing it to develop is greater even than the monstrous evil of war?' His answer is an unhesitating yes. The questions are then posed whether all this might not be said by a pagan moral philosopher, and whether the Christian should not respond to that call which is higher than justice and earthly loyalty. Temple's answer reveals his understanding of the relation of Gospel and Law. The Gospel does not destroy but fulfils the Law and the Prophets. So Christianity does not sweep away all wisdom attained apart from it. The kingdoms of the world have their place by God's appointment. They are not the same as the Kingdom of God, but they have powers and rights which are to be exercised in obedience to God's laws. 'To check the aggressor and to set free the oppressed are ways of doing this.' So too, if the Gospel fulfils the Law we must not fail to discharge our elementary obligations. 'We must pay our debts before we give away our goods in reckless generosity.'

This argumentation partly reappears in a letter Temple wrote to a young friend in November 1939, but it is even more theological. The move from the absolute to the relative realm comes about because the order of things has departed from the rule of God. 'So we are involved in an entanglement due to the sin of mankind, including our own, in which the best thing we can do is still a bad thing. None the less it is right to do it, because it is the best possible. And so we have got to do it and be penitent while we do it. That is the only hope I can see of both resisting injustice and securing that justice comes out of it. Where the method of redemptive suffering is possible and the people concerned are capable of rising to it, it is no doubt the best of all; but there is no way that I can see in which we could redemptively suffer so as to change the heart of Germany and deliver Poles and Czechs; and if there is, our country is not yet anything like prepared to do it. So once again we have to do the best we can, being what we are, in the circumstances where we are – and then God be merciful to us sinners!'[7]

Here, then, Temple clearly sees the necessity to retain the way of justice and law, even though this falls short of the way of redemptive suffering. But if the Marcionite tendency is in effect repudiated, so also, here and elsewhere, are the Manichaean and the Pelagian. Both involve the question of the relationship of the individual Christian to society and the state.

As early as 1912 Temple wrote of the social or political necessity for compromise, 'arising from the fact that we are members, whether we will or no, of the society in which we live; and certainly it seems to me 'that our capacity to raise th it society depends upon our being veritable members of it, working for the highest things which we can work for in it, but not cutting ourselves off from it, not standing aside and giving good advice from the touch-line.' A thoroughly Christian nation would refuse to fight if only its own interest were at stake, but the Christian citizen of a state which has not yet reached that pitch should not refuse to fight, 'because if he does he may be putting himself entirely out of touch with the great stream of life which at the moment may be a far nobler thing than any practicable alternative'. The problem of motive enters in here. 'Perhaps the noblest character of all is the one that would refuse to fight; but the man who is ready to give up his own life for the sake of his country's gain, or in obedience to his country's command, is clearly a better man than one who shirks fighting on the ground of self-interest, and there is a serious danger that a man by attempting to force the highest will, as a matter of fact, only encourage the lowest.'[8]

Temple's queries concerning the effect and the motivation of opting out of society were to recur in both wars, and he does not mince his words. In *The Challenge* he remarks that it is absurd to be neutral at Little Trumpington when England is at war, for the pacifist is protected by the Navy and will also share in the fruits of victory. To refuse to recognise one's membership of a country at war is to rebel. In 1939 Temple described the pacifist as in a sense a modern representative of the monastic principle. Just as not all Christians are called on to be monks or nuns, neither should all Christians be pacifists. 'If all Christians took that course, there would be no Christian impulse behind the civic enterprise of justice. I have been urged to receive the evil of the Nazi regime into my own soul as a redemptive sacrifice, instead of resisting it. But no one has told me how I am to do this. The actual effect of our all turning pacifists would probably be the continued obliteration of the Polish and Czech States and the avoidance of any diminution of our own material wealth.'[9]

So too in 'A Conditional Justification of War' he recognises the way of the monk and of the Christian citizen as two ways of Christian obedience. But if a pacifist merely refuses to fight then he enjoys the immunity and food provided by the Armed Services, so he has made a very slender witness to the supremacy of love. He should go further and contract out of the advantages as out of the obligations of the secular order of society. Those who do this – for instance, by sharing the lot of the very poor in order to bring them new strength and hope – really are pioneers of a better order. But those who accept the common obligations of men are also pioneers. 'The Kingdom of God uses the service of both – of the Good Samaritan and the Good Centurion.'[10]

The other form in which Temple's anti-Manichaean thrust appears is in his treatment of the question of force. True, Christ could not win His Kingdom by force. But we are left with the fact of the existence of force, and the issue with the pacifist can be put in the form: Is the true Christian principle the abolition of force or its consecration? In the Church Assembly in 1932 Temple posed this question to pinpoint the difference between himself and a pacifist speaker. His own view was for the consecration of force, as of all other powers possessed by man. This meant using the means of force only in ways agreed, either by the national community or the community of nations, for the maintenance of its own general law. So too in 1941 Temple said force was an indispensable element in the ordering of life. To consecrate force is to subject it completely to law, the law which should be expressive of the highest welfare of mankind at large, and must be continually revised to that end.[11]

Temple's accusation in 1935 that pacifists had Pelagian tendencies undoubtedly arose from his strongly held belief in the limited yet indispensable role of the state. The issue is set out remarkably well as early as 1914.[12] Can the state obey the Christian law at all? 'Has self-sacrifice any real meaning when applied to communities, and if so is it in their case a virtue?' And if the Christian law is held to be inapplicable or unattainable by a state, what is the individual Christian to do? Most Christians, says Temple, reject pacifism; for the nation is not prepared to accept it; and in any case the war would go on, evil forces would triumph, and heroic sacrifices would fail of result. Men sense their solidarity with the nation, and so give it their utmost support. 'In adopting this attitude they do not feel that they are compromising Christian principle. A nation has a real existence. It, as well as the individual, has a contribution to make to the Kingdom of God. The individual cannot live wholly to himself ... Nevertheless it does seem to involve us in ... the entanglement of sin ... A sinful man *cannot* live the life of Christ; a sinful nation *cannot* perfectly obey His law; and the citizen of a sinful nation *cannot* escape altogether from his nation's sin.' Temple quotes St. Paul: 'Wretched man that I am, who shall deliver me from the body of this death?'

Temple is at his most explicit on this matter in correspondence he had in 1944 with Mr. Derek Fane, who had written to him on the question of pacifism and ordination.[13] In his first reply Temple wrote: 'I believe that there are Christians who are called to personal pacifism and to give the special witness which this carries; but if they go on to say that *all* Christians ought to be pacifists, I believe that they are involved in profound theological error – and that of such a kind as to be disastrous to the cause of Christian civilisation.' Fane's position is that pacifism is either right for everyone or for no-one, otherwise it cannot be standing for any objective standard of right. He presses Temple to say where a competent and authoritative statement of the 'profound theological error' can be found – one which is neither a bare statement of the opposing view, nor a statement of theological principles with which Fane and his pacifist friends agree as fully as anyone. Temple's reply is succinct. There is no formal pronouncement of the Church. 'But the error in question consists in one or other of two lines of thought which may also be combined. One is the notion that the National State ought in its dealings with other National States to act upon principles that would be proper for Christian individuals to adopt for the guidance of their conduct; the other is the notion that Christians can and should detach themselves from their civic obligations when these require them to do as citizens what they would not do as isolated Christian individuals. There is a theology of the State which involves obligations for Christian citizens, and it seems to me that as a rule my pacifist friends have a theology of the Church but no theology of the State at all.'

Because of his theology of the state Temple can refute the view that what is morally wrong cannot be politically right. He can also distinguish between fighting for the Kingdom of God and fighting for a Christian civilisation. 'If you look at the New Testament carefully there can be no doubt that there is a theology of the State as well as of the Church, and that it is our duty to do as citizens in support of the State things which it would be inappropriate to do as Churchmen in support of the Church and its cause. The soldiers are therefore quite right when they say that war is not Christianity, but they would be quite wrong if they went on to say that therefore Christians ought not to fight. The duty to fight is a civic duty which, if the cause is good, Christianity accepts and approves, but it is not a duty which has its origin in Christianity as such.' The nearest he came to obliterating this distinction was in his Enthronement Sermon at Canterbury, where he favoured the utmost effort to win the war, not only to keep open the possibility of a Christian civilisation but also to prevent the destruction of the Ecumenical Movement, on which he set high hopes.[14]

Temple has no illusions about the dangers of resorting to force. It is very hard, he says, to extract justice from strife; passions evoked by war blind vision and distort judgement; victory will not result in pure justice, but it can result in something far nearer justice than a Nazi domination. 'No positive good can be done by force . . . But evil can be checked and held back by force . . .' And he had no doubt that it was vital to pursue justice by force if necessary.

One of his most forthright statements came in 1935, only a few days after his remarks about the heretical tendencies of pacifism. It well illustrates the anti-Pelagian dimension. Speaking at Pontefract he replied to a letter in *The Times* from the pacifist C. E. Raven. He agreed that the goal was peace; the problem was the way. 'Of course the ideal of mutual love holds for all men and women and for all human groups.' Converting the world to the Christian faith is the primary task. 'But if, while that process of conversion is incomplete, the Christian calls nations to act by love only, when justice is still insecure, he is likely to receive immediate applause but to produce no actual result. Love of neighbour is very hard for individuals; for nations it is much harder. God's grace makes each possible for those who seek that grace; but till nations, as nations, learn to do this, the law of love is beyond their reach. The virtue that can be effectively established is justice, and I have no doubt at all that we must hasten the coming of the Kingdom of love at this stage by pointing to it as the only true object of man's hopes, by calling all men to the practice of Christian faith and religion, whereby alone those hopes can be fulfilled, and meanwhile by bending our energies to establish for its sake the rule of justice among nations.'[15]

Temple used one other line of attack on pacifism. Again it is theological in its root. He believed that some pacifists subscribed to the view that physiological life is absolutely sacred. This would, says Temple, be a Hindu or Buddhist position, but not a Christian one. For it rules out giving one's life as well as taking another's. But if the Christian is not to count his life dear, then as compared with some other things loss of life and taking it are a small injury. The New Testament word for 'life' has the deeper connotation of personality capable of eternal life, not merely life in the animal sense. War is certainly horrible; but so is a Nazi concentration camp, or the suppression of national community. The question is therefore: How can I prevent the greatest imminent evil or promote the greatest practicable good? And Temple warns about emotions playing us false: 'We cannot in the proper sense *think* about this except by achieving such a measure of detachment as to seem cold-blooded; the alternative is to be swayed by feelings, and then we easily think that to be most wrong which we feel to be most disgusting – which may have very little to do with the moral issue.'[16]

Temple was never prepared to rate suffering as the principal form of evil. The root evil lay in Nazi tyranny which was destroying European civilisation; the issue was a matter of justice for nations and individuals; it posed the question whether the form of civilisation which had grown up out of the Christian doctrine about God was to have wider scope or not. Nor was he willing to look on war itself as the principal evil. 'So far as I can see, we shall be playing upon the surface if we regard war itself as the evil rather than as one form in which the evil of the world is peculiarly obvious, when it occurs.' The real disease was not war itself, but selfishness and self-seeking; true peace could be secured not by the prohibition of force, but by instilling the root principle that we are members one of another.[17]

It is difficult to convey the strength of Temple's conviction that pacifism as a universal principle was a serious error. The gulf he felt between pacifists and himself is perhaps best appreciated by words of almost bitter disappointment spoken in 1941. 'Is it not true that the peace movement in the period following the last war was desperately weakened by an attempt to compromise between those who were persuaded that force must be used, and even ought to be used, and those who believed that it ought not?' It was no good pursuing a common goal by diametrically opposite means, even if it was sad to part company in practice with those whose goals were the same. 'With all friendship for those who must disagree with us, we must say "If you can win a majority, go your way; if not, we must go ours".'[18]

The word 'friendship' is not a vacuous term. Temple was well respected in pacifist circles. Early in the Second World War he helped to gather a group of pacifists and non-pacifists whose prime aim was to affirm their ultimate unity in Christ. To this end they produced a statement 'Towards a Christian Britain' and then the book *Is Christ Divided?* Temple consistently held the view that some Christians were called to be pacifists. It was a one-sided testimony, which counter-balanced the tendency towards sheer materialism and worship of force; it bore witness to the un-Christian character of war, to the supremacy of love, and to the world-wide family of God.[19] This was similar to the vocation of some to point to a pure ideal of social relationships in fellowship and love, which probably could not be translated immediately into any political programme or picture at all. He quotes St. Francis's vocation to embrace holy poverty. However, says Temple, St. Francis never said everyone ought to abandon worldly goods; and it would have been 'a stark dereliction of duty' for Pope Innocent III to join the Franciscans. Temple seems to have been influenced here by Jesus' 'double principle' – in the world but not of it. His way of doing justice to both and finding 'the line of true adjustment' is to reject pacifism as a universal principle, but to respect 'personal pacifism'. However, Temple soon realised that this position was no satisfactory synthesis in the eyes of pacifists. In *Is Christ Divided?* he admitted that 'the difference is profound and incapable of adjustment'.[20] He had immediately in mind here the pacifist who based himself on an absolute imperative, but equally he could find no adjustment with those like C. E. Raven who differed from him more at the level of the effectiveness of the rival positions. The book brings out well both the strength of the two positions and the impossibility of synthesis. In fact Temple's treatment of pacifism is a good illustration of the way his propensity for Hegelian synthesis can take the edge off the dilemmas which Christianity is uniquely equipped to recognise. I shall develop a critique of Temple on pacifism in a moment, and pursue it through into a consideration of the way he relates love and justice in Chapter 15.

Temple's respect for personal pacifism made him a staunch defender of the recognition of conscientious objection in both world wars. The issue, as he saw it in 1916, concerned the adjustment of the duty and rights of the state and the duty and rights of the individual. He upheld the duty of the individual to follow his conscience, in the sense of his deliberate judgement with regard to the right course to follow. But the state also had a moral judgement to follow. If there was a clash, each party ought to respect the other, and remember that conscience is fallible. The state should sift out true conscientious objectors. Many objectors were devoted servants of the country, and it was only through individuals that progress was made. Since the state could only deal with acts and not with motives, it should say ' "I believe that you are wrong. I believe that I have the right to say that you must either defend your country or cease to be a member of it. But I will not say this. I will appoint you to work unconnected with the war;

work disagreeable and not well paid; so I shall test those who are acting by a genuine moral judgement. And you, if you are honest, will make no complaint." ' Consistently with this position Temple argued the following year that the state had the right to debar conscientious objectors from voting; but it was not wise to do so, since conscientious objection had already been recognised by the state without threat of subsequent disabilities, and many objectors were vigorous workers for a better ordering of society. More fundamentally, there was a danger of Britain, like Germany, making the state supreme in the moral sphere. The first duty of the state was not to secure its own safety but to recognise the authority of Christ. We should therefore be more lenient and respectful to the conscientious objector who had interpreted Christ's claims differently from the state.[21]

Temple's basic position on pacifism is convincing. He does, however, grant himself too easy a victory. He does not quite reckon seriously enough with competent pacifist thinkers and he reveals one persistent weakness.

It is, first of all, by no means certain that one can simply divide pacifists into those who stand by absolute principle and those who balance estimates of greater and lesser evil. The pacifist G. H. C. Macgregor, for instance, in *The New Testament Basis of Pacifism* (1936), believes it absurd to renounce *all* use of force, including the maintenance of order by civil authority.[22] His central point is that, since the moral order is one whose basic principle is love, only those social sanctions are justifiable which are ultimately redemptive, that is, designed to win men back from evil to good by evoking from them a response to the appeal of love. The tension between the laws of the Kingdom of God and the forces of evil reaches breaking point in the matter of war: war is wrong because it essentially contradicts the principle of love, so stultifying the specifically Christian method of meeting evil. We shall never affirm to others that the moral order is one of love by blowing them to pieces.[23] Macgregor insists that pacifists do not passively practise non-resistance, as if it were the essential principle of Christian ethics. The injunction in the Sermon on the Mount not to resist evil is followed by the positive commands 'Love your enemies' and 'Be perfect as your heavenly Father is perfect'.

Furthermore Macgregor's case does not rest on isolated texts; like Temple he considers the total impression of Jesus' deeds and words, and he finds confirmation in St. Paul. At the centre is love of neighbour, rooted in God who loves all men impartially and sets an infinite value on every individual. This love of neighbour is to be interpreted in the light of Jesus' own way of life and above all in the light of the Cross.[24] With this vantage point and a professional approach to exegesis (he was Professor of Biblical Criticism at Glasgow) Macgregor concedes that the episode of the two swords (Luke 22.36–38) may imply the disciples had carried swords on their journeys for self-defence, but he rightly maintains that Jesus' words must not carry too much weight. They may be metaphorical or ironical, and cannot be taken as an endorsement of armed force. Similarly Jesus' reply to Pilate cannot be taken simply to mean it would be right to fight for an earthly kingdom, but not for spiritual truth; for surely the Christian is to practise here in the world an ethic which is not of this world.[25]

We can perhaps already see what is Temple's persistent weakness. It is a tendency (not consistent, but persistent) to assume a comfortable fit between the Kingdom of God and the kingdoms of the world. The questionableness of all forms of coercion, and especially war, does not find adequate expression. This can be amply and simply illustrated.

First, it is precarious, even with the qualifications he uses, for Temple to say that the law of love commands fighting, or that killing is absolutely right in certain circumstances. Granted the necessity of choosing the least evil course of action and of implementing it decisively, it is vital to be constantly reminded that the action is in a profound sense a contradiction of the law of love. Temple fares better when he reminds us that even when we do the best we can in the circumstances we still need to be penitent and seek God's mercy.[26]

Secondly, Temple is inclined to stress the continuity of Law and the Gospel by recourse to the word 'fulfilment', and to suggest that Law must be secured before we respond to the Gospel. He once wrote: 'Sound doctrine and experience alike assure us that the stage of the Law must precede that of the Gospel, and that, though the Gospel carries us far beyond the Law, we need the foundation provided by the Law to be secure before we can truly respond to the Gospel.'[27] As Macgregor points out, Temple's wording easily plays into the hands of the militarist, who will fight another war to secure righteousness as a basis for the Gospel. In fact, however, the New Testament shows the Gospel being offered to Jew and Greek *before* the Law is secure, and moreover as the only way of establishing the Law.[28] Temple is more profound when he recognises frankly (as we shall see) that, even if proximate justice is a necessary precondition for love, nonetheless perfect justice can only be had as the product of the perfect love of God in men's hearts. Certainly something more profound than a comfortable two-tier concept of the relation of Law and Gospel, righteousness and love, is required.[29]

Equally suspect is Temple's phrase 'the consecration of force', which is advanced against the supposed Manichaeism of pacifists.[30] We can agree that the universe is sacramental and that force is a feature of it, which must be used according to God's will. But we need to remember that in the Second World War the fruit of consecration was the bombing of dams and the crippling of the German war effort. We may concede a relative legitimation of such acts, but to speak of consecration is to invest acts of war with a false aura, and to weaken defences against those more questionable acts of military 'necessity' which Britain in fact shamefully committed.[31] Temple is on safer ground when he notes the capacity of self-interest to masquerade as justice. Our consecrations may be corrupt![32]

Fourthly, Temple is ill-advised to speak of pacifists as being rebels against their membership of society.[33] Quite apart from falsely impugning the motives of many pacifists, Temple underplays the tensions which arise between loyalty to God and Caesar. A pacifist like Macgregor certainly would endorse a Christian impulse behind the civic enterprise of justice. His agony is that in the matter of war the claims of Caesar and God collide. As he sees it, he puts God first and his loyalty to the universal Body of Christ above loyalty to the national community.[34] His case is a strong one, and it will not do for Temple to come down quite so simply in favour of the 'good centurion' and to find a 'line of true adjustment' by rejecting pacifism as a universal principle but respecting 'personal pacifism'.[35] It is Temple, rather than the pacifists, who reintroduces the concept of the monastic minority.

They would rightly claim that pacifism was the way of the pre-monastic early Church as a whole, and say it ought to be a way for all Christians alike to-day.[36]

The pacifist case, however, does not carry conviction. Temple is fundamentally right to assert that in his day there was no option but to weigh up alternatives and choose the lesser evil, which in 1939 was war. The alternative would have been total Nazi domination of Europe, implying mass executions and the annihilation of all European Jews, to say nothing of the prostitution of values and the corruption of countless minds. It is, alas, vain to claim, as the pacifists did, that the third possibility between war and submission was to obey Christ's call to the way of the Cross, either because our faithful obedience could precipitate an inrush of God's power to transform the situation, or simply because Christ's way is the Way of Crucifixion – and through it ultimate victory.[37] Even if it is true that Jesus did not calculate consequences as His hour of death approached, one cannot deliberately ignore consequences and in the name of love of neighbour court the death and corruption of millions, least of all against their will. Temple was right: it was not a moral requirement that the British nation voluntarily undergo self-sacrifice, since that would do nothing to rescue subjugated Europe.

CHAPTER 13

WAR

In both World Wars Temple offered some theological reflection on the causes of war which led him to make suggestions about the spirit in which Britain should face it. In a sermon preached in February 1916 Temple branded as sheer superstition the idea that God deliberately caused the war to punish men for sins such as drunkenness or impurity or Sabbath-breaking. The causes of war lie in human wills. 'All the way through [the] Gospel of St. John we are taught that a judgement of God is not a deliberate act of His intervening in the world to make guilty people suffer, but an automatic product of His Presence and Revelation. So we shall think of this war. It is, indeed, a judgement upon the world of sin ... The sin which led immediately to the outbreak of war we may believe to be mainly in one nation, but the root is to be found among all peoples, and not only among those who are fighting, but neutral peoples just as much. The punishment for that sin comes through the moral order which God has set up in the world, an order which reacts upon those who break it.' Clearly Temple believed it was fundamentally the doctrine of God that was at stake. So too in 1940 he says the Gospel message that God is love must be a message of judgement as well as consolation; for it pronounces doom upon every selfish purpose or person or nation. 'Under that judgement and that doom we now stand.'[1]

Temple never gave a detailed analysis of the causes of the wars. As we have already seen, he was sometimes inclined to see a direct causal connection between competitive trade and war. Yet he consistently singles out nationalism as the central issue. During the First World War the chief foe is idolatry of the national state by Germany. He thinks the moral principles of Bismarck were simply national egoism and the superiority of the state to all obligations. In 1943 the diagnosis is the same: since the Middle Ages one department in life after another had claimed autonomy. 'So the State came to be thought of as an end in itself – a doctrine long held in Germany and nakedly proclaimed by the Nazis: the idolatry of the State.'[2] This criticism was not directed at Germany alone.

Britain's own patriotism was tribal. Any patriot should remember that Christ died neither as a soldier nor for his country. Temple's consistent view was that there could be a Christian patriotism, but it entailed always checking loyalty to one's own nation by recognition that 'we are members one of another', and that every other nation has its own place with its own excellencies to contribute.[3]

The only answer to the crisis was a return to Christian belief, he said. In our enjoyment of life we had thought that what we had learnt to value must be prized by all sane men. The trouble with the Nazis was not that they did not practise what they preached. Their actual standards were perverted. For Temple the only ground of confidence in our values was God as Christ had made Him known. Yet the paradox of modern English culture was that though it was largely Christian in quality, it regarded faith in God as a dispensable indulgence. Neglect of God naturally led to violation of His law; the first need was to return to God. It was astonishingly silly to say that a man's religion was a private affair between him and his Maker; and we were not going to extirpate fervent Nazi belief by a 'mild haze of cautiously held opinions.'[4]

It is little wonder therefore that Temple persistently called his fellow-countrymen to penitence. He was a leading figure in the National Mission of Repentance and Hope in 1916. The call is most insistent in the hour of victory or when the tide is turning in Britain's favour. In his editorial in *The Challenge* immediately after Armistice Day he stresses the responsibility which rests on the British, and wonders whether they have really learned their lesson and repented. At Christmas 1942 he quotes the Miserere (Psalm 51) and warns of the danger of pride and forgetfulness of God.[5] For Temple penitence is a necessary attitude in facing the massive suffering which the war entailed.

Nothing correspondingly roused Temple more than self-righteous talk of reprisals. He would have only the minimum of suffering inflicted on the enemy. True, Britain's duty in the World Wars was to fight, and that meant fighting effectively. Yet that did not give her *carte blanche* to inflict whatever suffering she liked. In an editorial of 1915 Temple deplored high-level and therefore indiscriminate bombing. It was not true that any methods of warfare would do. 'Men are not logical machines and they have not such perfect control of their own psychological mechanism that they can permit themselves to commit outrages in war and yet remain as morally sensitive as ever when peace returns.' We should not minimise risk to our lives without taking moral considerations into account. Temple distinguished reprisals (injury inflicted in proportion to injury received) from retaliation as a policy of preventing further injury to the defenceless. But he doubted whether either would be effective. Above all we had to bear in mind the purpose for which we were fighting: 'Our capacity to advance the cause of international law will be enormously increased if out of respect for it we have submitted to outrages which we were only able to prevent by imitating our enemies' disregard of that law.'[6]

Fearing degeneration of character, Temple's watchwords are steadfastness, vigilance, discipline. Not only must men show no hatred. 'The religion of Christ is the defiance of what – apart from it – seems to be nature.' We must love and pray for our enemies. Love of enemies was quite compatible with severity, but there was an immense difference between severity and ill-will, as the behaviour of Christ to his opponents showed. Similarly, any prayer which denied the Germans had the same right of approach to God was unacceptable. The Lord's Prayer was the model, for in war-time Briton and German could have knelt side by side and meant the same thing as they said it.[7] Temple was certainly aware of the immense difficulty of combining severity and sensitivity in the name of love. This is most apparent in his correspondence with Marshal of the Royal Air Force Sir John Salmond, who complained that Temple's reported regret over necessary military operations was likely to sap men's strength of will in a hard and ruthless task. Temple's reply contained these words: 'It is of real importance to maintain, as far as one can, sensitiveness to the horrors of war even while one is facing them. I do not the least believe that it diminishes the readiness for endurance or for thoroughness, but it does something to counteract the inevitable hardening tendency of war of which the final result is as expressed in Shakespeare's terrible line, "All pity choked with custom of fell deeds".'[8]

The suspicion must remain of a discrepancy between these fine words and Temple's reaction to the bombing of Germany in the

Second World War. He saw the bombing of dams and cities as legitimate acts of war. He drew on Catholic tradition to distinguish between causing something by direct intention and causing it incidentally. Repeated pressure, especially from Bishop Bell of Chichester, came over the systematic bombing of whole cities area by area. One correspondent said of the bombing of Berlin, 'If we accept this, there is nothing we shall not accept – we shall no longer be fighting for any ethical standards.' Temple fended this off by saying he had no evidence of deliberate attacks on an area which was not a real military objective; total war had made the distinction between combatants and non-combatants almost non-existent. Temple satisfied himself too easily with assurances from the Air Ministry that communities were destroyed only if that was necessary to cripple the German war effort, and he was slow to realise the probability of a discrepancy between official directives and practice.[9]

Temple's concern for the relief of suffering earned him very wide respect. He personally showed his support for Poles by speaking at the Anglo-Polish Christian Circle.[10] It was however to the case of the Jews that Temple devoted the greatest energy in the relief of suffering. As early as 1933–34 Temple had collected evidence about the concentration camps, submitted it for examination by a High Court Judge, and written a personal appeal to Hitler. It was eventually received and acknowledged by the German ambassador to Britain, Ribbentrop. Temple was always watchful about signs of anti-Semitism in Britain, and in 1938 joined with others to write a letter of assurance to the Chairman of the Jewish Board of Deputies, Neville Laski, repudiating anti-Semitism as wicked folly. During the war he became President of the Council of Christians and Jews. Twice he pressed hard the case of the Jews in the Lords. His chief protest was against any shelving of responsibility by delay in decision. Men's obligations are decided for them by the contingencies which they did not themselves create and very largely by the actions of wicked men. 'The priest and the Levite in the parable were not in the least responsible for the traveller's wounds as he lay there by the roadside, and no doubt they had many other pressing things to attend to, but they stand as the picture of those who are condemned for neglecting the opportunity of showing mercy.'[11]

Temple also gave what encouragement he could, limited though it was bound to be, to the German Confessing Church. In January 1943 he preached at Pastor Niemöller's birthday service in the German Lutheran Church in London. Here he honoured the leaders of the Confessing Church, thanking God that the one effective centre of resistance to Nazi oppression in Germany had been the Christian Church. He did however express regret (somewhat unfairly with hindsight) that they had not protested so far at the extermination of Poles and Jews. 'It has been protest in self-defence rather than protest on behalf of outraged justice and of brotherly love.' What was at stake was not the survival of an ecclesiastical institution but the capacity of the Christian fellowship to give fearless testimony to Christian truth. By contrast Christians in Holland had condemned the treatment of Jews. But it was to those who had resisted Hitler that he looked for the re-education of the German nation after the war. 'I set great hopes upon those people in Germany who through this time have been suffering bravely and constantly for the truth, persecuted and oppressed, and who will be recognised afterwards as having alone been loyal to what would have saved their nation from disaster.'[12]

CHAPTER 14

PEACE

1. *The First World War*

Much of Temple's early thought about peace reveals an unsatisfactory juxtaposition of sober realism about international politics and flights of idealism about the capacity of the Church to raise the human race towards the Kingdom of God. Take a sermon of January 1915.[1] Temple acknowledges that there is some worth in peace construed as 'mere neutrality', where nations exist over against each other and only avoid war. But he soon rises to a rhapsody on the Church and the Kingdom of God. Religion, he says, starts with God and sees how in the light of revelation all the solution of human problems is to be found. It is the church's task to inspire the nations with a sense of their relations to one another. 'The Church's task is simply to turn men's attention and the nation's attention away from the things that have to be divided among men to those things which become the property of all ... We are co-operative already in the things that really matter. In the love of God we are united; we only need to find it out.' True, the Church should support schemes for international arbitration; but they can only carry authority where the nations agree to settle their differences by law. And 'what court or authority can dominate the nations sufficiently to make them feel that what unites them together is more precious than anything which separates them? There is only one ideal that can do that, the ideal of the Kingdom of God ...' These words do not really reckon with the intractable problem of the egoism of groups and institutions, even less with the highly ambiguous nature of the Church as an institution called to mediate God's judgement and salvation in history, yet composed of imperfectly redeemed sinners and prone to egoism itself.

It is in fact sometimes the very sense of man's predicament which drives Temple to his highly idealistic antidote. In *Christianity and War* he takes a depressed view of man's capacity for loyalty wider than national. The Church is neither One, nor Catholic, nor Holy. The need is for a united international society devoted to Christ, reviving the Christendom of the Middle Ages but free from its failure, that of using 'the world's methods for God's purpose'. True peace must consist in the recognition of all nations as parts of the one Kingdom of God realised on earth. The Church 'by binding its members to itself, while leaving them still fully citizens of their own countries, would aid enormously their desire to rise a little nearer to the ideal of Christ and draw their country with them.'[2]

These flights of idealism did not blind Temple to the necessity of facing complex realities as peace became a possibility. He was particularly forceful about the notion of forgiveness. The duty of forgiveness implied the duty of repentance and restitution by the guilty. 'To deny this is to repudiate the foundation truths of Christianity.' We should not barter away the issue we held in trust through unwillingness to endure to the end. In any case, it was easier for Britain to be magnanimous because she had not suffered as much as Russia or France. We could not afford to detach our interests from theirs or forfeit their friendship and thereby the best hope for peace. 'An insecure peace will enthrone militarism in every nation in Europe, till the fabric of European civilisation goes down in a new and vaster catastrophe.'[3]

This prophetic fear was not an isolated occurrence but a nagging anxiety. He could see that a League of Nations would be no necessary panacea. Alliances in the past had often been formed at the expense of liberalism. There was the danger that the nations constituting such a League might actually check the growth of freedom, or break up the League itself. Another danger was that the League might be controlled by a ring of international financiers. 'We earnestly desire,' Temple concludes, 'the establishment of this League of Nations; we wish it all possible success; but we dread above all things its failure, for if it is established and fails, the whole cause of peace and international goodwill must of necessity be put back for many generations.'[4]

In October 1918 Temple commented on the German peace proposals. At one point he was crucially at variance with Lloyd George and the mood of the country. 'We must consider all doubtful matters from the point of view not so much of our own estimation of justice, as of the peace and prosperity of the world for a generation yet unborn ... We must, above all things, be careful not to satisfy any passion of our own at the cost of involving them in any repetition of this world disaster; and we must remember that nothing is so likely to damage the peace of the world as the inclusion in the settlement of any terms which seem to any of the peoples involved a humiliation or an outrage. We all of us need humility; but humiliation is seldom the road to it. What we want is a peace of which German citizens of A.D. 1950 or 2000 will be prepared to say, "That was a settlement dictated by no self-interest in any quarter, but by justice alone".'[5] Temple hoped for an international court to try those directly responsible, but again warned it must be an impartial court.

2. *The inter-war years*

Humility by humiliation was the impossible way Lloyd George and the British electorate chose to travel. Intoxicated with the idea of hanging the Kaiser and extracting £6,600 m. reparations, Britons can hardly have noticed Temple's warnings. His article of July 1920 advocating 'moral opportunism' called for imagination, for self-sacrifice, and for thoughts to be fixed 'not on satisfying abstract justice, but on promoting the highest welfare of humanity in the days to come.' The people pursued the short-sighted policy of crippling Germany; Temple pointed out that to keep Germany poor was to prevent Britain herself from reaching her own highest wealth. He denied this was a piece of pure expediency. 'The economic law is merely an expression of the law of God, who made us so that if one member suffer, all must suffer with it . . .' A policy of stern retribution could do nothing but stiffen German resolve to fight again as soon as ever a chance of success emerged.[6]

Temple was distressed by incessant talk of Germany's guilt. In July 1922 he pleaded for the cessation of all argument about war guilt. Germany was indeed the aggressor, but the guilt was that of all Christendom. Besides, all talk of guilt obscured the fact that all European nations were inevitably interdependent, in more than an economic sense. Ten years later he was still pleading. He preached at Geneva before the international Disarmament Conference, including the words: 'One clause there is in the existing treaties which offends in principle the Christian conscience and for the deletion of which by proper authority the voice of Christendom must be raised. This is the clause which affixes to one group of belligerents in the Great War the whole guilt for its occurrence . . . We have to ask not only who dropped the match but who strewed the ground with gunpowder.' The sequel was a flurry of critical correspondence, which Temple answered in a preface to the sermon on its publication. The prize piece of misrepresentation was by Sir Austen Chamberlain, who took Temple to say that all nations were equally guilty, and lectured him on Christian morals. Perhaps this indicates the degree to which men were addicted to 'abstract justice'. Certainly it brings to light a dilemma which Temple never found it possible to resolve. 'If you fasten on a point like the War Guilt Clause,' he wrote to his brother, '. . . a lot of people forget (or never read) what you actually say, and attack you for something else. But if you only state principles, without any concrete application, no one knows that you have said anything at all.'[7]

Temple's watchword is: 'If you want peace, prepare for peace, not war.' But how was one to prepare for peace? Temple's thinking about the League of Nations shows the continuation of both idealistic and sober thinking. On the one hand, he says the message of the Christian Church to the nations of Europe is, Seek ye first the Kingdom of the God of love. Even the best scheme for the League of Nations will fail unless there is the spirit of dedication which no political machinery can call forth. On the other hand, particularly as the efforts for peace proved futile, Temple increasingly threw the emphasis on the relative value of the machinery. Any international tribunal might indeed show partiality; but the alternative was appeal to force, which did not even aim at impartiality or justice. In fact, the League of Nations and the Permanent Court of International Justice represented 'not a derogation from the sovereign rights of the national State, but the fulfilment of the State's essential principle. For the essence of the State is the subordination of all force to the authority of Law, and it is only through the League and the Court, or some strictly analogous organisation, that this subordination can be effected in international affairs . . . It is mere folly, and blindness to the laws of cause and effect wherein God's judgement is manifest, to suppose that mere good-will, apart from any appropriate organ of activity, can prevent disputes from issuing in war.'[8]

In an article of 1935 we find that the strands in Temple's thinking are beginning to fit into a more coherent structure. The ideal remains of the Church uniting men in a fellowship to which all natural divisions are irrelevant. It is to uphold certain basic principles: God as the Father of all men and the King of all nations; the importance of the individual; and the family of mankind. However, when it comes to practical policy, one complicating factor is the fact that 'all natural societies or groupings of men are animated by a measure of corporate egoism more intense than that which animates their component members as individuals.' For this the only cure is the conscious acceptance of Christianity. Until then 'the problem of Christian statesmanship is therefore to find the way in which national egoism may be subordinated to, and if possible made to serve, justice, peace and goodwill. For such a task we have no infallible guidance . . .' Temple suggests that no nation should judge its own cause; that competition in armaments should cease; that therefore the League of Nations should be strengthened. Even if we did not obtain what we considered justice from the International Court, we would get the benefits of an ordered community. Individual nations and the international community could then mutually defend each other. So too, a few months later, Temple could write: 'It is vain to ask of nations, such as they are, that they love one another – that is to say, that each will treat the interest of the others as on a level with its own apart from any further inducement. But it is possible to establish a measure of external justice among them, securing such conduct as love would prompt by making departure from this injurious to self-interest . . . We must use [political adjustments and contrivances] for what they are worth, while our spiritual attainments are so small. But the only true security for peace is in the goodwill of mutual love; and mutual love among men is the fruit of love of God in their hearts, and cannot spring from any other root.'[9]

Temple constantly urged the British Government to act through the League of Nations. He deplored the way the Government had waited until the League ruled that there should be an embargo on arms to Japan, because of its aggression against China, and had then imposed its own embargo on both Japan and China. One consequence could be that if all sizeable nations declared embargoes, smaller nations might have difficulty in

securing arms for their own defence. In indulging their virtuous
sentiments great nations would then have increased their own
preponderance. Any form of isolated action therefore did harm.[10]
Much worse was to follow. By August 1935 Temple was
writing to *The Times*, urging upon the Government the principle
that Britain should leave no doubt about her determination to use
the machinery of the League if other states would join us. The issue
was Italy's attack on Abyssinia. Temple half-expected the League
to call on member states to use force on behalf of Abyssinia. But no
call came, and by 1937 he was deploring the massacre of men,
women and children as a reprisal for an assassination attempt on
Italy's chief official in Addis Ababa. Failure to protest, he said, was
tantamount to acquiescence. 'Without protests standards
imperceptibly change; that which yesterday all agreed to regard as
permissible to no civilised power becomes to-day the accepted
commonplace, not alone of colonial rule but of war everywhere.
Tomorrow we may be the object or victim of the methods we
have allowed, by acquiescence, to become permissible.'[11] But
neither the League nor the British Government would act with
sufficient determination to prevent the deterioration of the
situation. They were equally ineffective over Spain. In 1936
Temple rejected Franco's claim to be representing Christianity,
and he feared a dictatorship in alliance with a reactionary Roman
Church. The following year he deplored the bombing of
Guernica, supported an appeal for funds to evacuate Basque
children, and finally joined in sending a manifesto to Franco,
warning him that wars started for high ideals could degenerate into
a bitterness which obscured or even replaced the original causes of
war, and urging him to make clear to the world the reasons which
he deemed sufficient for the continuance of the war.[12] Inevitably
there was no response.

Temple was one of the main disturbers of the policy of
appeasement. There is however no doubt that he did welcome
Neville Chamberlain's assurance of 'peace in our time' after the
Munich conference. But his letter to *The Times* shows that it was a
qualified welcome. In particular he saw that even if Germany had
some ground for grievance over the case of Czecho-Slovakia, there
was bound to be terrible hardship in the immediate future. He
supported a plea that Britain should give out of taxation an

estimate of the cost of one week's war to the Czechs as a contribution to resettlement.[13] His support for this suggestion – almost a species of charitable 'ambulance work' by the guilty – is an index of Temple's desperation. All that remained was the collapse of the promised peace.

3. The Second World War

A study of Temple's thought in the period of the Second World War reveals the deployment of most of the positions he had built up over twenty-five years. He repeatedly criticised the Versailles Treaty: it had created a real sense of grievance by humiliating Germany. In correspondence in *The Daily Telegraph* he demonstrated against criticism that the Allies had agreed that the Peace Treaty of 1919 should be based upon the Fourteen Points of President Wilson's address, but had then failed to keep their word. Temple warned against a repetition of vindictiveness. This was bound up not only with the question of peace aims but also with war aims. He was adamant that there could be no peace with Hitler's regime, not because it was undemocratic but because it was utterly untrustworthy. But if we could assure German opponents of Hitler that there would be no vindictive settlement, there was a chance that the German people themselves might eventually overthrow Hitler. In February 1940, at the invitation of the Primate of Norway, Temple was able with others to confer with leaders of the Scandinavian Church and agree that it would be right for Britain to enter into negotiations with Germany if the Czechs, Slovaks, and Poles were guaranteed independence and included with others in a congress to negotiate a definitive peace. Temple's consistent policy was a dual one: defamation of the Nazis but justice to the German people.[14]

We can see the development of Temple's thought about love, power and justice from three contributions he made. They show increased penetration of thought about the application of Christian concepts to harsh realities.

The first concerns a settlement with Germany after the war.[15] Temple distinguishes first between an interim and a permanent settlement, and secondly between corrective justice (sub-divided into retributive, deterrent and reformative) and distributive justice. Temple gives two reasons for making an interim settlement: first, passions could cool and dispassionate judgements be formed – in a period of five years men would be able to see what are the real problems; secondly, preparation for a general peace conference could go ahead through the collection of facts and consultation. All nations defeated or occupied by Germany should have a voice, with neutrals as assessors. The interim settlement should be in part penal, to avoid any condoning of German actions. 'It must be made clear to all German people that such aggression brings calamity to the aggressor as well as to his victims. This is required by justice, and is, I think, a necessary preliminary to the re-education of the German mind vitiated by years of Nazi propaganda.' Temple believes the penal element of the truce should be such as to touch the national and political rather than the personal and economic life of the people; only so would it be relevant.

Temple denies that this is contrary to the Christian principle of free forgiveness; for forgiveness, to be real, must be costly; and secondly, no nation has ever been Christian in a degree that makes free forgiveness applicable to it, so 'infliction of a just penalty is nearer to Christian righteousness than such action as seems to condone the wrong.' In a note Temple stresses that free forgiveness is in fact conditional. The first condition is repentance in the sense of the change of heart which leads us to take God's view of the world instead of our own – the reversal of our original sin, which it is not in our power to effect. Secondly, there must be no condoning of evil. This condition is fulfilled on the Cross, since there we see what man's injury to God really was and is. 'It is only when forgiveness is accompanied or preceded by such agony that it is altogether right. That is why St. Paul says that the Cross enables God to be just while He forgives, to forgive while remaining just. No man can quite reach that height. No nation can come near it, nor ever will be able to do so while History lasts. For History is the record of man's entanglement in sin; and though in the final consummation sin will be done away, that consummation lies beyond the historical process. So we have not got to consider what perfectly righteous England might achieve, but what is the best that sinful England may hope to do.'

As for a permanent settlement, all thought of corrective justice must be eliminated. It must aim at distributive justice, 'all nations, including Germany, taking part on equal terms in the negotiations, and all having equal claim to consideration and their fair share in organizing the common life for the common good.' The embittering conditions of a penal peace must be avoided, for any penal element would, as the years passed, press upon citizens not guilty of the crime.

Temple could see in 1940 that any settlement with Germany would raise the question of the effectiveness of any future League of Nations. An important article appeared in *The Fortnightly* in May 1940 entitled 'Principles of Reconstruction'.[16] It begins with a statement of five relevant principles. We are already familiar with the content of three: of men as children of God, of personality as sacred, of men as members of one family. Significantly, Temple's fourth and fifth principles relate to sin and to nations. Men are self-centred; deliverance can come only by the active love (grace) of God calling out surrender and trust (faith). 'So far as this has not happened or has incompletely happened ... they need to be restrained in their self-assertiveness and induced by appeals to their self-interest to respect justice in their mutual dealings.' Nations exist by God's providence; national loyalty is by its own nature wholesome, but is infected by self-centredness. 'Thus if there is to be any approach to a brotherly fellowship of nations before all men are converted to a life of perfect love, it must be by the same method of so organising their relationship to one another that national self-interest will itself urge justice in action.' Thus, guided by realism elevated to a principle, Temple thinks that, short of the leavening influence of an effective universal Church, the way forward best lies in the organised co-operation of groups of people sufficiently close in tradition and interest for this to be voluntarily accepted, yet sufficiently disparate to introduce some effective checks and balances. He suggests the Danubian group; the Czechs, Slovaks and Poles; Scandinavia; and Great Britain, France and the 'Benelux' countries. Temple is searching for something practicable, intermediate between complete national autonomy and a general federation.

These local federations would be included in a more comprehensive League of Nations. A critical question was whether the authority of the League should be moral only or also coercive.

Here Temple is clearer in his negative than his positive views. We had to get rid of uncertain sanctions, either by making them certain or by abolishing them. Experience had taught us not to leave the application of sanctions to sovereign states.

The third significant contribution of Temple was made in a House of Lords debate in December 1943 on the Allied Conferences.[17] It was perhaps his greatest demonstration of realism. Temple claimed that there was much confusion over power politics. 'The *Machtpolitik* of Germany . . . has so alienated people who have any hope of seeing politics based on a moral foundation that they have become unwilling to recognise any permanent place for force in the organisation of the world, and there has come to pass a desire to regard power as a passing factor which the progress of the world will dispense with. Therefore it seems to some of us of very great importance, if we disagree with that, to lay the foundation clear that power, though it is not an aim to be rightly accepted as the governing principle in our policy, is none the less a fact in the world, and will continue to be a fact in the world, which must be recognised and controlled.' Thus Britain's desire for a balance of power in Europe cannot be an end in itself, but it is an indispensable condition for any worthy goal, because no nation which feels itself threatened can devote itself wholeheartedly to the tasks of peace in a co-operative spirit. The whole British Commonwealth should remain strong. Many friends in Europe had felt deserted by Britain in the period after 1918. If this time we helped to maintain a balance of power, a good neighbour policy might be built up which would include even Britain's present enemies. Our aims should therefore be, in order, first to provide security against aggression, even if that involves surrendering some of our sovereignty; secondly, the social welfare of all peoples, partly under the auspices of a new League of Nations encompassing much more than the political field; thirdly, to diminish the excessive significance of political frontiers, which curiously had been a product of the growth of democracy.

There can be no doubt that Temple's sense of the harsh reality of life is more marked in his last years. There was however no total change. He had appreciated the necessity of compromise at least as early as 1912. And there is no abandonment, even in his latest writing, of lofty aspirations; the hope for an effective international

Church grows with the development of the Ecumenical Movement.[18] There does appear to be a more coherent structure or groundwork to his later, as compared with his earlier, thought, centred on the concepts of love and justice. In the next chapter I shall co-ordinate Temple's views on love and justice and consider the adequacy of his position with particular reference to Reinhold Niebuhr.

CHAPTER 15

LOVE AND JUSTICE

In his handling of pacifism Temple repeatedly used parallel pairs of concepts: love and justice, Gospel and Law, Church and state. These are plainly models which enabled him to orient himself in this issue. We need therefore to pursue our critique of Temple into the area of his basic models. Let us concentrate on instances of the use of love and justice, whilst bringing in the other pairs to provide further illumination. First, then, what was Temple's position over the relationship between love and justice? Since he never wrote a systematic exposition of this we have to construct an answer out of a large number of scattered references. We shall do this for the period 1934 to 1944; for it was only in these years that Temple gave persistent and explicit attention to this topic, and it is on the relatively stable and coherent position he then held that he can most fairly be judged. We shall then go on to consider the challenge presented to him by Reinhold Niebuhr ('the troubler of my peace'), and see how successful Temple was in responding to him, given his own background in the Anglican tradition.[1] First, however, let us see Temple's position over the relationship between love and justice.

(a) *The basic relationship of love and justice*
Justice is not identical with love: it does not exhaust the meaning of love. Love *transcends* justice. For justice is a virtue relevant to the realm of claim and counter-claim; but where love is established these claims simply do not arise. This does not mean that justice is something contrary or alien to love, which love mitigates or softens.[2] Nor does it mean that love can leave justice behind. For love *presupposes* justice as a virtue applicable to the relations between groups. Similarly, the Gospel does not negate or leave behind the Law, but rather presupposes it. This is the basis of Temple's complaint of Marcionism in the pacifist position.[3]

(b)   *The problem of group relations*

Groups have acquired a novel prominence through the development of man's control of nature. People are now bound together in units which are both larger and more closely knit. It is precisely in the mutual relations of groups that the chief problems of modern life are found. Love in the hearts of individuals would ease group relationships, but it could not settle them. Can the law of love be directly applied to groups? Temple cites the case of Christian ratepayers who created goodwill by asking for an increase in the rates in the interests of slum-clearance. Such an application of the law of love is, however, all too rare, and this prompts Temple to ask whether this rarity is because of a remediable selfishness in individuals, or whether there is some obstacle in the very nature of corporate relations, and, if so, whether this is an ordinance of God or a product of man's corrupt nature.[4]

As an answer to these questions Temple first holds that quite apart from complications due to sin, social relationships do modify the content of duty. Thus it might be noble for a bachelor but blameworthy for a father to undertake a risky form of social service. But Temple devotes most space, in various places, to the factor of man's entanglement in sin. Neither individuals nor groups are able to fulfil the law of love. In nearly every social institution, policy, or action, we find evidence of the two foundations of society of which Plato writes in the second book of *The Republic*: the positive principle of mutual need and help, and the negative principle of competing selfishness.[5] On the one hand man's membership of groups, such as his citizenship, is part of God's purpose for him. On the other hand, groups are prone to an egoism far more intense than that of an individual. Voluntary associations may exhibit self-concern, but it is especially a danger with natural communities from family to nation. All these are inevitably self-regarding. They generate a devotion which has no object outside of them. This is particularly true of a nation; for it is able to appeal both to the altruism and to the egoism of its citizens. The effects of this exorbitant egoism can be mitigated only if the members of the community feel they have a loyalty to a wider group. Family egoism is effectively checked by national loyalty. But there is no effective check on national egoism, and it can be demoniac.[6]

Groups, therefore, and especially nations are far less amenable to the law of love than individuals. To call on nations to act by love only is likely to produce no actual result, when large numbers of citizens are wholly or partly unconverted, and when nations as nations do not seek God's grace. The way of redemptive suffering, whilst ideally best, would in the conditions of Europe of 1939 be completely impracticable and ineffectual.[7]

A further complication is that groups function through representatives, who act as trustees for the interests of the members. It would be ridiculous for a Trade Union committee to prefer the employers' interest to that of the workers. It would be wrong for a businessman to jeopardise by a quixotic pursuit of ideals the interests of his work-force – or even of his shareholders. Similarly, the Government acts as a trustee for the nation. A nation is neither a mere aggregate of its citizens nor is it an entity apart from them; it is themselves acting collectively in an experienced fellowship which includes past and future generations. Those who make decisions in its name are not like the will of a single individual; rather they resemble trustees administering an estate which is not their own.[8]

(c) *Justice as the way of love in group relations*

Temple poses the question, Does the law of love in its fulness, including the claim of self-sacrifice, apply to groups? His answer is: In an ultimate sense – yes. That law is the expression of the nature of God, and therefore universal in its scope. The ideal of mutual love holds for all men and women and for all human groups. The Christian statesman and the Christian citizen should have before their minds the Kingdom of God and His justice as the only standard of their conduct. However, the claims of love can be urged irrelevantly and ineffectively. The application of the law of love is indirect and limited. It is indirect in the sense that a group like a Trade Union has no obligation, and as a rule no right, to be generous. Rather, its duty is to promote the interests of the workers justly. 'But both employers and employed are rightly called upon to act as servants of the community, and to be guided in relation to the community by the spirit of love.'[9]

Temple elucidates by offering an interpretation of the two great commandments. The first is absolute: towards God the demand is for an absolute surrender. But love to our neighbour is relative and limited: we are to love him as ourselves. 'In no case is the agent called upon to prefer the interest of his neighbour to his own; he is required to put them on a level, and this will include the assertion of his own interest if this is not being put on a level with the neighbour's. But for the community which includes alike the man and his neighbour, both may be required to sacrifice their private interest, while for God, His Truth, and His Kingdom, an absolute and unlimited sacrifice may be demanded.' Temple thus incorporates into his interpretation the concept of wider loyalties checking narrower loyalties. The whole irresistibly leads to the idea of the impartial tribunal, which will listen to the claims of rival groups and adjudicate between them in the light of the community's interest.[10]

The way of love thus lies not through altruism, but through reasonable claim and just award, in short, through justice. Justice is the true form of love at the level of groups. So long as men are organised in groups with diverging interests, so long must love express itself first in justice. We cannot leave the influence of the Gospel without effect on the vast area of human groups until almost all men are devout Christians. The Christian citizen has to dedicate himself in the power of love to the establishment of justice. An axiom here is that the Gospel fulfils and does not destroy the Law: we must not so respond to the Gospel as to fail to discharge elementary obligations.[11]

(d) *Two different priorities; the necessity of approximation and compromise*

Temple's position here involves two kinds of priority. The first is a priority in terms of value. The Christian is always eager to rise to the full height of the vision he has been granted in his most exalted spiritual moments. He will judge all he does or attempts by the highest standards. However, he must reckon with the fact of sin and 'work with the material in hand. Men do not love the highest when they see it; they are much more likely to repudiate it with disgust and to crucify or otherwise rid themselves of anyone who proclaims and embodies it.'[12]

This leads to the second priority, one in terms of indispensability. The most fundamental requirement of a government is not the expression of love, or even of justice, but that it should supply some reasonable measure of security against murder, robbery and starvation. Internationally a balance of power is indispensable if nations are to co-operate in the tasks of peace. Here, then, the priority is that of securing certain minima. Furthermore, any advance from there will rest on a clear recognition of the factor of sin. The feasible task of governments is to establish a measure of external justice, that is, so to order life that self-interest prompts what justice demands.[13]

All this is plainly a policy of gradual approximation to justice; our task is to mould society so that the nearest approximation to justice is actually established. It is a view which allows of a positive approach to that which falls short of the ideal. For instance, healthy business and commerce are in accord with the Christian principle of life. But in fact they are infected with egoism, and the Christian businessman is right to compromise. He must have his principles or ideals. In the face of sin, he must neither abandon the ideal, nor compromise to the point where witness to the ideal becomes ineffectual. He must work steadily for the gradual purification of commerce, remaining in the business world. He must not so follow an ideal as to allow himself to be driven from the market; nor must he simply withdraw from business, thus leaving it a prey to men of no ideals.[14]

This view is grounded in an understanding of how nature and grace are related and how God deals with fallen nature. Temple's sacramental Christian philosophy forbade any separation of nature and grace, as if Church and state rested on totally different principles. It is this which prompts him to detect Manichaeism in the pacifist position, and leads him to use the phrase 'the consecration of force'. Grace is manifest in the order of nature; the Church's principles do have political effects. And even if we say that nature is so fallen as in no way to manifest its Maker, the Gospel forbids us to say that God has abandoned it. In fact, we have to distinguish between God's will pure and simple and God's will in the face of a fallen world. The world is God's creation. His will for it, considered absolutely, is that it should correspond to His own nature of holiness and love. In fact the world is corrupted, though not wholly. But we cannot say that where love fails God has no care for what happens except that men should live in a fallen world as if it were not fallen, or behave as if they were not fallen themselves. Rather, God has a purpose with which men who know themselves fallen may co-operate, using their fallen nature as in part the instrument for its own recovery. In other words, in the circumstances God wills compromise, and to refuse to compromise is to fail His cause.[15]

In sum, it is not those who compromise, but those who pursue ideal courses, who are most likely to pay only lip-service to Christian principles. Often those who make most progress towards an ideal are those who advocate moderate courses of action. 'Its assertion of Original Sin should make the Church intensely realistic, and conspicuously free from Utopianism.'[16]

(e) *The two different priorities in corrective justice*

The tension between the two kinds of priority is evident in Temple's thinking about corrective justice, notably in the Clarke Hall lecture, *The Ethics of Penal Action* (1934).[17] The essence of punishment, according to Temple, is that it is the reaction of a community against a member. The community has three interests to consider. Priority must go first to the maintenance of the community's own life and order. To this end retribution and deterrence are the chief means employed by the state. Deterrent penal action is necessary to social well-being. However, it acts on an infra-moral plane. It interferes with the liberty of some citizens in order that the general liberty of all citizens may be the more secure. But it ignores the personal quality of the offender, treating him as a means to the good of others. It does, however, whether threatened or actual, have a moral influence. 'To say that you can make folk good by Act of Parliament is to utter a dangerous half-truth. You cannot by Act of Parliament make men morally good; but you can by Act of Parliament supply conditions which facilitate the growth of moral goodness and remove conditions which obstruct it.' Moreover, deterrence plays on men's sense of shame, which, being rooted in regard for others, has positive moral value. Deterrence is thus indispensable; but it is morally justifiable only if it is subordinate to other forms of penal action.

Retribution is superior to deterrence, because it is more truly moral. It stands for the truth that it is 'the first moral duty of the community ... to reassert the broken moral law against the offender who has broken it.' It treats the offender as a moral agent (and 'to deny individual responsibility is to deny personality'). In the interests both of the community and the offender the community must assert its antagonism towards his evil will. Refusal to condone must have priority over forgiveness.

However, the criminal is never only a criminal and nothing else. He is a human being, and here we reach the need for reformative processes, which are 'less indispensable but more positively valuable'. Here Temple invokes his Platonic view of human development towards maturity of character, linking it with Christianity: 'Every man truly is that which God's eternal knowledge apprehends, and this includes the effects upon him of all the work of grace. We are not what we appear, but what we are becoming; and if this is what we truly are, no penal system is fully just which treats us as anything else.'

Thus on the one hand the interest of the offending member comes last in the community's priorities in terms of indispensability; on the other hand, the priority in terms of value is for the development of the potentiality of the offender in the context of restored relationships within the community.

These ideas on corrective justice are, as we have seen, applied by Temple to international relations. Checking the aggressor, setting free the oppressed, underlining the failure of Prussian militarism, establishing checks and balances of power – these are the primary aims. Yet a balance of power is not an end in itself; it is an indispensable foundation for building peace.

Similarly, there is a real place for retributive justice. Towards Hitler and the German people the international community must express its repudiation of their actions. There must be no overlooking of wrong. God, in Christ, does not overlook wrongs. But whereas He takes them into Himself we do not have the spiritual power to do that. 'If we dream of that we deceive ourselves, and the result ... will be a condoning of evil, and that is worse than all.' We must lean in the direction of refusal to condone, rather than grant cheap forgiveness.[18] There are, however, two *caveats*. The first is that retributive justice can easily lapse into vengeance. Hence we find Temple's criticism of the Versailles Treaty, and his fear of reprisals in the Second World War or a vindictive peace after it. The second *caveat* is that retribution is not enough. We must look beyond to reformative and to distributive justice. Temple hopes that, in the case of Hitler, restraint and retribution might lead him to a new way of thinking about life and the claims of others; in the case of the German nation the hope is for conversion and re-education internally, and for a full place in the family of nations. The retributive element must give way to the distributive. This does not mean that past actions will be forgotten in the estimation of justice, though defeat itself would probably be sufficient punishment for Germany; and in any case individuals have long since realised that it is worth forgoing 'abstract justice' in order to obtain the benefits of an ordered community.[19] The aim would be a good neighbour policy amongst all; hence Germany must take part on equal terms in negotiations for a permanent settlement. Thus, just as the ultimate priority with the individual offender is his restoration to the community's life and the development of his potential, so the international offender is to be restored to its rightful place in the community of nations, and share in organising the common life for the common good.

(f)   *Justice according to need: Temple's personalism*

In his book *Agape: An Ethical Analysis* G. Outka points out that though everyone agrees that justice is in some sense the rendering to each man of his due, Christian writers on *agape* and justice do not distinguish very carefully between possible conceptions of justice. Is justice giving everyone the same regardless of circumstances? or giving similar treatment to similar cases? Is it rewarding each according to deserts? or giving to each according to needs? Temple never discusses these distinctions. It is, however, clear that his sensitivity to the factor of circumstances would rule out 'to each the same thing'. 'Similar treatment for similar cases' on the other hand, with its inbuilt questioning of privilege, is implicit in Temple's thought. More strikingly, Temple treats 'to each according to deserts' as a lower form of justice than 'to each according to needs'. He would no doubt agree with Honoré's dictum: 'All men considered merely as men and apart from their conduct or choice have a claim to an equal share in all those things, here called advantages, which are generally desired and are in fact conducive to their well-being.'[20] Here we touch on Temple's personalism. Justice is to be understood in terms of personal life rather than of purely economic wealth. Hence Temple's views on the profit motive and the just price. Hence too the accent on individual freedom, on worker participation and the running of industry, and on more equal educational opportunity, which would include the development of a critical ability to raise questions about the justice of any prevailing social order. Correspondingly paternalism and charity are to be avoided, since they militate against the achievement of justice in this sense.[21]

(g) The limitations of the quest for justice

Temple's repudiation of utopianism can be elucidated further by asking whether perfect justice could ever be attained. The answer is, of course not. (By perfect justice Temple presumably means a situation where all receive their due according to their needs but without any thought of advancing claims.) We are a very long way from the stage of justice where men are willing to put their claims, arising from their divergent interests, on a level. Beyond that there is the need for groups to be drawn together in an organisation based on their common interest. Even this state should not be confused with the love of which the Gospel speaks. Co-operative justice is in full accord with love, but love is the highest and only quite adequate manifestation of spiritual unity. What is more, perfect justice is a *product* of perfect love, not a stage on the way to it. 'There is little hope that a man will in fact be consistently just, unless he is inspired and upheld by a love which has its source in the love of God.' Nothing short of conversion, spiritual discipline and worship of God are required if love and peace are to be secure. Nothing short of an effective universal Church can really cure the egotism of nations.[22]

The Christian must therefore be a real churchman if he is to be an effective citizen. His first concern in relation to others will be conversion. But he will also do what he can to remedy a defective social system, because the social witness of the Church is both a preparation for the Gospel and a consequence of it. And, without relenting in his efforts, he must rid himself of 'the Pelagian notion that we can "build" or "extend" the Kingdom of God, except so far as the proclamation of the Gospel may be the occasion of its extension through the opening of the hearts of men to the manifested love of God . . . When the Lord Christ comes it is not to crown our efforts by the establishment of the perfect co-operative commonwealth; it is to "put down all rule and authority and power", and so, having vanquished all enemies (the last is death), to become subject to the Father, "that God may be all in all". In other words, the goal of Christian hope is not any kind of social or political achievement, and its realisation depends on the cancellation of that bond of mortality which is the prime condition of all our endeavours here.'[23]

In formulating his position on love and justice Temple undoubtedly drew extensively on the work of Reinhold Niebuhr (1892–1971). Niebuhr developed his own understanding of love and justice in response to the American Social Gospel (a rough equivalent of optimistic Anglican social thought) and liberal pacifists. His early social thought was in fact much shaped by the Social Gospel, and he always acknowledged its contribution in correcting the individualism of American Protestantism. But he came to reject as illusion liberal ideas about the possibility of building a new society through education and moral persuasion; liberal circles reflected a middle-class optimism based on ignorance of the more intolerable injustices of society. His years in Henry Ford's Detroit led him to use Marxist analysis and observe, 'An industrial overlord will not share his powers with his workers until he is forced to do so by tremendous pressure. The middle classes, with the exception of a small minority of intelligentsia, do not aid the worker in exerting this pressure. He must fight alone.'[24]

For some time in the 1920s Niebuhr was himself a pacifist, even serving as national Chairman of the pacifist Fellowship of Reconciliation. Yet he was always troubled, not sure whether his pacifism was 'the result of nausea or of a genuine understanding of the moral issues involved in international strife.' It was mainly the social and industrial strife which pushed him to break with pacifism. His wrath was directed against those pacifists who saw the Cross as a strategy for the successful solution of political conflicts. This was disastrously to compound political naiveté and heresy. The political naiveté was that it irresponsibly gave the advantage to tyranny, and in the name of love issued in a perverse lovelessness for the victims of tyranny. Theologically it treated Jesus as a hero who challenged us to try harder. It proclaimed a Renaissance faith in man, and by abstracting war from the rest of reality, falsely believed it could be mastered by men of reason and good-will.[25]

In opposition to this kind of pacifism, Niebuhr insisted that Jesus' ethic was a perfectionist one. The Sermon on the Mount proclaims unambiguously an ethic of non-resistance. This must not be converted into an ethic of non-violent resistance, which Gandhi was popularizing at the time. True, there is a discrimination to be made between violent and non-violent resistance, but it is only a matter of degree, and neither is to be confused with the absolute renunciation of force seen to perfection on the Cross. Niebuhr believed that it was not the Renaissance view of man which illuminated man's collective existence, but the Reformation doctrine of man's sin and the justifying grace of God. For Niebuhr the power of the Gospel was that it dealt with the condition of all men, who were sinners entangled in the violation of the law of love.[26]

It was here that the Lutheran background of Niebuhr came into play. His father was a minister of the Prussian Union Church, which contained Lutheran and Reformed elements. He emigrated to the United States, and Reinhold was born there and brought up in what became part of the Evangelical-Reformed Church, into which he was ordained. In his running battles with various Christian groups Niebuhr had much to say in criticism of the Lutherans. He particularly deplored the way in which Lutheranism had allowed the sacred and the secular to become separated, and his own ideas about love and justice were a conscious corrective. Yet it remains true that Luther's thought about Law, grace and perfection was influential in his break with liberal pacifism. John Bennett says there were early theological influences which brought a different shading into Niebuhr's understanding of Christian social teaching than could be expected from those who had always lived on soil prepared chiefly by Calvinism or by sectarian versions of Christianity. He thinks that it is in part this influence from Luther which made it difficult for Niebuhr to communicate his convictions about perfection or about Law and grace to the majority of Christian liberals living in the U.S.A.[27] Let us now see his basic convictions about love and justice.

Niebuhr construes Christian love (*agape*) essentially as *self-sacrifice* in contrast to mutual love (*eros*) which, he claims, always has the root of selfishness in it. It is true he does speak of love in terms of mutuality: 'The law of [man's] nature is love, a harmonious relation of life to life in obedience to the divine centre and source of his life.' But that is an ultimate state, and Niebuhr's preoccupation is with the confrontation of that law of love with this fallen world. Heedless, uncalculating love must entail self-sacrifice in this life. 'The perfect disinterestedness of the divine love can have a counterpart in history only in a life that ends tragically because it refuses to participate in the claims and counter-claims of historical existence. It portrays a love "which seeketh not its own". But a love which seeketh not its own is not able to maintain itself in historical society.'[28]

This means that it is impossible to construct a social ethic out of the ideal of love in its pure form. Perfect love leads to the Cross; historical society must rather seek justice. Yet if Niebuhr denies the direct applicability of love to the world of contending claims, he still insists on its relevance. How then are love and justice to be related? Love and justice are plainly not identical; for love is heedless and sacrificial, whereas justice is discriminating and concerned with balancing interests and claims. The law of love has a transcendent eschatological reference which is related *dialectically* (that is, in a positive yet negative way) to this life.[29]

First, love *fulfils* justice by transcending it: it goes beyond the general provision for need prompted by a sense of justice to meet the other man's particular needs. 'Love is the end term of any system of morals. It is the moral requirement in which all schemes of justice are fulfilled ... because the obligation of life to life is more fully met in love than is possible in any scheme of equity and justice.' Secondly, love *requires* the pursuit of justice. Justice is not alien to love; it is the way in which love must find expression in complex human relations. But thirdly, love *negates* justice because 'love makes an end of the nicely calculated less and more of structures of justice. It does not carefully arbitrate between the needs of the self and the other, since it meets the needs of the other without concern for the self.' Whatever our achievements in the realm of justice, they always stand under the judgement of love. The laws of justice, since they take sinful self-interest for granted, 'are therefore always in danger of throwing the aura of moral sanctity' upon that sinful self-interest. 'They must consequently stand under the criticism of the law of love.' 'There is no justice ... which can be regarded as finally normative. The higher possibilities of love, which at once is the fulfilment and the negation of justice, always hover over every system of justice.' Love is not only 'the source of the norms of justice' but also 'an ultimate perspective by which their limitations are discovered.' Yet love also *redeems* what remains incomplete and distorted by sin. It is in this sense too that love fulfils justice. Indeed, draughts of love are necessary if justice is not to degenerate into something less than justice.[30]

The positions of Temple and Niebuhr on love, justice and pacifism are virtually identical, yet there remains a difference, which is to be related to their different backgrounds. As we have seen, Temple's disposition, stimulated by pre-1914 optimism and British Hegelianism in particular, was always to look for harmony and synthesis. This colours his interpretation of St. John's Gospel, which heavily emphasises Christ's Incarnation (1.14) and His drawing of all men to Himself when He is lifted up (12.32). In Temple's theology we find no sharp distinction between love as mutuality and love as sacrifice. Sacrifice, he wrote, is not always painful; that depends on the response. 'Sacrifice expressing a love that is returned can be such a joy as is not otherwise known to men.'[31] Behind this language lies the central though unobtrusive motif of the complete mutuality of self-giving among the Persons of the Trinity, which for Temple must be a model for the relations of men to God and men to men. The painful sacrifice of Christ, as we saw in Chapter 5, is the means by which God brings men back to a right relationship with Himself, and is made effective in the Eucharist, where we continue to receive Christ's offered life, so that we can give ourselves more completely to God. The goal is the

Communion of Saints, to be brought to perfect harmony and peace in eternity. We should also recall Leonard Hodgson's testimony to Temple's own spirituality which lifted his colleagues into a realm where he habitually dwelt and which was the source of his own courtesy, patience and love of justice.

It is clear in Temple's social ethics that the dominant note in his understanding of love is mutuality. This is evident in his preoccupation with fellowship. The goal for Temple is a world completely in fellowship with God and completely at harmony with itself. The restoration of the offender to the fellowship of his society, the resolution of conflict between Capital and Labour, the creation of a true community of nations under the guidance of a truly ecumenical Church – at every point mutuality is the goal, and also the criterion for each step along the road.

The obvious temptation for Temple was to assume a direct connection of sacrifice with the social order. At first he seems to have succumbed, though even by 1914 he had begun to doubt whether communities could practise sacrifice. During the 1920s he was uncertain and ambiguous. On the one hand he would call on Labour to practise brotherhood and forgiveness towards Capital, as if *agape* were a strategy for success in a sinful world. Yet he could also praise sacrificial constáncy during a strike in pursuit of claims for justice. By 1939 Temple explicitly abandoned any idea that self-sacrifice was an ideal with direct application to society, and by 1942 it is left to individuals to practise it voluntarily. Understandably Temple never had the time to reach a coherent reformulation of his Christian philosophy. His frequent talk of fellowship appears to preserve some of the old optimism and gives the impression of a smooth upward movement from total selfishness to perfect mutuality. Sometimes, however, he emphasises man's entanglement in sin and warns against utopianism. It is here that he comes nearest to saying that love negates justice. Sometimes he comes perilously close to severing love and justice. One is reminded of Reinhold Niebuhr's comment in 1943 that English social pronouncements seemed to be taken from the pages of the old American Social Gospel, yet in practice Christian radicals could make the shrewdest analysis of social and political forces, and understand the persistence of egoistic impulses and conflicting interests.[32]

Niebuhr was able to achieve a more co-ordinated position than Temple. It defends us against optimistic belief in smooth upward progressions, whilst at the same time clearly asserting the relevance of *agape* to the social order in two distinct ways: love acts as an indiscriminate criterion, in the sense that it exposes the way all our achievements of justice fall short of the law of love and stand in partial contradiction to it; love also acts as a discriminate criterion, in that it can suggest ever greater approximations of justice to itself. Robert Craig is basically right when he remarks that Temple sees smooth continuity between justice and love, between state and Church. Craig asks 'Can the problem of the "Two Cities" really be solved by saying that there is a simple convergence of duties for the Christian citizen in his dual capacity [as a citizen and a churchman]?' Temple speaks too easily of the way of love lying through justice, too little of the tension in the soul of the Christian citizen. He fails 'to insist sufficiently on the sin and contradiction of love inherent in political organization.' Niebuhr by contrast succeeds where Temple fails in his insistence on the dialectical relationship of love to justice.[33] In the last chapter I shall elaborate on Niebuhr's position, trying to show that his basic dialectical framework provides the correction which Temple was seeking in his Christian philosophy from 1937 onwards. It is not however a position which is entirely free of difficulties, and we must end this chapter on a cautionary note. The difficulties are not fatal to the framework, but rather reflect Niebuhr's trenchant polemicism and require a stronger emphasis on one aspect of the framework.

Niebuhr's social ethics has been repeatedly criticised, particularly for an alleged pessimism. It is claimed by Macgregor that he propagates a doctrine of human depravity, sunders the natural and redeemed, and has an eschatology which makes the Kingdom of God wholly future.[34] That these claims are unfair is amply shown by Gordon Harland's careful work, *The Thought of Reinhold Niebuhr*. He certainly was hopeful provided men made an accurate reading of the dynamics of divine grace and man's finitude and sin. It must be conceded, however, that in his trenchant polemicism Niebuhr laid himself open to such criticisms, and at certain points his thought is imbalanced. First, he made too sharp a separation of *agape* as heedless sacrificial love and mutual love, which he tended to dub *eros*. In typical vein he wrote that mutual love is 'always arrested by reason of the fact that it seeks to relate life to life from the standpoint of the self and for the sake of the self's own happiness.' One can understand the charge that Niebuhr's conception of mutual love is neither mutual nor love. In a rather different vein (but in the same work) he writes that 'mutual love (in which disinterested concern for the other elicits a reciprocal response) is the highest possibility of history; . . . such love can only be initiated by a type of disinterestedness (sacrificial love) which dispenses with historical justification.' As Paul Ramsey rightly remarks, in that case mutual and sacrificial love are types of disinterested concern for the other and are therefore both genuine love.[35] Certainly there will be perfect mutuality only in the completed, transcendent Kingdom of God. But we must beware of so stating this that we run down the possibilities open to the self in historical existence. It is true that love heedless of the self is needed to initiate reciprocity, but mutual love, where the self counts for one among many, is a genuine goal which finds a considerable measure of attainment in history.[36]

Secondly, as a reflex perhaps, Niebuhr distinguishes too sharply between the capacity of individuals for love and justice and the capacity of groups. Macgregor asks whether groups cannot generate a genuine *esprit de corps* which lifts them above the sum of their individual members.[37] Whilst the balance of historical evidence favours Niebuhr (and he was particularly good on how self-interest corrupts fellowship) he does tend towards a dogmatic pessimism about group behaviour.

Thirdly, Macgregor's riposte does pose the age-old problem of utilitarianism: is there not a point where, in the name of the sanctity of personality, we cease making calculations of utility? Neither Temple nor Niebuhr satisfactorily dealt with this problem. Temple had his defence works in his ethical stance of principles, as we saw at the beginning of Chapter 11, yet ran into difficulties over the bombing of Germany. Niebuhr seems in fact to have been a pragmatist who came to decisions almost intuitively. But pragmatism can easily capitulate to a current undemanding ethic. 'There is a point in the questioning of pragmatism. If politics is the art of the possible, who will aspire to the impossible? And if no one tries for the impossible, how will we know the limits of the possible?' Does Niebuhr's doctrine of sin lure us into settling for the mediocre?[38]

I think a broad eschatological framework like Niebuhr's can offset these dangers if the emphases are right. On the one hand it should act as a defence against complacent acquiescence in the mediocre, because it gives a clear place to the constant pressure of the divine grace, exposing our failings and drawing us on to envisage and establish greater approximations to love. A perfectionist ethic must encourage a utopian strain of thought (and Niebuhr himself always had more patience with utopians than with those who separated religion and politics). This is all the more important when (as perhaps today) the most widespread human failings are not so much overweening ambition and the lust for power as boredom, frustration, and quiescent despair. On the other hand this same framework can call in question all utopias (the cultural religion known as 'the American dream', which Niebuhr knew best, is only one), because they forget that the final consummation of history lies beyond the conditions of the time process. It can also give a staying power in the quest for justice which utopians often lack, and head off descent into the opposite danger of cynicism. Niebuhr's pragmatism always did operate within a theological framework, centred on the Cross, and he tried to pilot his way between utopianism and cynicism, but there is unfortunately an excessively negative impression given which needs correction. Reinhold Niebuhr's own life is perhaps the best refutation of the critics, as it is an eloquent testimony to the positive dynamism of his thought.[39]

PART IV

CHRISTIAN SOCIAL ETHICS TODAY

CHAPTER 16

A FRAMEWORK FOR CHRISTIAN SOCIAL ETHICS

The time has come to gather together the results of our enquiry and develop a framework for Christian social ethics. It is important to be clear what is and what is not possible. It is not possible to produce a definitive framework. The Bible presents us with the raw materials for a social ethic, but not in such a way that they can be readily systematised. We have to work out what are the fundamental motifs in Scripture, recognising that we shall not be able to do justice to all the evidence, and that modifications of the framework will therefore be necessary. Similarly, our Christian experience of living in the world will prompt adjustments. What is claimed for this framework is that (i) it is consistent with the dominant motifs of the biblical witness; (ii) it presses us squarely to face the social problems of our day and grasp its opportunities; (iii) it is prompted by the study of the work of eminent people in the field of Christian social ethics across a wide denominational spectrum; (iv) it has advantages over certain other ways in which Christians have related their faith to social order. This last point will mainly be taken up in Appendix I, in order to avoid overloading the chapter itself. The framework is now set out in five sections, each ending with a summary.

1. *The dialectical method*

The dialectical method entails a constant oscillation between overall understanding and concrete experience. At any one point in time we have an understanding of reality (both of fact and of value) which has been steadily built up by a reciprocal process: we use our understanding of reality to interpret our concrete experience of living, and we allow our reading of experience to modify that understanding (pp. 17, 134).

If our understanding of reality is from a Christian perspective, the process will be an interaction between our understanding of the Christian faith, recorded in Scripture and mediated through centuries of Christian experience of worship, prayer, reflection and action (the tradition), and our concrete experience of living.

Temple tends to short-circuit the functioning of the method. In his philosophy he has a fixed concept of Christianity which is not properly checked against other positions or the facts (pp. 45f., 134f.). In his social ethics, at least up to 1926 and sometimes beyond, he over-emphasises moral ideals and does not sufficiently face empirical constraints and the factors of power, conflict and self-interest. This reflects the Hegelian legacy, with its assumption of a rational universe waiting to be synthesised by rational human beings (p. 134). It is when he guides the thorough enquiry into unemployment (pp. 145f.), operates the model of love and justice (ch. 15), and recognises the large scale irrationality of the world from 1937 onwards (pp. 62–64), that he most faithfully operates the dialectical method.

The word 'dialectical' is not important in itself, and can be doubly misleading, because we have also been speaking of a dialectical relationship of love and justice, where 'dialectical' is used in a rather different sense (p. 198), and because it suggests the peculiar dialectics of Hegel. Though I shall continue to use it here for the sake of consistency, other words or phrases are preferable, such as 'the reciprocal method' or 'the method of interplay' or 'the method of oscillation' (pp. 17, 134).

The method is very important for its concreteness (p. 134). It acts as a corrective to the view that social ethics starts with high-level abstract principles which then have to be applied to situations. Widespread though this supposition is, it is far from satisfactory. This is partly because human beings and their world are dynamic and changing (pp. 116f., 138–140). In addition, from a Christian perspective it cannot be satisfactory because of the concrete way God reveals Himself to us (pp. 116, 133, 137). The concreteness is evident as soon as one reflects on the sheer fact that the form of the Gospels is basically narrative: the recounting of historical events (pp. 139f.). Moreover it is a very earthy story. Jesus is born in humble circumstances, exposed from the start to the world's indifference or harassment. The story culminates in His horrific death, procured by an unholy conspiracy of self-interested power groups. It is in and through these harsh events that Jesus is either worshipped or reviled.

Temple has an understanding of how God reveals Himself which is thoroughly consistent with the dialectical method. In the chapter on natural law we saw that for Temple the primary medium of revelation is events, not propositions (pp. 115f.). In *Nature, Man and God* he writes that the mode of revelation which fits what we know of God is a coincidence of divinely guided events with minds divinely guided to apprehend those events. 'The essential revelation is an act of God apprehended in a complete living experience, in which subjective and objective factors are both active; it is not capable of isolation from that experience, and is only renewed so far as the experience itself is recovered or renewed.' It is the living God Himself who is revealed. The Bible and creeds are secondary to that revelation. The Bible is the record of the revelation, but not the revelation itself. The creeds are doctrinal 'inferences drawn from that revelation in the context provided by the rest of experience; and their spiritual value is not in themselves; it is in the directions which they offer for recovering the experience from which they spring.'[1]

The dialectical method, especially if it were not freed from the Hegelian matrix, could easily seem an exercise strictly for intellectuals who love to make smooth syntheses. Temple's reference to revelation 'in a complete living experience' is a reminder that it is the whole person who is involved, not just the intellect. The story of Job in the Wisdom Literature of the Old Testament confirms this insight and can scotch the idea of smooth syntheses. Job suffers the loss of family and possessions. The 'comforters' descend upon him, endlessly ringing the changes on the doctrine that the righteous prosper and the unrighteous come to grief; suffering therefore implies sin in the sufferer. The reader has already been admitted to the courts of heaven and knows that Job is innocent, and that his suffering is to test whether there is genuine devotion to God on earth. Job knows that he is innocent. He threshes about for a fresh understanding of his God. God must be unjust, a relentless persecutor, a capricious tyrant, a ruthless warrior. God must be just, and ultimately reveal Himself and vindicate Job. In making these judgements Job appears to carry within him the doctrine of his comforters. There is an acute conflict between his understanding of God hitherto and his present experience. The great revelation at the end of the book does show that the friends were right in their assertion of God's transcendence and of the need for Job to accept the limitations of being human and to seek God in humble trust. But they have resolutely been keeping piety and reality apart and have failed to speak the truth about God. Job has passed the test of disinterested devotion to God, and he is brought to a deeper insight into the mysterious relation of man and God, before whom he repents in dust and ashes.

The practice of the dialectical method could involve such a traumatic reappraisal. Christians should certainly not suppose that the revelation in Jesus Christ dispenses them from such a possibility. The outstanding paper at the Malvern Conference of 1941 was from Donald MacKinnon. It contained many clues about deeper foundations for theology and social ethics, and it still repays study. MacKinnon was critical of an easy-going Christian sociology based on Creation and Incarnation. Creation is a mystery, and there was no necessity that God should have brought us into being. The Incarnation is not the disclosure of universal cosmic principles, but the manifestation of the divine Word in the harsh particularities of human existence. It is the Cross which reveals the final secret of the relation of man and God. On this basis MacKinnon attacked the lust after synthesis and any glib talk of reconstruction after the war. Every individual should first feel the almost unendurable tension between the Kingdom of Grace and the kingdom of the world. Whereas Temple thought that Malvern had put the Church on the map again, MacKinnon asserted that the Church is a question and a scandal. It is no refuge from insecurities and questionings, yet we strive to make it just such a refuge, and this is the supreme betrayal. The Church is an eschatological society, bearing witness to the triumphant Passion of the Son of God. Death and Resurrection are the rhythm of its life, in a deeply disturbing sense. For the conflict once played out between Caiaphas, Pilate, Iscariot and Christ is continued within the Christian and within the Church.[2]

To summarise:
1.1 Christians should seek God's will through a continual interplay between their understanding of the Christian faith, drawn from Scripture and the tradition, and their concrete experience of living.
1.2 Revelation is an act of God apprehended and renewed in a

complete living experience. The price for the recipient may well be drastic reappraisal and repentance.

2. A dramatic vision, embracing love and justice

It was only in the last ten years of his life that Temple really practised the dialectical method, by facing up to the harsh realities of the world. In Part I we saw how between *Christus Veritas* (1924) and *Nature, Man and God* (1932–4) Temple moved to a much tougher view of evil (pp. 53–57). From 1937 he was dissatisfied with his attempts to fit experience together into a harmonious system on the basis of the Incarnation. No rational Christian map could be made of an evil and irrational world. The emphasis of *Christus Veritas* and *Nature, Man and God* seemed all wrong. They had given too much the impression of a static system. Temple offers us ingredients of a different emphasis: a theology of Redemption rather than a theology of Incarnation; the Word as a dynamic force of judgement rather than a static principle of rational unity. The impotence of man to save himself calls for the work of divine grace. The world must be changed by Christ into something very different before a Christian map is possible. The task of the Christian is not to explain the world (as if the Kingdom were already fully here), but to convert the world in the light of the future coming of the Kingdom (pp. 62–64).

Temple's ethical idealism, and especially his social principle of sacrifice, also wilted under the pressure of events and the impact of Reinhold Niebuhr (pp. 67–69, 200). It was not enough to preach ideals and intensify the will to pursue them. It was necessary to grapple with alien ideologies and recognise the world was a place of egoisms and competing centres of power. Temple urges Christians to 'restore hope to the world through a true understanding of the relation of the Kingdom of God to history, as a transcendent reality that is continually seeking, and partially achieving, embodiment in the activities and conflicts of the temporal order' (p. 71).

In Chapter 10 we noted the conditioned nature of our moral reasoning and the constant danger of absolutising relative insights (pp. 118–120). We concluded that chapter by saying that a thoroughly revised natural law will have an eschatology which reflects the ambiguities of history and will deal with the themes of finitude, sin, conflict and power. To use the language of Helmut Thielicke, it will articulate the fundamental motif of the dramatic tension between this age and the age to come, between the Kingdom as already realised, and the Kingdom as yet to come (pp. 120–125).

Temple was right in 1942 to refer to world history on the analogy of a drama, where the full meaning of the first scene only becomes apparent with the final curtain, and we are in the middle of it (p. 64). He came nearest to an adequate framework embracing these various emphases in his handling of love and justice (pp. 187–196). Nearer still was Reinhold Niebuhr (pp. 196–203). The words love and justice can easily sound cold and abstract. So it is important to appreciate Niebuhr's dialectical understanding of the relationship of love and justice is rooted in a dramatic reading of God's dealings with the human race in judgement and mercy, culminating in the Cross.[3]

In the biblical view history does not have a rational unity of its own; any unity it has is given it by the sovereign God. To redeem His fallen world, God enters into a covenant relationship with a particular people, Israel. He promises faithfulness and vindication to Israel, but He also demands faith and righteousness from her. Israel's election gives her no special security. Indeed, she is exposed to the temptation of making herself the centre of history. She succumbs to idolatry. History is not therefore merely the arena where God exercises dominion; it also discloses the depth and universality of evil as men deny that dominion. History is a dramatic contest between all men and God. The prophets were especially sensitive to man's rebellion against God. The ultimate problem of the meaning of history in their eyes is how history can be any more than judgement, that is, whether God's promise of redemption for history can be fulfilled at all. Certainly for them the Messianic age was never to be the natural culmination of the historical process, but the result of gracious divine intervention. (We can illustrate Niebuhr's point by reference to two passages. First, in Psalm 51 the psalmist acknowledges that God is righteous in His judgement, yet he appeals precisely to God's righteousness mercifully to rescue him: 'and my tongue shall sing of thy righteousness.' Secondly, Hosea 11 daringly hints at the extreme tension in God Himself in the face of Israel's sin. Because He is a God of righteousness, He cannot condone Israel's transgressions; yet in lovingkindness He bears the pain of her sin and pardons and restores her. In both cases there appears to be a resource in God beyond His demand for justice, which is inseparable from it, yet stands in an uneasy relation to it.) For Niebuhr the good news is that in Jesus Christ God overcomes the contradictions in history, not by destroying the 'wicked' and vindicating the 'righteous', but by bearing the evil of all men. Suffering innocence, which from our standpoint highlights the problem of history's moral ambiguity, becomes the answer to the problem. The suffering love of Christ is the love of God who bears the sins of the world and overcomes its contradictions by taking them upon Himself. This is the ultimate dimension of God's sovereignty. The Cross exposes and condemns the power of human sin (and the best as well as the worst in history is involved in rebellion against God); but it also reveals the greater power of sin-bearing love to reconcile and redeem.

In the light of the Cross Niebuhr considers the relation of the Christian to the grace and power of God. Grace for Niebuhr is not only God's power in us (the dominant accent in Temple) but God's power over us in judgement, mercy and forgiveness. On the one hand grace is effective in us – there are indeterminate renewals of life and significant realisations of the Kingdom of God. On the other hand the contradictions of life remain; man is still in rebellion against God (even the Christian); he falls under the power of God in the form of judgement, and must rely on God's power of mercy and forgiveness. All good is tainted, every structure of justice incomplete, all achievements need divine mercy. History remains ambiguous to the end: the Kingdom is in a sense present, but it is yet to come in its fulness. We live 'in the interim', between the first and second coming of Christ. It is in this way that heedless self-sacrificing love remains permanently related to social life, demanding justice, negating it in judgement, and yet redeeming it in mercy.

Such a vision captures more successfully than Temple the glory and the tragedy of the human race as we know it in our experience. The articulation would surely be even better if it made explicit what is left implicit but plainly presupposed, namely, the

Resurrection of Jesus Christ and the gift of the Holy Spirit.

It is a vision which is also faithful to the dynamics of the New Testament. It reflects, for example, the intensely dramatic quality of St. John's Gospel, so beloved by Temple. The Word, one with God in the beginning, and bringing life and light to the world, is always in conflict with the darkness. The Word becomes flesh. Those who receive Him are given the power to become sons of God; yet when He comes to His own, His own do not receive Him. The whole Gospel, as is obvious to anyone who reads it aloud, is a series of dramatic encounters between the Word and a wilfully uncomprehending world. God's purpose is to bring salvation to the whole world; yet the world with a few exceptions chooses darkness, and incurs the judgement of the Word. The climax is the Passion, where mutually hostile groups briefly unite through fear, cynicism and expediency to rid themselves of a threat. Here Jesus Christ, having loved His own, loves them to the end (13.1), in an act of perfect human self-giving which is at the same time the supreme revelation of the glory of God. Cross and Resurrection almost form a single event, both revealing the glory. Furthermore, the gift of the Spirit is inseparable from both. It is symbolised by the blood and water flowing from Christ's pierced side, and by His breathing on the disciples on the evening of Easter Day (19.34; 20.22). Through the Spirit Jesus draws all men to Himself (12.32). The Spirit is with us for ever, guiding us into all truth (14.16; 16.13). His presence, however, is no genial offer of comfort. He continues also the work of convicting the world of sin and judgement (16.7–11).

This vision is also faithful to St. Paul, who dramatically speaks of the tragic predicament of man as a debtor and slave to sin and death, of the self-emptying of Jesus Christ in His Incarnation (Phil. 2.5–11, 2 Cor. 8.9), and of His victory won on the Cross as He strips the principalities and powers and triumphs over them. Through this justifying work of God and through the Resurrection and the gift of the Spirit the promised new age is inaugurated. Yet Paul knows that the powers of the old age are still virulent, and he looks forward to the consummation, when Christ will put all enemies under His feet, even death, and God will be all in all. The Christian meantime belongs to both ages: he is by the grace of God already justified; yet he still cries out, 'Who will deliver me from the body of this death?' (Rom. 7.24). God has reconciled us to Himself in Jesus Christ and given us the ministry of reconciliation; yet we are still called on to be reconciled to God (2 Cor. 5.1, 18, 20).

To summarise:

2.1 At the heart of Christian social ethics lies a dramatic vision of the way God relates to the world and human history. The Old Testament is the story of God's dealings with a rebellious people in judgement and mercy. The story reaches its climax when the God of love becomes incarnate in Jesus Christ. In deed and word He proclaims the Kingdom of God and seeks to draw all men into a loving relationship. He is wilfully rejected and crucified. He rises from the dead. The Holy Spirit is given and the new age ushered in. Jesus Christ, through the witness of the Church, draws all men to Himself, but the powers of the old age are still very active, even among Christians. There are significant realisations of the Kingdom, but there is also the continuing need for the work of transforming divine grace, judging, forgiving and converting the human race.

2.2 Since God shows unbounded care for each one of his children, *love transcends justice*, in the sense that it goes beyond the general provision for human need and meets the needs of particular individuals.

Since God demands nothing less than justice, *love requires justice*. God's redemption of the world cannot be effected by glossing over or condoning man's injustice.

Since the sacrificial love of God, seen to perfection on the Cross, exposes the injustice of all men, *love negates justice*. All our attempts at justice are under judgement; for all are reflections of a sinful order of claim and counterclaim. Moreover all our attempts are partial and conditioned, and need exposure to save them from the danger of being absolutised.

Since the love of God constantly reconciles and redeems, *love redeems justice*, saving justice from degeneration and opening up fresh possibilities of renewal and of greater approximations to justice and love.

3.   *Persons*

We have already seen that persons are creatures who apprehend the world and God in and through their historical experience, and that they stand in a dialectical relationship to God. We now articulate the further dimensions of persons implicit in the notions of love and justice.

From our experience of life we know that the world is fundamentally dynamic (p. 116). Objects are not really unchanging essences with changing particulars. Nor are persons really immortal souls with physical bodies. They stand in an open relationship to objects and other persons (pp. 52, 117). They share fully in the dynamism of the world. Not only are they constantly acted upon, but they have the capacity themselves to modify their environment and their self-understanding (p. 116). They encounter new challenges (p. 132), and creatively take practical decisions (p. 118). They continually engage as whole persons with one another in a common life which is an experiment and an adventure (p. 127).

Within this dynamism of persons it is possible to detect certain constants – dimensions of personality without which personal life as we know it would be inconceivable. They embrace both fact and value, since they are facts of our present human existence and need to be maintained and fostered for any meaningful future existence. They are sometimes called principles (pp. 126, 136f.), necessary *a prioris* of human existence (p. 132), or basic values (pp. 140f.). They are:

i.   the freedom and dignity of the individual;
ii.   the sociality or fellowship of persons;
iii. the need to serve the community or the common good. (e.g.
      pp. 34, 52f., 111f., 128f.).

Covering basically the same ground are such trios as freedom, justice and solidarity (Honecker), or freedom, equality and participation (Huber and Tödt) (pp. 141–145).

It is because of the fundamental nature of these dimensions of personality that we attach such importance to institutions like promise-making – what have been called the covenants of life, which assert so forcefully the sanctity of personality (pp. 128, 130). These dimensions also shape our understanding of the state and law. The state is under God and exists to promote the freedom of individuals, the friendship of persons, and the common good. It is not just a dyke against anarchy. Law-making is a rational activity with these same ends in view (pp. 112f.).

The Christian faith, in confirming these dimensions of personality, gives them a deeper context. Thus the freedom and dignity of persons are grounded in the fact that they are created and loved by God. They are made in His image, implying that they always stand in God's presence and are called freely to respond to Him and to have eternal fellowship with Him. The sociality of persons is rooted at its profoundest level in the very nature of God as Trinity. For if persons are in the image of a triune God, then surely they are all equally made for love of God and each other, and the goal is the completed Communion of Saints. The requirement for responsible (and if need be costly) service is grounded not only in the same doctrines but also in the life of the servant Messiah, and is endorsed by the great symbol of the Church as the Body of Christ, where we are members one of another and each member serves the whole with whatever capacities God gives (pp. 52f., 58–61, 77, 109).

The Christian faith can also correct certain misunderstandings of these dimensions. It may, for instance, call in question the individualistic view of freedom as an inborn quality, and in line with our dramatic vision embracing love and justice it may stress man's entanglement in sin and his inability to save himself. True freedom is then seen as a gift from God, who remains faithful to His promises. As such it is also inescapably a gift of freedom for responsible loving service to the neighbour (pp. 142f.).

These constants of human personality can never be articulated in final form. Both the Christian faith and our changing experience of human life will bring new insights and correctives. We shall learn from the natural sciences more about the capacities and limitations of human life. The social sciences will certainly shed new light on the nature of personality and on the mechanisms by which we distort it. Literature and the arts, indeed almost all disciplines, can contribute towards an integrated understanding of persons, but the dialectical method will ensure that this is never a completed task (especially pp. 138–140).

To summarise:

3.1 Persons are dynamic and changing, standing in an open relation to the world and to each other. Within this dynamism it is possible to detect certain constants:

the freedom and dignity of individuals;

the sociality or fellowship of persons;

the need to serve the community or the common good.

3.2 The Christian faith provides a deeper context for these constants in the Trinity, God's creation of man in His image, the life of Jesus Christ the Son of Man, the Church as the Body of Christ, and the goal of eternal fellowship with God in the Communion of Saints.

3.3 The Christian faith can also correct certain misunderstandings of these dimensions of personality.

3.4 Drawing on the Christian faith, experience and the several disciplines we must aim at an integrated understanding or persons, while recognising that the dialectical method will ensure this is never a completed task.

3.5 The role of the state is to promote the freedom of individuals, the friendship of persons, and the common good. It is to do this directly itself and through support of the natural groupings of people.

3.6 Law is a rational matter, to be framed in the light of the constants of human personality.

4. *Natural morality and the Christian faith*

Whilst rejecting Thomist natural law with its two-tier scheme, we should still accept the validity of natural morality. There is a genuine knowledge of good and evil, acquired through human reason and recognised by human conscience, independent of the Christian revelation. The Bible itself endorses this conclusion. The image of God in man persists after the fall. The Gentiles know certain moral norms in their conscience without the Christian revelation. St. John teaches that judgement falls on those who flout the moral order God has set up in the world. Redeemed man is transformed and renewed, not totally re-made. Certainly man is completely dependent on God for his knowledge and acts of goodness, but not thereby dependent on the Christian revelation.

There is 'common grace', sustaining the possibilities of love in all men (pp. 108f., 121, 171).

Since morality is fundamentally objective and moral discourse rational, then natural morality can form a bridge between Christian and non-Christian, enabling them to communicate, find common ground and co-operate. This is vital in an increasingly pluralistic world (pp. 49f., 108–110).

However, if we practise the dialectical method we shall find that a synthesis or integration of natural morality and the Christian faith is not easy (pp. 122f.). Whilst it is logically true that whatever is rational morality must be Christian morality (the strong point of Catholic theology), in fact actual men and women each develop, more or less consciously, a world view of which their morality is an integral part. They have an ideology, in the neutral sense of 'a pattern of beliefs and concepts (both factual and normative) which purports to explain complex social phenomena with a view to directing and simplifying socio-political choices facing individuals and groups.'[4] Though rational discussion of these world views and ideologies is possible, to say that rational morality is Christian does not carry us very far. What is required is the kind of programme recommended by Huber and Tödt, which starts out from the concrete situation reflective of world views and attempts a positive yet critical dialogue. In such a dialogue the Christian may well receive fresh illumination and insight, and may be moved to correct imbalances in his understanding of the Christian faith. Yet he will also be sensitive to points where his perspective diverges from those of others. Common ground is often easiest to achieve at a practical level. Beneath the surface may well lie disagreements in substance or emphasis, which, even if not fatal to agreement, cannot be ignored. Again, this dialogue is a process which can never be complete.

This point can be reinforced if we return to the Scottish theologian N. H. G. Robinson, whom we left in Chapter 10 endorsing natural morality. Robinson wants at the same time to give full weight to Barth's insistence on the sovereignty of God. It is no use, he says, juxtaposing Christian morality and ordinary morality or superimposing the one on the other. There cannot be two independent moral claims on the Christian life. We have to reckon with the final authority of Jesus Christ. To treat Him merely as an example is not enough. Christ does not just happen to be supreme at the moment, perhaps to be superseded by a better example; His supremacy is valid for time and eternity. Furthermore, though Christian morality enters upon ground already occupied by general morality, this does not mean that the Christian simply accepts what he finds there. General morality can be radically distorted. At the most fundamental level its pervasive defect is that it is divorced from its origin in God. It may also be distorted in respect of the detailed content of moral law, or simply because it is articulated in the form of law, divorced from the Gospel. Furthermore, general morality tends to concentrate attention on the individual moral agent. Yet the human situation to which morality belongs is a social situation, and it is surely an over-simplification to treat it as if it were nothing more than the sum total of atomic situations, in which individual affects individual. If there is an ethical goal of fellowship – and Christianity regards the highest good as fellowship – then general morality is ill-adapted to contain it. This individualism tends to abstract the moment of moral choice from complex human experience and the historical process, as if it were an element of the eternal. On the other hand, when it does take account of movement and change, it is very prone to move towards the doctrine of automatic moral progress. This is very evident in the philosophy of T. H. Green. General morality, then, needs to be supplemented by a doctrine of history, and by a doctrine of divine remedial activity whereby the total moral sphere is restored in its integrity. Robinson's plea is for 'mutual recognition as between the claim of morality and the claim of divine revelation, and mutual integration in a manner consonant with the remedial character of the revelation.' Man's autonomy must be seen as an autonomy which is responsive to God.[5]

These words clearly support our rather complex relating of natural morality and the Christian faith. They also point back to our dramatic vision, centred on God's redemptive act in Jesus Christ, as well as reminding us of dimensions of personality. Furthermore they encourage the practice of the dialectical method in a search for an integration of natural morality and the Christian revelation.

To summarise:
4.1 There is a natural morality, valid independently of the Christian revelation.
4.2 Since morality is fundamentally objective and moral discourse rational, natural morality can form a bridge between Christian and non-Christian, enabling them to communicate, find common ground and co-operate.
4.3 Nevertheless a synthesis or integration of natural morality and the Christian faith is not easy. A positive yet critical dialogue can lead to mutual illumination and correction in the search for an integration of the two, consistent with the remedial character of the Christian revelation.

5. *Making decisions*

'The right thing to do is the thing that is the best in the circumstances' (p. 127). With Temple we reject a preoccupation with absolute moral rules (p. 126) and the straight implementation of an ideal (p. 33). The absolute that is required is conscientiousness in making moral decisions. We need to consider circumstances as far as possible and adjust or compromise in the face of them. This does not imply total accommodation to circumstances. We must always have in view the goal of the development of persons in community, and not compromise to the point where witness to that goal becomes ineffectual (p. 191). We must uphold the sanctity of personality and not flout the obligations which it imposes (p. 128).

It is therefore going to be impossible to read off decisions by a process of deduction or simple casuistry from ethical norms, whether derived from Scripture or reason. Because God's world is both a changing and a fallen world, and because of our own finitude and sin, there is going to be uncertainty in our decision-making. The moral life is inherently an experiment and an adventure (pp. 117f., 127). We are called creatively to find meaning in the world, and to shape it by our responsible decisions (pp. 117f.). Though it will often be clear from a Christian perspective what courses of action are unacceptable (p. 150), or at least highly questionable, we can expect a plurality of responses

from among Christians (p. 132). Disagreements are to be expected.
There is clearly no incompatibility between all this and what we
have said about the dialectical method or about persons. But how is
it to be interpreted in the light of our understanding of the relation
of love and justice? Certainly our scheme of love and justice is
utilitarian. In the face of circumstances love requires compromise
in the form of the pursuit of justice. The danger is that we
compromise more than we ought and become content with our
compromises. Temple is prone to say that if a thing is right in the
circumstances it is absolutely right (pp. 158, 168). This danger can
be guarded against only if we remember also that love negates
justice and love redeems justice. In the light of heedless love all our
attempts at justice stand under judgement and the need for mercy.
Our chief attitude to compromise must be a permanent sense of
misgiving, even horror. Otherwise we degenerate towards a state
of insensitivity where all pity is indeed 'choked with custom of fell
deeds' (p. 173). Temple's accent on the sanctity of personality is a
vitally important defence against this degeneration, especially if it
is grounded not only in the fact that each person is a child of God
by creation, but also in the heedless love of God in Christ on the
Cross.

This interpretation of Temple's ethical stance has an important
implication. That stance (pp. 126ff.) seems to presuppose a
comfortable fit of Plato, utilitarianism and Christianity. However,
in the light of the Cross there can be no comfort. As we have seen,
the Christian faith is not susceptible to such an easy integration
with natural morality.

At the end of Chapter 11 we commended the search for middle
axioms – recommendations intermediate between principles and
programmes which are arrived at by bringing alongside one
another an analysis of the empirical situation and the total
Christian understanding of life (pp. 148f.). We focussed on middle
axioms, not for their own sake, important though they are in the
work of Boards of Social Responsibility, but because they
illustrate the process of relating experience, empirical disciplines
and Christian faith, in short, the dialectical method. This process is
equally applicable at whatever level of church life members engage
with social questions from a Christian perspective. Indeed the
more one argues for the dialectical method, the more important it

is that reports of Boards do not merely provide illumination for ordinary people, but are informed by their experience and reflection. Temple was quite right to say, as we saw in Part I, that the task of thinking out problems afresh is one which can be successfully undertaken only in the closest relation with the experience of those who are exposed to the daily pressures of the economic and political struggle (pp. 71f.). There is a great need for the development of strategies which encourage people to come together to help each other to live their faith in the social arena with greater confidence and support. This is the primary place where the dialectical method needs to be implemented. Appendix II offers some guidelines for the functioning and composition of groups of this kind. Appendix III imagines such groups using the framework outlined here to consider the problem areas which Temple himself engaged in – industrial relations, unemployment, economics, international relations – in their present-day form. In each case a number of questions are set out which are prompted by the framework.

To summarise:
5.1 It is necessary to take account of circumstances in making moral decisions.
5.2 We must always have in view the goal of the development of persons in community and the sanctity of personality.
5.3 The danger of comfortable compromises can be offset if we remember that love negates justice and love redeems justice. Compromise must entail an attitude of misgiving, even horror.
5.4 Decisions are to be made by bringing alongside one another an analysis of the empirical situation and a total Christian understanding of life. On this basis Boards of Social Responsibility should pursue the search for middle axioms. But the task of thinking out problems must be undertaken only in the closest relation with the experience of those who are exposed to the daily pressures of the economic and political struggle. The primary place for decision-making is in local groups, whose members help each other to live their faith in the social arena.

This framework obviously needs expansion. Much more of Temple's Christian philosophy could be included within it. I have concentrated on sketching co-ordinates of a framework suitable for today, which would in fact do justice to Temple's insights in the last years of his life. There is, however, something more important than co-ordinates and expansion.

It has been said of Reinhold Niebuhr that he offered not so much an ethic with a clear content for generating decisions, but rather a spirituality. Plainly Niebuhr does offer content – an understanding of the way God relates to His world – which can offer guidelines for decisions. Our proposed framework aims to do no less. However, a framework is mere dry bones unless it is grounded in a living experience of God – in short, in a spirituality which enables us to enter into the movement of God's dealings with His world. Our framework is clearly not one which yields easy answers. We shall be faced with agonising choices, even with horrifying compromises. The nuclear problem is the worst, and there is no prospect of it disappearing in the foreseeable future. How is it possible to live at all in such a world without going mad? Niebuhr, for all his furious social activity, was first and foremost a preacher and pastor with an impressive spirituality. It was one which was centred in the Cross, and returned again and again to the conviction that ultimately we are not called in the least to justify ourselves but to accept the justifying love of God in Christ, and live serene in the knowledge that the forgiving and merciful God is powerful enough to overcome all our sin and confusion.

Temple's spirituality was more obviously sacramentally based. Wherever he was he could look out on the world and know that he was in the presence of the God of love. The focus of this sacramental world was the Eucharist. Here we receive Christ's offered life, so that we can give ourselves more completely to God. Here God makes effective the redeeming work of Christ, drawing men back into a right relationship with Himself, and so with each other (pp. 59f.). But let us leave Temple serenely reading to an embattled committee in a small chapel in Switzerland (pp. 14f.): 'They that wait upon the Lord shall renew their strength; they shall mount up with wings as eagles; they shall run, and not be weary; they shall walk, and not faint.' 'I am the vine, ye are the branches. He that abideth in Me and I in him, the same bringeth forth much fruit; for without Me ye can do nothing ... As the Father hath loved Me, so have I loved you; continue ye in my love ... This is

my commandment, that ye love one another, as I have loved you.'
Herein lies the secret of Temple's spiritual greatness. Herein too lies
our hope for a world of love and peace and joy.

APPENDIX I

It is an obvious fact that there is perpetual and often stormy disagreement about the relation of the Christian faith to social order. There are no doubt many reasons for this. A very important one is the character of the Bible itself. The Bible does not readily yield a systematic social ethics. It was compiled over more than a millennium and reflects changes in historical circumstances and in the understanding of God and His relation to the world. It is by no means easy to disentangle what is culture-bound from what is of enduring validity. The critical issue of the relation of the Old and New Testaments has not been resolved. It is not clear exactly which ethical aspects of the Old Testament have continuing force in the New, and how they are affected by their new context. If we focus only on the New Testament, we find it does not give us a single theology. Today most New Testament theologians handle the synoptic evangelists, St. John and St. Paul separately. Even a single writer (St. Paul is a good example) may have many strands of thought which are far from easy to harmonise. The more obviously ethical content of the New Testament does not have a straightforward interpretation. It is found in a variety of forms of literature. For example, there are not only injunctions and exhortations, but beatitudes and parables. Moreover, how all this is related to the narrative and doctrinal material is not obvious. Jesus' ministry undoubtedly involved Him in social problems, but He did not advance a clear social ethic. His pronouncements are *ad hoc*, the outcome of running battles with His adversaries. The centre of His message was presumably the inbreaking of the Kingdom of God in His own person. His life and teaching were a challenge in the first instance to His own people. They do have universal implications; but how that is to be worked out socially is not defined. Nor was the Church of the New Testament chiefly concerned with social issues outside its community. It is therefore not surprising that controversy rages today over the relation of the Christian faith to social order.[1]

Another important reason for disagreement is the different

situation in which we live from biblical times. Ethical problems constantly arise which were simply unknown then, many of them because of the rise of technology. Moreover, the complexity of the technical issues and our very pride in our technological virtuosity may well often blind us to the ethical dimensions of these problems. Coupled with this is the undoubted fact that how we read the signs of the times is likely to be affected by our position in the social scale, whether we are in a job or out of a job, white or black, woman or man.

This book has approached some of these problems, not in an abstract systematic way, but through a critical evaluation of one man, seeing whether his method was adequate to the biblical witness and to the situation before him. I have suggested that what the Bible primarily gives us is a dramatic vision of God's relations with the world and persons, focused in the life, death and resurrection of Jesus Christ. That vision should lie at the heart of any Christian understanding of reality we build up by the dialectical method, and should include broad guidelines, centring upon our understanding of persons. Any Old Testament material and any imperatives in the New Testament need to be read in the light of the central indicative of what God has done in Jesus Christ. This approach should deliver us from any legalistic recourse to moral absolutes, and free us for decision-making which is responsive to the situation and faithful to the spirit of God's dealings with us.

The framework I have offered has naturally been worked out in dialogue with many ways of relating the Christian faith and social order, only some of which appear in the body of this book. It will already be clear that I am most in sympathy with Reinhold Niebuhr. Among the representatives of the Anglican tradition I rate Temple, John Macquarrie and Ian Ramsey very highly, and among Roman Catholics those who are seeking a revised moral theology in the light of Vatican II, notably Josef Fuchs, Dietmar Mieth and Charles Curran. I also appreciate those Lutherans like Wolfgang Huber and Heinz Eduard Tödt who have reflected deeply on the way their tradition allowed the sacred and the secular to become separated. By turning back to Luther himself, and also by learning from the Confessing Church, they have arrived at a position very similar to Niebuhr's.

The reader is entitled to know more about other ways of relating faith and social order, and this appendix comments on a few further examples. It can only be very selective. It will concentrate on two which respond to Temple explicitly, and two others which have attracted much attention in recent times. I cannot hope, however, to do full justice to them in a few sentences, especially the last two.

Most of those who criticised *Christianity and Social Order* and Temple's speeches of 1942 sharply separated Christianity and social affairs. To discomfort them, Edward Hulton ended an article in the *Picture Post* with a little quotation: 'We have merely made a clear-cut division between politics, which has to do with the affairs of this world, and religion, that is concerned with the affairs of another world'; and he then added: 'These are the words of Hitler.'[2] The perennial problem of those who would separate Christianity and social order is that they play into the hands of unjust regimes because they have no purchase on the world of politics. This was largely the position of pre-Nazi Lutheranism. The two kingdoms had become two entirely separate spheres. 'Love requires justice' is essential if those inclined to separation are not to wander beyond the pale of an acceptable Christian social ethic.

In England, with its strong Protestant tradition, it is still very common to hear the cry 'Religion and politics don't mix', as if the separation of the two were self-evident and the only alternative their identification. This position is usually associated with the conviction that the Gospel is addressed only to individuals. The ethical content of the Bible is generally seen as rules for the conduct of individuals in private life. The Calvinist inheritance, however, drives the English to reconnect religion and politics. This is generally done by demanding certain Christian attitudes in public as well as private life. Individuals are to be disciplined, responsible and honest. Sometimes policy itself is shaped so that these virtues will be strengthened in national life, whereupon politics takes on the character of a moral crusade.

This position is rarely articulated in an explicit and coherent manner. It remains a string of loosely connected presuppositions. Of course, it is not wholly false. A distinction between religion and politics is necessary. Jesus does lay stress on the response of the individual to the Gospel. The ethical content of the New Testament is more readily applicable to the individual and to small groups than to collectivities. The virtues mentioned are genuine Christian virtues. The weakness lies in what the supporters of this view fail to say. There is no mention of the Church as the corporate Body of Christ, called to incorporate all human beings. There is no recognition of the essentially social nature of persons. There is no sensitivity to the Christian themes of power and self-interest, operative especially within collectivities. There is no sustained attempt to explore the implications of the Cross for a reading of human history. These are broad criticisms of a general type. There may be few who hold the position in detail, but I do not think I have set it up as a caricature to knock it down. Certainly the type is no less powerful for being amorphous.

It will, however, be helpful to look at two specific examples of this general type. I would stress that neither neatly fits; each has to be evaluated for what it is in itself. Both comment on Temple, and both have been influential.

The first is Hensley Henson. Henson was a master of language. Though given to verbose rhetoric, he had the knack of exposing the woolliness of others in one uncomfortably sharp sentence. A good example is his criticism of COPEC's apparent wish to impose a Christian ethic by law on a post-Christian nation. Yet Henson was not careful to listen to what the victims of his criticism were actually saying. His own position neglects important aspects of the Bible and is defective in its understanding of the social situation. This can be seen if we explore an apparent inconsistency in Henson.

Henson accused the members of the Standing Committee in the 1926 miners' strike of meddling in economics and politics, and yet himself condemned strikes of miners and railwaymen from the pulpit. He criticised Temple and the other bishops for boldly adventuring into political and economic controversy under their official episcopal titles without mandate from their dioceses, yet signed his own letter about the strike to *The Times* 'Herbert Dunelm (Herbert Hensley Henson).' Henson not only claimed that Archbishop Davidson's appeal from the Churches was bad economics. It also gave impetus to the tendency 'to substitute for religious teaching a declamatory sentimental socialism as far

removed from sound economics as from Christian morality.'
Henson held that economics is entirely autonomous: religion and
morality can have their effects only within the limits prescribed by
economic law, which is final and inexorable. He appeals here to St.
Paul's sequence of the natural and the spiritual in 1 Corinthians 15.[3]
Behind this lies a position which Henson later propounded in the
Gifford Lectures of 1936, *Christian Morality*. Here he wrote that
'Christian morality . . . is the morality inculcated by Jesus Christ,
and illustrated by his example', and that 'the authority of Jesus is
final because it is limited to the sphere of personal morality.'[4] Here
lies the explanation of the apparent inconsistency. When morality
has respected economic law, it does have relevance in the economic
and political sphere, but only at the level of the individual.
Henson's hostility to strikes arises either because they are bad
economics, or because they are bad morality, in that they involve
men breaking their contracts of employment and resorting to
intimidation of their neighbours. This is a quite inadequate
reconnecting of the two spheres of religion and economics, for it
abstracts morality from the realities of the social context, and so is a
species of the individualism N. H. G. Robinson condemned. We
saw earlier that Temple cited freedom of contract as an instance
where freedom may be complete in principle but negligible in
result. That shows a sensitivity to wider issues of power and
conflict which is essential for an adequate pursuit of justice. Henson
is important as a gad-fly of others, but does not offer us a plausible
alternative.[5]

The most comprehensive historical work on the social thought
of the leadership of the Church of England is Dr. Edward R.
Norman's *Church and Society in England, 1770–1970*. It is very
stimulating, largely because of his challenging attacks on the
received uncritical interpretation of the Christian social tradition
from Maurice to Temple. The attacks are prompted in part by his
sharp historian's eye for social realities. Yet his evaluation is also
undoubtedly shaped by his own implicit theology. Let us consider
Norman's handling of Temple himself.

Norman's remarks on Temple up to about 1924 are
uncomplimentary. Temple is an instance of one general conclusion
of Norman's study, that 'the social attitudes of the Church have
derived from the surrounding intellectual and political culture and

not, as Christians themselves seem to assume, from theological learning.' Temple's vision can in the end be stripped down to the educational one of giving everyone the opportunity of attaining the intelligentsia's material and cultural standards. His social ideas came not from his philosophical (or, it is implied, his theological) thinking, but from the Christian Social Union tradition, which was a faithful reflection of the values of the intelligentsia. Norman plainly thinks he has uncovered not simply a historical but a disreputable phenomenon. True, in places he is neutral about this. He expects churchmen to borrow from secular culture, and Christian ethics to be shaped by contemporary non-Christian influence. He even says that 'this is, no doubt, the way of all truth; it takes on the form and the idealism of the intellectual preoccupation of each generation.' But he is certainly writing pejoratively when he notes the almost exact fit of current values with theological interpretation. Temple is further criticised, with partial justification, for an academic moralism which was far too impressed with ideas and out of touch with reality. Indeed, his passion for social justice 'was all ideas, resting upon an innocent awareness of the real nature and expectations of working-class life in England.' One manifestation of this academic moralism was Temple's indictment of competition and his recourse to 'more systematic collectivist politics' to secure a society resting primarily on co-operation. It was only after 1924 that Temple began to realise that social questions did not have easy solutions.[6]

Norman's second set of remarks on Temple tells us that after his translation to York in 1929 he 'continued to sober up.' He made some impressive contributions to Christian sociology (*Men Without Work* is cited), which was at least 'a serious attempt to define distinctly Christian principles of society, derived from Christian doctrine, and not just an attempt to conflate Christianity with secular social ideas.' Temple became more realistic in his judgements. He became more cautious about diagnosing the causes of economic crisis, and about applying political solutions to social problems. There was no such thing as a Christian social ideal, no illumination from the Gospel about technicalities such as social credit.[7] Temple stressed more emphatically the priority of the individual over the state: here was an instance of churchmen diverging from secular humanism. There was an increasing prominence given, according to Norman, to the Church's real and legitimate function as a source of general principles, not applications to economic and political questions, and to the 'priority of Christian conversion, before the solution of the world's evils should be attempted.' And so comes the accolade we would scarcely have expected initially: Temple represented 'the most balanced and intelligent thought of the moderate left.'[8]

Norman's contrast between the earlier and later Temple is certainly overdrawn. For example, the earlier Temple was not simply a starry-eyed idealist. Even Norman admits that as early as 1917 Temple's Collegium was condemning full state socialism and stating that 'no artificial changing of the framework of society would succeed if the members of that society remained unchanged.' COPEC saw the tension between prior individual conversion and prior reformation of social structures. Moreover, we have seen how Temple agonised over the problem of war and the Christian in 1914. At the other end of Temple's life Norman underplays the importance of social witness to him as a preparation for, as well as a consequence of, the Gospel.

The intriguing question is whether we can track down the source of this overdrawn contrast. A major difficulty with *Church and Society in England, 1770–1970* is that, though it is subtitled 'A Historical Study', it is pervaded by an elusive theology as well. Norman's judgements on Temple are shaped as much by his normative presuppositions as by his historical research. The presuppositions understandably lie hidden in this book, but they surface more clearly in his 1978 Reith Lectures, *Christianity and the World Order*.[9] The overwhelming thrust here is towards a separation of religion and politics. In his fierce antagonism to the supposed politicisation of Christianity he associates the spiritual primarily with the transcendent, the unearthly and the timeless; there is a corresponding tendency to dub secular values 'material'. Of the Incarnation it is surprisingly said that the visible and the unseen worlds were briefly joined. Norman harps on the relativities of this life to the point where he rejects Christian espousal of social principles, and even speaks of the worthlessness of all human expectations. He also drives home the contrast between the personal and the social. True religion is to do with the inward soul of man; the teachings of the Saviour clearly describe a personal rather than a social morality. Norman seems to want politics to be a calculation to balance interests, or a convenience for satisfying the need for basic order, not a moral enterprise aiming at justice. He appears to believe that all political outlooks are equidistant from the teachings of Christ. It is this separatist position which has surely affected the animus with which Norman attacks Temple up to 1924.

On the other hand Norman agrees in the Reith Lectures that biblical teachings do have social consequences. Christians will engage not merely in charitable palliatives but in corporate and political action; they will co-operate with others to promote the eradication of agreed injustices (though apparently co-operation with the world is always on the world's terms). It is here that the distinction between politicisation ('the internal transformation of the faith itself, so that it comes to be defined in terms of political values') and engagement in politics comes into play. Unfortunately no clear guidance is given in the Reith Lectures about how the Christian faith bears upon social issues. The separation of religion and politics triumphs, qualified by one direct link only, the doctrine of sin. The doctrine of sin dominates Norman's mind because for him it has been a neglected first principle of the traditional theological view of man (the only place in *Church and Society in England, 1770–1970* where his theological position is quite evident is over original sin).[10] Further, Norman hankers after *distinctly* Christian principles, and it is the doctrine of sin which for him marks the distinction between Christianity and humanism. In this perspective Norman approves of the later Temple because he was not politicised, and he even exaggerates the extent to which he moved to a 'realist' position.

Norman's own position, then, turns out to be inconsistent. He fails to make an adequate connection between Christianity and politics. Moreover, to relativize this life so thoroughly and to isolate the doctrine of sin is to invite a false realism. For it can easily blind men to the legitimacy of aspirations for a more just social order, and relieve those in power from the duty of remedying injustice. David Jenkins appears to be right in his judgement that Norman reflects a defective view of how God relates to the historical process as its Creator and Redeemer. 'Doctrinally and spiritually speaking it would seem that Norman will not allow

God to get close enough to history and does not allow himself to get close enough to human beings as they struggle, hope and fail today. He seems to want to go back to an imagined past of detachment and remote transcendence. Christians can surely, in faith, only go on.' For Jenkins the transcendence of God is experienced in the midst of history. The Christian tradition is not static, but develops through a living encounter with God under the pressures of the contemporary. Faithfulness to this God therefore requires a profound sensitivity to the contemporary, even in its most secular form, and in particular a passionate concern for those whose humanity today is negated. And that inescapably entails a concern for politics. This is how Christians must seek to discern and respond to God's will. 'Without an element of this discernment of and response to God mediated through the pressures of the contemporary ... "traditional" Christianity fades from a response to the living God to a cultic practice maintained by initiates and little related to a Gospel of salvation addressed to the whole world out of experience of a living God ...'[11]

We can certainly be grateful to Dr. Norman for reminding Christians of several strands of their faith. He is right to insist on the transcendence of God and the vital distinction between religion and politics. It is easy to tackle political questions in excessively moral terms and to invest too many expectations in politics. Norman is right to remind us of God's address to each individual and of the reality of sin. However, all that is valid in Norman was clear to men like Temple, Oldham and Niebuhr in the late 1930s and 1940s, and already in Niebuhr's case formed part of a far more adequate Christian social ethic.

Comment on Karl Barth is necessary because of his leadership in the Confessing Church during the Nazi era, and because his ideas are always stimulating and are still very potent, for example in the reshaping of the doctrine of the two kingdoms and in discussion of the peace question. Yet comment here must end in suspended judgement. For there is a major debate about the relation between Christianity and politics in Barth's thought and action, and I am not competent to carry it further, even less to resolve it.[12]

It is widely agreed that up to the First World War Barth was theologically liberal. He was also a religious socialist. His observation of the condition of the industrial proletariat during his pastorates at Geneva and Safenwil in Switzerland made him strongly critical of capitalism. For Barth, true socialism is the Kingdom of God. God's socialism certainly transcends man's struggles for socialism; but it also includes them. A number of disappointments led Barth to rethink both theologically and politically. In early August 1914 he read a proclamation by ninety-three German intellectuals supporting the war policy of the Kaiser. Among them were almost all his revered theological teachers. He was scathing about the way the German war machine was backed by a war theology which harped on the motif of sacrifice. Moreover the German socialist parties did not shrink from taking part in the carnage. Barth realised that he could no longer follow the ethics and dogmatics of his liberal teachers. He became committed to the search for deeper theological foundations, which would foster Church renewal, and in turn be the mainspring of a better political practice. Politically Barth was frustrated by the failure of liberal efforts at social reform, and he seems to have moved further to the left. In 1915 he joined the most left-wing party in Switzerland, and was active establishing unions and organising strikes. He made frequent use of Marxist ideas and enthused over the Russian revolution of 1917. It is little wonder he was nicknamed the 'red pastor'. The main point at issue in recent debate is how far it was politics which precipitated and shaped his theological change.

The second edition of Barth's commentary on St. Paul's letter to the Romans, published in 1922, shows us the scale of his rethinking, and it brought him a chair in Reformed theology at Göttingen University in Germany. He emphasises the infinite difference between God and man. In order to clear the way for the infinite sovereignty of God, he propounds a dialectical way of conceiving God's relation to man, whereby every affirmation about God must be counteracted by an equal and opposite negation. In particular Barth stresses that man cannot by his own efforts establish an immediate relationship with God; that would be merely self-justification and therefore sin. There is no point of immediate contact with God, as the liberals claimed, either in individual experience or in history. Natural theology and natural law are false trails. Only God can bridge the chasm between himself and the world, and he does this through his self-disclosure in Jesus Christ, coming vertically from above, as it were, in judgement and grace.

This shift had repercussions on Barth's political thinking. He could see that there was a danger in saying that God's socialism includes man's struggles for socialism. It could lead to a brazen identification of the two, and so to man's exploiting God for his own purposes. Barth now withdraws direct religious sanction for socialist politics. Even socialist revolution stands under judgement when confronted with the sovereignty of God. It is God who brings in the wholly new, and God's revolution is the absolute limit to all human revolutions and a judgement upon their sin. This insight was aided by Barth's disenchantment with the course of the Russian revolution under Lenin.

Here also there is dispute. Some claim that Barth turned his back on politics. Did he not himself deny every theological affinity to Marxism and liberalism, and did he not declare that politics was fundamentally uninteresting and a game of relativities? Others, however, quote his words, 'I have always been interested in politics,' and claim that he never ceased to believe true socialism was the Kingdom of God, and that his radical revolutionary direction was maintained. It was rather that for a variety of reasons he concentrated on his central theological task, and that the radical turn of his theological thinking led him to become more soberly pragmatic in his politics. This should not be interpreted as passive complacency about political affairs.

A further theological shift in Barth is evident in 1931, the year he produced the book it gave him the greatest satisfaction to write, his study on St. Anselm. Inspired by Anselm's use of analogy, Barth moves from a dialectical theology with a severe emphasis on the infinite distance between God and man, to an analogical theology. The notion of analogy presupposes the distance between God and man, but it stresses the possibility of making affirmative statements in theology. For Barth this possibility is grounded in God's gracious decision to reveal himself to man.

The method of analogy enables more positive connections between the Christian faith and the political realm, and this was to be vitally important in the stand against Hitler. Though at first Barth's emphasis was mainly on the defence of the Church and the Gospel against the encroachments of the Nazis, he presently attacked the wider effects of their policies – the arbitrary justice, the denial of spiritual values and the extermination of the Jews. Rebelling against the separatist version of the Lutheran doctrine of the two kingdoms, he now developed an analogical model in *Gospel and Law* (1935), *Justification and Justice* (1938), and *The Christian Community and the Civil Community* (1946). The two kingdoms are related as two concentric circles, with Christ himself at the centre of both. The inner circle is that of the Gospel and the Church, the outer the political. There are analogies between the life of the two circles. For example, we are told that since the Church lives from God as the light lit in Jesus Christ, the political corollary is that it will be the sworn enemy of all secret policies and secret diplomacy. The Church, moreover, witnesses that the Son of Man came to seek and save the lost; it will therefore concentrate on the poor and the oppressed and choose the political movement likely to lead to social justice.[13]

The common view is that neither the dialectical Barth nor the analogical Barth arrives at a satisfactory way of relating the Christian faith and politics. The dialectical Barth is too negative. He stresses the transcendence of God so heavily that he loses touch with the concrete realities of life. When he swings over to the model of analogy, he may provide clear positions for moments of great crisis, as in the Barmen Declaration of the Confessing Church in 1934, but he does not offer much help for the relative decisions which are the inescapable requirement of political life. Thus Reinhold Niebuhr pictured Barth travelling in a religious airplane at so high an altitude that he gives us no guidance for discriminating choices. The result is political irresponsibility and complacency. One aspect of this criticism is that Barth maintained a negative attitude to natural theology and natural morality. This led him on the one hand to neglect the necessary task of empirical analysis, and on the other to attempt to move directly from the Bible to clear directives for social action. The result, it is held, is a certain arbitrariness. It would, for instance, be just as possible to argue that because God is often a hidden God, secret diplomacy is commendable. There are also, as we have seen, problems about the Church as such throwing in its lot with a political movement.

The contrary view, however, is that Barth was always interested in the connection of Christianity and politics, and that he succeeds in being no less empirical and analytical than his critics and in making those connections. His refusal to condemn Communism outright after the Second World War in the way he had condemned Nazism was not a sign of arbitrariness, but was based on a shrewd appraisal of both systems.

A further complication is that in the *Church Dogmatics* Barth sponsors a rather different ethics, one of the divine command. Christians are humbly to listen to the command of God in each particular situation and obey it. The intention of Barth is to safeguard God's sovereign freedom and warn man against supposing he possesses some basis apart from God, perhaps in enduring principles and rules, from which he can make his moral decisions. Yet how are we to distinguish true from false hearing of the command of God, unless we already have some criteria? Does the freedom of God not look remarkably like arbitrariness? And how does an ethics of the divine command relate to the model of analogy?

We must await further developments in this debate. Barth's critics may exaggerate, but it is hard to resist the conclusion that he suffers from serious deficiencies, and we should perhaps follow those German thinkers who, whilst immensely influenced by Barth, do not believe that he offers an adequate model for Christian social ethics. It is instructive to look at Huber and Tödt. It is no accident that, like Barth, they use the concept of analogy. They can appreciate Barth's criticism of the separatism of pre-Nazi Lutheranism. However, they retain a Lutheran perspective which, like Niebuhr's, offers a more complex understanding than Barth of the relationship between the two kingdoms. As we saw, they take a positive yet critical stance towards natural morality, and they are keen that Christians should engage in analysis, using the insights of the various disciplines. For all their sparring, perhaps Niebuhr and Barth were not so far apart if we focus on their insistence on God's transcendence over, and judgement of, all politics, and on their affirmation of positive connections between Christianity and politics.

The impact of Barth on a whole generation of thinkers in Christian social ethics has been immense. We have already seen how the Christendom Group were trying to respond to him. They were engaged in deriving a Catholic sociology from dogma. Barth's rejection of natural morality caused complications, but his strong dogmatic stance tended to reinforce their deductive approach. On a wider front the thought of the World Council of Churches was almost dominated by Barth and the Biblical Theology movement from the 1940s right up to the Geneva Conference on Church and Society in 1966. This conference marked a major shift in the centre of gravity from Europe to the Third World. Since then Biblical Theology has been just one strand in the burgeoning political theologies of Europe, America, and especially the Third World.

The political theologies which have sprung up in the last few years are very valuable for many of their insights. They are strongly critical of some consequences of the Enlightenment: the relegation of religion to the private sphere, the production of abstract systems and theories of human life, the adulation of technological virtuosity, the reduction of the human person to a socially conditioned entity. The Roman Catholic J. B. Metz, for example, is encouraged by the spirit of Vatican II to attempt positively yet critically to offer a theological enlightenment of the Enlightenment and its subject, the middle-class citizen.[14] Political theologians rightly recognize that all our theology takes place in a social and political context. Anyone who thinks he is exercising neutral non-political reason is probably conforming to the *status quo*. Metz sees that the task of the Christian is not to produce an even more comprehensive theory of human life, but to practise the faith in and through concrete historical situations. This entails solidarity with those who are oppressed and denied their humanity. For a person is not an isolated individual; persons are made for solidarity; identity can only be won through social struggle. The contribution of Christianity goes far beyond moral exhortation. Formally it is rich in story and narrative (a form which is thoroughly concrete against all abstractions). It publicly preserves an eschatological memory of a God who is the subject and meaning of history, and who liberates people to become subjects and persons themselves. All the powers within history lie under the eschatological proviso of God, that is, they are relativised and judged in an ultimate sense by God. In particular the Cross underlines the importance of suffering (thus calling in question the 'woe to the vanquished' attitude of the oppressor) and offers a ground for the hope of future freedom.

Liberation theology is particularly good at exposing the violence embedded in the structures of society and at showing how technology can powerfully reinforce it. The Church itself is deeply implicated in this oppression. Liberation theology's call to Christians and the Church is to break out of complacency or a fastidious (and spurious) clinging to innocence, to feel the sufferings of the oppressed as intolerable, and to enable the marginated to take a positive grip on their own destiny and to create change themselves, thereby recovering their humanity. Quite understandably it calls for the play of imagination in envisaging and anticipating social goals, over against mere extrapolations made from within the presuppositions of a rationalised technological present.

All these insights of theologians like Metz, Moltmann and Gutiérrez are to be welcomed.[15] None of them is incompatible with the model of the relation of religion and politics which emerges from a critical study of Temple and Niebuhr. There are, however, tendencies (within liberation theology in particular) which give rise to major reservations. Let us concentrate on the connections between theory, praxis and theology.

Gustavo Gutiérrez describes the theology of liberation as 'a critical reflection on Christian praxis in the light of the Word'; or, more extendedly, theology is 'a critical reflection from and about the historical praxis of liberation in confrontation with the Word of the Lord lived and accepted in faith.' This looks quite acceptable. It appears to suggest that the Word provides criteria for reflection on praxis. Yet in liberation theology praxis itself has a primacy in a way that is disturbing. Liberation theologians are in reaction against abstract theology, which they believe has been a persistent perversion in the West. They do not, however, simply recommend that we start from the concrete situation. We are to start from a commitment. For Gutiérrez, liberation theology is a theological reflection 'based on the Gospel and the experiences of men and women committed to the process of liberation in the oppressed and exploited land of Latin America.' This commitment is one which takes its origin not from theological ideas (for that would be to revert to abstract theology), but rather from the social sciences – in fact, from Marxism. Only so can the biblical message be genuinely understood.[16]

It is quite legitimate to have some sympathy with this approach. It is indeed unsatisfactory to think of theology as an abstract system of ideas which is then applied in practice, and of ethics as a set of abstract absolute norms. It is true that much Christian social ethics in the West has drawn grand ideals ostensibly from the faith, and failed to get to grips with questions of power and conflict in society. It has therefore fallen into ideology, in the bad sense of a scheme of thought which deflects both beneficiary and victim from facing up to and dealing with historical realities. Latin Americans are peculiarly well placed to see the terrible effects of such ideologizing. Roman Catholic liberation theologians on the one hand criticise their Church for its acquiescence in the *status quo*, its backing of pseudo-Christian traditions and values which are really petit-bourgeois, its formal ties with the state, and its defence of its own prestige and power. On the other hand they are totally disenchanted with development economics, with its bland assumption that resources will 'trickle down' to the poor. It is understandable that in their situation they look on a Marxist interpretation as the only one which makes sense.

The reaction, however, has created difficulties of its own, which liberation theologians have yet to address in a thorough way. First, there is a cluster of problems in resorting to Marxism. In the degree to which Marxism succeeds in being scientific, Christians should accept it. But how scientific is it? One test lies in its power of prediction, and here it has not been conspicuously successful. At a far deeper level, however, it is plainly more than a science (more, too, than an economic theory), and at this point the Christian may well have much more to say. Marxism certainly has an ethical passion, and advances views about man and history which come into conflict with Christianity. Liberation theologians, in reaction against passive acceptance of the *status quo*, are prone to speak of man being a free agent of history, one who can make himself responsible for the transformation of social and political structures. It may be good Marxism to speak of autonomous man in this way, but is that compatible with a Christian understanding of freedom? Not if we follow Huber and Tödt. Liberation theologians also make use of the concept of utopia, not in the sense of an illusion or an unattainable vision, but in a Marxist sense: utopia is already present in the struggle against oppression, anticipating a future which is assured to those who commit themselves to the revolution. But how far is such a view about the forces inherent in history compatible with eschatological notions of Christian hope founded on grace? An exercise of 'decoding' is plainly called for. The basic point here is that there should be a dialectical process, whereby theologians relate as positively as they are able to such an ideology, but also retain a critical role over against it. If the dialectic is abandoned, then theology is simply subsumed under ideology.

Liberation theologians tend only to nibble at these questions. We can believe that they genuinely want the Christian faith to challenge every ideology in the name of the truly human. But they hamper themselves through their phobia of all abstract theology. They seem to believe that the only alternative is to take a Marxist interpretation as their departure point. But they thereby forfeit any real capacity to criticise Marxism from a Christian perspective.

Secondly, and as a reflex, when a Christian perspective is involved, it seems persistently to be distorted by prior commitments. Thus several, in their exegesis of the Exodus story, maintain that originally the role of God was secondary to that of Moses. The Israelites in bondage in Egypt became conscientised and found their political leader in Moses before there was any intervention by God. For this there is no evidence. Furthermore it is questionable whether the syndrome of oppressor–oppressed is an adequate key for understanding Scripture, and whether the Exodus should have the prominence it is given by liberation theologians. Though it is of determinative significance for Israel and is a motif constantly reinterpreted in both Testaments, it is questionable whether it can bear the weight put upon it. The Kingdom of God seems to have a far greater claim to centrality. It is doubtful in this connection whether some liberation theologians do justice to the novelty of the event of Jesus Christ. An importance facet of this is the self-giving love of Jesus which took him to the Cross. Segundo's commitment to revolutionary praxis leads him drastically to transmute sacrificial love (which Niebuhr correctly reads as heedless of self) into 'efficacious love'. The quest for social and political justice appears to distort the dynamics of the New Testament generally: the injustice of man to man is treated as more fundamental than the rebellion and impiety of man towards God.

These distortions have wide ramifications. It is hard to resist the impression that we are offered not so much a Christian theology of liberation as a general salvation history under which Jesus Christ is subsumed. In their antipathy to a dualistic, privatised reading of Christianity, liberation theologians assert the indivisible unity of history. The salvation Christ offers becomes then a paradigm rather than something unique. A symptom of this tendency is the way in which all the oppressed are elevated to the status of a Messianic community. This not only fails to recognise the inalienable uniqueness of Jesus himself as the Messiah. It also raises major questions about the nature and place of the Church.

For anyone with a grain of imagination and sympathy liberation theology, and political theology in general, are quite intelligible phenomena of the late twentieth century, and raise very important questions. They cannot be simply written off as passing trends or as manifest error, and they are likely to have lasting repercussions on the theological scene. At present, however, such answers as they offer invite many reservations, and we must wait and see how these theologians rework and develop their thought and practice.[17]

APPENDIX II

I remarked at the end of Chapter 16 that the primary place for the implementation of the dialectical method is at the local level, where people can come together to help each other live their faith in society with greater confidence. There are many Christians who find it difficult to see how their faith can be a resource to them in daily living, especially if they belong to large institutions. Some find they are caught up in rapid change and face an uncertain future; others are conscious of a tension between a Gospel of love and the rules within which they are expected to work, perhaps as a foreman or a manager. All too often they find that few of their colleagues are Christians, and that their parish is concerned almost exclusively with the domestic aspects of Christian living. To combat feelings of uncertainty and isolation there needs to be a continuing network of support within a diocese or district, as part of its concern for pastoral care and mission. Ian Ramsey, for example, as Bishop of Durham appointed in 1969 a theological consultant in industrial and social affairs, Margaret Kane, who among many other activities set great store by gathering together groups of people whom she knew to be struggling to make connections between faith and life.[1] It is a critical test of understanding and commitment how fully such a post is backed through diocesan structures as a whole, and whether importance is accorded to the creation and sustaining of a network of support.

Local groups of this kind will no doubt vary a great deal; each must decide by trial and error the best way of operating. It is however possible on the basis of limited experience to suggest a number of rough guidelines which can serve as a check-list.

In the first place it usually helps to start out from the quite specific life situations of the members themselves. They join because they are puzzled or excited by some problem or opportunity in their experience. No book, not even the Bible, will speak so directly to their condition that they can study it and go away satisfied. And the obvious form in which to present these situations is the story: the narrative form, as we saw in Chapter 11, is of central importance in the Christian faith. It is no accident that this is the form of the Gospel and is central to the Eucharist, and it is a natural way to articulate concrete Christian experience.

Members are unlikely to tell their story unless they feel safe within the group. They may well be afraid of looking foolish, perhaps because they are not very articulate, or because they have a residual belief that there is an unambiguous answer to be read out of Scripture which they have stupidly failed to spot. They may also fear that they will be given a moral harangue which leaves them feeling chastened but none the wiser about what they ought to do. It is of critical importance that the storyteller is allowed to present the story exactly in the way he or she wishes, and that the other members simply listen, use their imagination, and enter into the story. It may well have affinities with hundreds of other situations, but it is this particular situation which is to be grasped. The first questions of the audience must be for clarifications. Only then should they contribute what they can from their own experience. They may recount similar experiences, or draw upon insights from the disciplines, or widen the perspective beyond the local, or suggest which part of the Bible or Christian tradition might throw particular light on the story. The chief object is to help the storyteller to interpret the situation better, make personal connections between faith and life, and decide what are the next practical steps to be taken. No one else can or should perform those tasks, and the group would deserve to collapse if the storyteller were threatened with the loss of freedom and responsibility.

The composition of the group is of great importance. All the members must positively *want* to make connections between faith and life. As a matter of commitment and courtesy they should be willing to attend regularly, and it helps to decide at the outset precisely how many sessions there will be. It is best if a group can achieve a balanced representation. It is an advantage to have both clergy and laity together, helping and understanding each other better. The laity should predominate, since the main work of living out the Gospel in society, as Temple saw, falls to them. In any case the laity can often feel intimidated by the clergy, who generally enjoy a greater proficiency in speaking and theological learning. The group will also benefit from having members with varied experience of life and expertise in the disciplines, and that includes the expertise of the theologian. There is often a regrettable sense of divorce between universities and parishes, and a faith and life group can help to break this down, though the theologian may well need to acclimatise to an unfamiliar way of operating. That the group also needs to be thoroughly ecumenical scarcely needs saying nowadays; and indeed Christians repeatedly find that they have more in common with members of other denominations than with many of their own. In any case, in the matter of social action it is vital for Christians to think and act together, and not dissipate their energies in duplication. It is also vital that Christians find as much common ground as they can with non-Christians. The more pluralistic society becomes, the more necessary this is. Not only is this practical sense, but also Christians do not have a monopoly of ethical or religious wisdom, nor has the Church in history consistently distinguished itself in its defence of human dignity. Christians must therefore combine with people of other faiths and none, learning from them and taking to heart their criticisms. Moreover, non-Christian members of the group can save Christians from using esoteric language and remind them of a fact they often overlook: the Church exists primarily not for itself but for the sake of the world.

APPENDIX III

If we adopt the framework proposed in Chapter 16 and turn to the problem areas which Temple himself engaged in – industrial relations, unemployment, economics, international relations – what might we say about them in their modern form? No concrete answer can of course be given here. We can however mention a number of questions which are prompted by the framework.

In *industrial relations* we have to understand the outlook of those engaged in the industrial process. What factors have historically shaped their present attitude? How do they perceive their present situation? What are their fears and aspirations for the future? Here the social sciences can be particularly helpful.

We have also to ask about the economic pressures on industrial relations. What is the economic state of the industry? What are the varying options for the future which are in any sense feasible? What are the unavoidable constraints? The economist can provide an analysis of the immediate situation, setting it in a wide economic perspective.

How can the development of persons in community best be fostered in this situation? Who are the persons involved beyond those immediately engaged in the industry? What common interests and agreements already exist between the parties? What are the configurations of power? Where can one detect the operation of self-interest, and what degree of justification does it have? Which party's humanity is under the greatest threat from the power and self-interest of others? Are the 'unavoidable' constraints generated by a powerful self-interest, and if so are they therefore avoidable after all?

What arrangements, then, can be worked out which (a) build on existing common interests, (b) harness self-interest in order to arrive at a greater approximation to justice, and (c) give compensating power and benefits to the weakest party? What is the most disturbing point of this compromise, and how can we work towards a situation more compatible with the Christian Gospel?

Any group which studies the *unemployed* today is likely to find confirmation of the wisdom of Temple's social principles and of the inter-disciplinary and personal approach he used. The findings of the social sciences are particularly interesting. Confronted with the task of choosing the right perspective to understand the unemployed, sociologists and social psychologists are finding a symbolic-interactionist perspective particularly appropriate. This is because it focuses on the question of the self-image of the unemployed, as this is defined and re-defined in a network of social relationships. The importance of the sense of self-worth in the unemployed, inseparable from their relation to the community, is clear. Though this perspective is not in itself ethical, it does offer an interpretation of what is happening to human beings in society which is consonant with Temple's social principles. We therefore have an example emerging of what Dietmar Mieth referred to as an integrated understanding of persons.

At the same time there are factors in the 1980s that were not present in the 1930s: a technological revolution and certain limits to growth imposed by finite world resources. We have to estimate what are the prospects for employment, especially in the face of the microprocessor; what strategies can be developed for giving work to the maximum number of people. Above all we require a review of the longstanding so-called Protestant work ethic. It was a dynamic of the growth of capitalism, inculcating attitudes of discipline and hard work which were a mainspring of the success of earlier industrialisation. It required people to justify themselves by economically useful work. Yet if society today cannot offer such work to all who seek it, what is to become of the work ethic? How are we to revise it in a way which is appropriate to our present situation, and consistent with the development of persons in community?

Both industrial relations and unemployment rapidly carry us into questions of *economics*. We become involved in a critique of different economic systems. Are these systems simply morally neutral techniques for handling the economy? If they are more than this, can we develop moral critiques?

Let us take, for example, the prevailing economic system in the West, the free market, modified to a greater or lesser extent by government. Is this a neutral account of how one can generate maximum wealth? Has it in fact been more productive of wealth than any other economic system? If so, can it be justified solely on that ground? What are we to make of the moral criticisms that have been made of it? Is it a source of wrong human relationships? If it rightly emphasises the virtue of freedom, what kind of freedom is this, and how does it fare in promoting community or service to the common good? Does it in any case promote the freedom of the maximum number of persons, or only the freedom of a segment? If the latter, is there anything wrong in that?

This carries us on to questions of self-interest and power. If capitalism envisages a free market where each pursues his own interest, is it parasitic upon, and ultimately destructive of, virtues such as altruism and generosity, which are fundamental to human communities? Or does it rather open up the way for such virtues to be practised, free of all coercion, in the private sphere? Does it automatically distribute justly? If not, does that matter? Is there an ever greater concentration of resources in the hands of a minority in the community? If so, are the benefits of capitalism, material and moral, still worth the price, and are they obtainable only at that price?

This invites the consideration of other economic systems, actual or imaginary. One can raise equally searching questions about, for instance, the performance of state socialism. Economically, can a centralised, planned system be made to work efficiently? Ethically, can it safeguard the dignity of the individual? Does it necessarily promote community and the common good? As Temple saw, there is the problem of how to have any check upon those who wield the levers of power. What defence is there against incompetence or the corrupt pursuit of self-interest?

Christianity cannot ally itself with any economic system. That does not mean, however, that all economic systems are equidistant from Christianity. Each must be evaluated to see how closely it approximates to justice. And even the winner needs to be subjected to constant scrutiny, since it is capable both of improvement and degeneration.

The most burning question in *international relations* is obviously how under the nuclear threat we can move towards a safer and more peaceful world. Our framework clearly suggests that absolute pacifism is inadequate. It certainly bears witness to the ultimate demand of God that men love each other as He loves them. But the injunctions of the Sermon on the Mount cannot be simply carried out with success in a sinful world. Individuals may practise costly self-sacrifice, but it is generally beyond the capacity of groups as we know them in history. We need to aim at establishing higher degrees of justice, even if that is little more than a balance of power.

We need to face the task of analysing our present predicament. What are the basic types of weapons held and how are they deployed? What are the probable consequences of all-out nuclear war? What are the chances of a non-nuclear or tactical-nuclear war escalating into a full-scale nuclear war?

We need to try to understand the outlooks of the different powers, and the historical and geographical factors which have generated them. Here supremely we need to analyse the ramifications of the power of self-interest. Why is it that no agreement is ever reached which could lead to a reversal of the arms race? Is it just the negative aspect of mutual fear? Is it imperial ambition? If so, whose? Is it the desire to prove the superiority of an economic system? If so, whose? Is there an inbuilt momentum towards the development of ever more sophisticated weapons, a technological imperative reinforced by an imperative to generate jobs and profits?

Is it then possible to speak at all of a stable balance of power? Can we even talk of approximations to justice? When we reckon with the sanctity of personality, do we envisage any set of circumstances where war could be the lesser evil? Would war be possible without infringing the immunity of non-combatants and abandoning any sense of proportion between destruction and gain? (These two criteria for fighting are drawn from the traditional just war theory).

If our answer to this last question is no, is it possible to give a relative justification to the practice of nuclear deterrence, where we threaten to use nuclear weapons if the condition of an attack on us is fulfilled? Can this be a viable harnessing of self-interest to the avoidance of war?

More positively, are there common interests between the superpowers which can form a basis for closer ties? What can Christians do to build up positive relationships both within the arena of international politics and through the witness of Christian communities?

Our framework cannot provide ready-made answers to these questions, but it can, I suggest, point up in a sharp way the extreme precariousness of our position, whichever way we turn, and the dreadful agony of a choice between monstrous evils. It can drive us to look for all possible ways in which the sacrificial love of God can penetrate the vicious circles of fear and self-interest.

NOTES

The following abbreviations are used for works by William Temple:

C	Competition
CC	Citizen and Churchman
CD	Christian Democracy
CFCL	Christian Faith and the Common Life
CLF	The Church Looks Forward
CN	Church and Nation
CS	Christianity and the State
CSO	Christianity and Social Order
CTP	Christianity in Thought and Practice
CV	Christus Veritas
ECP	Essays in Christian Politics and Kindred Subjects
EPA	The Ethics of Penal Action
F	Foundations
FG	Fellowship with God
HNW	The Hope of a New World
J	Readings in St. John's Gospel
KG	The Kingdom of God
LL	Some Lambeth Letters
MC	Mens Creatrix
MWW	Men Without Work
NMG	Nature, Man and God
NP	The Nature of Personality
PC	Plato and Christianity
PR	Personal Religion and the Life of Fellowship
PTT	The Preacher's Theme Today
RE	Religious Experience and other essays
RSS	Repton School Sermons
SSTC	Studies in the Spirit and Truth of Christianity
TSPD	Thoughts on Some Problems of the Day
TWT	Thoughts in War-Time
UC	The Universality of Christ

Chapter 1: Temple's Home Background

The standard biography of Frederick Temple is the two-volume *Memoirs of Archbishop Temple* by Seven Friends, edited by E. G. Sandford. There is also the sketch of Frederick and William Temple in *Leaders of the Church of England 1828–1978* by David L. Edwards; and the early part of the biographical sketch of William Temple in Joseph Fletcher's *William Temple, Twentieth-Century Christian.*

[1] CLF 5.

[2] Sandford, I 3–4, 20, 24, 29, 36, 63; Edwards, 303–305; Fletcher, 237–239.

[3] Sandford, I 67–68; II 442–448, 487.

[4] Sandford, II 709.

[5] Sandford, II 467, 458; I 66.

[6] Sandford, II 423, 633; cf. I 295.

[7] Sandford, II 479.

[8] Sandford, II 472–473.

[9] Sandford, I 287, 223–224; II 606.

[10] Sandford, II 628, 635–636.

[11] Sandford, II 437.

[12] Sandford, II 692.

[13] Sandford, I 72–73.

[14] Sandford, I 97–114; II 563–565, 574–577.

[15] Sandford, I 222, 175.

[16] Sandford, I 197–198.

[17] Sandford, I 167–170.

[18] Sandford, I 183, 174, 218. The circumstances of the famous quotation about Temple are given on 179.

[19] Sandford, II 131.

[20] Sandford, I 296–297.

[21] Sandford, I 475; II 556–557, 708.

[22] Sandford, II 127.

[23] F. G. Bettany, *Stewart Headlam*, 67.

[24] Sandford, II 129–130.

[25] Sandford, II 126.

[26] Sandford, II 142–150; cf. 485 on conscience.

[27] Iremonger, 3; Fletcher, 240.

[28] Edwards, 311–313; Sandford, I 324.

[29] This is suggested by Fletcher, 241.

Chapter 2: Temple's Education

[1] Iremonger, 14.

[2] T. Arnold, *Principles of Church Reform*, 142 (edition of M. J. Jackson and J. Rogan).

[3] S. C. Carpenter, *Church and People, 1789–1889*, 64; *Principles of Church Reform*, 93; G. C. Binyon, *The Christian Socialist Movement in England*, 227; Hudson and Reckitt, *The Church and the World*, vol. III, 35.

[4] Binyon, 227; Carpenter, 61.

[5] G. M. Young, *Portrait of an Age*, 62–63.

[6] D. Emmet, in Iremonger, 527.

[7] PC, 90–91.

[8] RE 33–34, 51–56.

[9] Iremonger, 176.

[10] Iremonger, 538–539.

[11] Iremonger, 417–418.

[12] M. Richter, *The Politics of Conscience*, 35.

[13] Richter, 131, 102–107.

[14] Richter, 104–113, 173.

[15] Richter, 36, 109, 170, 38, 101.

[16] SSTC 42–43.

[17] Iremonger, 42–43.

[18] J. Fletcher, *William Temple, Twentieth-Century Christian*, 287.

[19] RE 3.

[20] Binyon, 162.

[21] The best account of the first phase of Christian Socialism is T. Christensen, *Origin and History of Christian Socialism, 1848–1854*.

[22] For a full account of the Divine Order see T. Christensen, *The Divine Order, A Study in F. D. Maurice's Theology*; there is a summary in *Origin and History of Christian Socialism*, 23–26.

[23] Christensen, *Origin and History of Christian Socialism*, 58.

[24] Christensen, ibid., 352, 365.

[25] For an account of Stewart Headlam and the Guild of St. Matthew, see Peter d'A. Jones, *The Christian Socialist Revival, 1877–1914*, Chapter V; also M. B. Reckitt (ed.), *For Christ and the People*.

[26] See Jones, Chapter VI.

[27] G. F. A. Best, *Bishop Westcott and the Miners*.

[28] Conrad Noel in *Socialism in Church History*, 257.

[29] Jones, 223, 197.

[30] For an account of the Church Socialist League, see Jones, Chapter VII.

[31] See I. Goodfellow, *The Church Socialist League, 1906–1923: Origins, Development and Disintegration* (Durham Ph.D. 1983).

[32] Jones, Chapter X.

Chapter 3: Temple the Educator

[1] Iremonger, 69–72, 486–487.

[2] Iremonger, 155, 160–161; R. Craig, *Social Concern in the Thought of William Temple*, 70–72.

[3] Iremonger, Chapter VII.

[4] 'The Church and the Labour Party' is in *The Economic Review*, April 1908, 190–202.

[5] Iremonger, 333–334, 128.

[6] Iremonger, 90–93.

[7] Iremonger, 74–77.

[8] Presidential Address, 16 October 1909, printed as a supplement to *The Highway*, December 1909; *The Constructive Quarterly*, March 1914, 188–190.

[9] Iremonger, Chapter VIII; *The Reptonian*, July 1912, and the Repton School archives; for Temple's view on the public schools, CN 182–191.

Chapter 4: Temple the Social Reformer

[1] Quoted by S. P. Mews in *Renaissance and Renewal in Christian History*, 363.

[2] Alan Wilkinson, *The Church of England and the First World War*, 230ff., 251ff.

[3] Iremonger, 171–179.

[4] *Christianity and War*, 10–13.

[5] e.g. *The Challenge*, 14 April 1916; 30 November 1917; Iremonger, 187–188.

[6] Iremonger, 179 and Chapters XIII–XVII.

[7] J. Oliver, *The Church and Social Order*, 23–24.

[8] Oliver, 25–28.

[9] Oliver, 28–33.

[10] Oliver, 48–52.

[11] Oliver, 52–55.

[12] Oliver, 41–45.

[13] *Chronicle of Convocation*, 1918, 349–353; Iremonger, 282, 291, 313–317.

[14] Iremonger, 322.

[15] Iremonger, 328–336; Oliver, 66–72.

[16] 'The Moral Foundation of Peace', *The Contemporary Review*, July 1920, 65–70; *The Pilgrim*, January 1921, 126.

[17] *The Pilgrim*, January 1923, 218–225.

[18] *The Proceedings of COPEC*, 200.

[19] H. H. Henson, *Quo Tendimus?* 78–135.

[20] Iremonger, 302–303, 324–325, 336.

[21] Henson, in a letter quoted by Norman, *Church and Society in England, 1770–1970*, 309; *Doctrine in the Church of England*, 16–17; Raven, quoted by Oliver, 68.

[22] E. R. Norman, *Church and Society in England, 1770–1970*, 279–281; Oliver, 72–77.

[23] Raven, quoted in Norman, *Church and Society in England, 1770–1970*, 282; Oliver, ch. 4.

[24] Iremonger, 512; Oliver, 106.

[25] Iremonger, Chapter XXII.

[26] Oliver, 98–100.

[27] V. A. Demant, *The Miners' Distress and the Coal Problem*; *The Religious Prospect*.

[28] v.i., p. 81.

Chapter 5: Temple the Christian Philosopher

The chief books on this subject are Jack F. Padgett, *The Christian Philosophy of William Temple*; Owen C. Thomas, *William Temple's Philosophy of Religion*; and Robert Craig, *Social Concern in the Thought of William Temple*.

[1] NMG ix.

[2] NMG viii.

[3] MC 7.

[4] MC 298, 1–4.

[5] CV vii–ix.

[6] NMG 44; Padgett, 55–59.

[7] MC 353; Padgett, 59–60.

[8] Padgett, 59–61, 170–173; NMG 410–411.

[9] NMG, Chapters I–II.

[10] Iremonger, 530–532.

[11] Padgett, 1, 61, 76, 117, 125; Thomas, 4; cf. W. G. Peck in *William Temple, an Estimate and an Appreciation*, 59.

[12] Padgett, 235, cf. 62; Thomas, 146, 154–158; Iremonger, 531.

[13] NMG 109–111, 202–212.

[14] e.g. CV 4–5; see Padgett, 68–70.

[15] NMG, Chapter XIX; Padgett, 70–71.

[16] NMG 498.

[17] NMG 132, 257, 490, 498–499.

[18] NMG, Chapter X.

[19] Padgett, 63.

[20] NMG, Chapter III.

[21] NMG 125–126.

[22] NMG 71–72, 497, 111, 77–78, 126, 146; W. R. Matthews, in *William Temple, an Estimate and an Appreciation*, 9.

[23] Padgett, 239.

[24] CTP 39–43, RE 247–248; Craig, 29.

[25] NMG 150–155, 168–169, 215; CV 28–29, 32.

[26] NMG 216–221.

[27] NMG 152–153, 253–254; cf. CV 16; Padgett, 76–79.

[28] CV 49; NMG 487, 234; Padgett, 80–82.

[29] Padgett, 83.

[30] NMG, Chapter IX, quotation from 242; see CV 203ff. for a sketch of these dimensions; Padgett, 87–91.

[31] CTP 59–60; CV 71; Padgett, 91–92, 96–97.

[32] NP 76; Padgett, 92–95.

[33] CV 254.

[34] NMG, Chapter XIV, esp. 385, 363–365, 369.

[35] NMG 366–368.

[36] NMG 372–376, 393–397.

[37] NMG 399–400.

[38] CV 234, 124–125; Craig, 59–64, 67.

[39] J xviii, xx, 17; NMG 478.

40 Craig, 16.
41 CV, Chapter XIV; J 48; F 254; Craig, 74.
42 CV 158, 163–170; NMG 494.
43 CC 87; CV 229–230.
44 CV 243; TSPD 150–151; CC 88–89.
45 NMG, Chapter XVI, quotations from 414, 422, 425, 424, 426.

Chapter 6: Temple's Last Years

1 *Doctrine in the Church of England*, 16–17.
2 The article was reprinted in TWT 94–103.
3 Iremonger, 537–538.
4 TWT 106.
5 HNW 10; cf. *Malvern 1941*, 12.
6 TWT 107.
7 Iremonger, 609.
8 TWT 100, 104–105.
9 *Malvern 1941*; *The Spectator*, 24 January 1941; Iremonger, 428–433;
Preston's article was in *The Modern Churchman*, April 1942.
10 *Malvern 1941*, 14.
11 TWT 26–27.
12 CSO (1942) 36–38.
13 CSO (1942) 35.
14 v.i. pp. 134ff.
15 Fletcher, 293.
16 Iremonger, 423–424.
17 Iremonger, 433; the critique of Aquinas is in RE 229–236.
18 See Iremonger, 569–578.
19 To be found in RE 243–255. I am grateful to Professor D. M.
MacKinnon for pointing out to me the importance of this piece in Temple's
own eyes.
20 H. H. Henson, *Retrospect of an Unimportant Life*, vol. III, 276.
21 *The Nation*, 11 November 1944, 585.

Chapter 7: Industry

1 Iremonger, 329.
2 RSS 174–177.
3 CN 80–85.
4 *The Challenge*, 8 September 1916; 8 February 1918; 10 May 1918; *Chronicle of
Convocation* 1918, 349–353.
5 *The Challenge*, 20 September 1918.
6 *The Challenge*, 8 September 1916.
7 *Chronicle of Convocation*, 1918, 344, 349–353.
8 MC 213–215.

[9] *The Challenge*, 11 January 1918.
[10] *The Challenge*, 10 August 1917; MC 223.
[11] *The Challenge*, 8 September 1916.
[12] *The Challenge*, 11 January 1918; *The Daily News*, 14 May 1918; *The Daily Herald*, 26 March 1921.
[13] *Chronicle of Convocation*, 1918, 349–353.
[14] *The Challenge*, 9 November 1917; *Chronicle of Convocation*, 1918, 349–353.
[15] *The Contemporary Review*, July 1920, 65–70.
[16] Oliver, 42–43; Cole and Postgate, 548–551.
[17] *The Pilgrim*, July 1921, 365–366; ECP 5–8.
[18] Oliver, 57–58, 78.
[19] ECP 9–18, in *The Pilgrim*, April 1923.
[20] Oliver, 79; Cole and Postgate, 577–578.
[21] *The Pilgrim*, October 1925, 1–7.
[22] Oliver, 80–82.
[23] *The Pilgrim*, July 1926, 362–372; see also ECP 48–57.
[24] *The Pilgrim*, October 1926, 1–7.
[25] *The Pilgrim*, January 1927, 123–125.
[26] CS 132–134.
[27] *The Times*, 12 April 1933.
[28] HNW 104, 54–55, 60–61.
[29] CSO 79–80.
[30] HNW 55.
[31] HNW 111.
[32] CSO 71–72, 74.
[33] HNW 61–62; CLF 158–162.

Chapter 8: Unemployment

[1] Foreword to the *Annual Report of the Community Service Council for County Durham*, 1936, as reported in *The Times*, 9 March 1936.
[2] PR 84; CV 223; cf. *Chronicle of Convocation*, 1918, 349–353.
[3] *The Challenge*, 10 May 1918; *Chronicle of Convocation*, 1918, 349–353.
[4] CS 98.
[5] *The Contemporary Review*, April 1932, 409–414, 'The New Problem in Economics'.
[6] Professor D. P. O'Brien of Durham University advises me that the economist whose work best fits the aim of the new school as stated by Temple is J. A. Hobson.
[7] Iremonger, 442–443.
[8] *The Times*, 23 January 1934.
[9] MWW ix.
[10] MWW xii.
[11] MWW x, 1–2, 26ff., 414–415.
[12] MWW x–xi.

[13] MWW 31, 3–5.
[14] Letter to *The Times*, 5 March 1934; Iremonger, 440–441.
[15] PTT 81–82.
[16] MWW 354ff., 371ff.; Iremonger, 442.
[17] CSO 12–13, 78.
[18] H. L. *Deb*. Vol. 113, cols 638–640 (21 June 1939).
[19] H. L. *Deb*. Vol. 123, cols 274–280 (10 June 1942).

Chapter 9: Economics

[1] *The Spectator*, 24 January 1941, 83–84.
[2] *The Pilgrim*, January 1924, 128; RE 206–207; *The Spectator*, 24 January 1941, 83–84; CLF 128.
[3] CSO 58–59.
[4] ECP 24–29.
[5] PR 60; *The Challenge*, 10 May 1918; CSO 15–16.
[6] KG 95–98.
[7] CLF 132–133.
[8] *The Fortnightly*, May 1940, 460; CSO 57.
[9] HNW 42–43, 50–51; *The Christian Century*, 9 October 1940, 1242–1244.
[10] CLF 153.
[11] *The Challenge*, 8 September 1916; CLF 127–128; cf. TWT 111–130.
[12] *The Christian Century*, 9 October 1940, 1242–1244.
[13] HNW 51–52; CLF 111, 122, 128.
[14] HNW 56–57; CLF 122; CSO 75; Iremonger, 438–440.
[15] HNW 52–53; 57–60; CSO 87–89.
[16] HNW 53–54; cf. CSO 82.
[17] HNW 55, 62.
[18] HNW 56; CLF 112; *The Fortnightly*, May 1940, 461; CSO 86–87; CLF 155.
[19] CLF 147–148, 154; LL 57–61; cf. CSO 88.
[20] CSO 31; CLF 150–152.

Chapter 10: Natural Law

The chief Roman Catholic works referred to in this chapter are
H. Rommen, *The Natural Law*.
J. Maritain, *The Rights of Man* (RM).
J. Maritain, *Scholasticism and Politics* (SP).
Charles E. Curran, *Catholic Moral Theology in Dialogue* (C).
Charles E. Curran, *New Perspectives in Moral Theology* (N).
Charles E. Curran, *Themes in Fundamental Moral Theology* (TF).
Charles E. Curran, *Transition and Tradition in Moral Theology* (TT).
Franz Böckle, *Fundamental Moral Theology*.

T. E. O'Connell, *Principles for a Catholic Morality*.
Richard A. McCormick, in Outka and Ramsey (eds.), *Norm and Context in Christian Ethics*.
John Finnis, *Natural Law and Natural Rights*.
Gerard J. Hughes, *Authority in Morals*.
I thank the Rev. Fr. Michael O'Dowd of Ushaw College for his comments on a draft of this chapter and part of the next.

1 A. P. d'Entrèves, *Natural Law*, 13.
2 K. Barth, *Church Dogmatics*, II.2, 517.
3 RE 230–231.
4 J. Macquarrie, *Three Issues in Ethics*, 91, 85.
5 N. H. G. Robinson, *The Groundwork of Christian Ethics*, 16, 42, 31–32, 134–137, 47, 210; cf. Hughes, 8, 24f.
6 K. Ward, *Ethics and Christianity*, Chapter 3; cf. Hughes, 88, 91.
7 H. Rommen, 166–175.
8 CC 73.
9 RE 231; CSO 60; HNW 57.
10 Rommen, 208f., 236–237, 242.
11 Maritain, RM 7–14. For a recent treatment of persons, community and the common good see Finnis, Chs. VI–VII
12 RE 231.
13 Rommen, 239–243, 220; Maritain, SP 109; cf. Finnis, 146, 169.
14 Rommen, 194, 168; cf. Finnis, Ch. X.
15 CD 38–39; CC 18; CS 8; C 201–202; CC 29; RE 247; J 361–362.
16 *The Listener*, 2 November 1944, 489, 492; *The Contemporary Review*, August 1928, 157; speech of 18 June 1941.
17 J. L. Lucas, *The Principles of Politics*, 332ff.
18 Bill McSweeney, *Roman Catholicism: the Search for Relevance*, Chapters 2, 3.
19 CSO 59–61.
20 NMG 82–88, 97–104.
21 RE 232–235. For a discussion of Temple's critique of Thomism see Victor White, O.P., 'Tasks for Thomists', in *Blackfriars*, March 1944, 93–117.
22 J. Macquarrie, *Three Issues in Ethics*, 44–46, 106–107.
23 Curran, TF 35, 37–38; Böckle, 190.
24 O'Connell, 151; Curran, TF 47, 59–63, 67–68; McCormick, 249.
25 Louis Monden, quoted by McCormick, 239; cf. O'Connell, 151.
26 Böckle, 208–209, 198.
27 Böckle, 192; Curran, TF 34; Finnis, 403, 34, Ch. V, 88, 96; McCormick, 239–243; O'Connell, 146.
28 RE 231–233.
29 Böckle, 190–191. See Finnis 13ff. on fact and value in the social sciences and their relation to natural law.
30 *Malvern 1941*, 14–15; RE 233–234.
31 D. B. Robertson (ed.), *Love and Justice: Selections from the shorter writings of Reinhold Niebuhr*, 46ff.

[32] H. Thielicke, *Theological Ethics*, I, Chapters 19 and 20.
[33] *The Documents of Vatican II*, 315–316 in Abbott and Gallagher edition.
[34] Curran, C 130–135; NP 65–68; TF 31, 148, 151–152.
[35] Curran, TF 146, 161; TT 127–129; C 125, 132–138.

Chapter 11: Principles

[1] NMG 267, 192–194; CTP 56–57.
[2] NP 73; NMG 168, 173, 177.
[3] e.g. NMG 180; CLF 142–143; HNW 93–94.
[4] NMG 177–178, 183.
[5] CTP 57; NMG 179–180, 183, 405.
[6] NP 74; CTP 57–59; CN 134–135.
[7] NMG 192–193.
[8] NMG 194, 190–191.
[9] CS 69, 83–84; RE 232–233.
[10] CSO 64; MC 195–198; NP 60.
[11] PC, Lecture II; FG 94–95; CFL 68–71; J 274, 283–285; cf. G. J. Hughes, *Authority in Morals*, 89.
[12] J. Macquarrie, *Three Issues in Ethics*, Chapter 2; P. Ramsey, *Deeds and Rules in Christian Ethics*, 20; Outka and Ramsey (eds.), *Norm and Context in Christian Ethics*, 54–55 (Outka), 70, 127 (Paul Ramsey), 363 (Basil Mitchell), 383–389 (Donald Evans); N. H. G. Robinson, *The Groundwork of Christian Ethics*, 274–278. On the limits of calculation and the importance of promises see Finnis, 111ff., 298ff.
[13] J. Fuchs, *Personal Responsibility and Christian Morality*, 115–152; cf. Böckle 194f.
[14] MC 39–40; UC 49, 59–60.
[15] Jack F. Padgett, *The Christian Philosophy of William Temple*, 272, 235.
[16] I. T. Ramsey (ed.), *Christian Ethics and Contemporary Philosophy*, 382–396.
[17] Dietmar Mieth, *Dichtung, Glaube und Moral; Moral und Erfahrung*. For an empirically-minded British approach to moral principles by a Catholic see G. J. Hughes, *Authority in Morals*.
[18] Martin Honecker, *Das Recht des Menschen*, Chapter VII.
[19] W. Huber and H. E. Tödt, *Menschenrechte*, 158–193; M. Honecker, 142–149.
[20] G. W. McDonald in M. Morris (ed.), *The General Strike*, 289–317; S. P. Mews, ibid., 318–337; Iremonger, 338–344.
[21] *The Financial News*, 5 October 1942; *The Economist* quoted in *Public Opinion*, 9 October 1942.
[22] J. H. Oldham, in W. A. Visser't Hooft and J. H. Oldham, *The Church and its Function in Society*, 209ff.; *Malvern 1941*, 10; R. H. Preston, *Crucible*, January 1971, 9–15; D. B. Forrester, in M. H. Taylor (ed.), *Christians and the Future of Social Democracy*, Chapter 3; R. H. Preston, *Church and Society in the Late Twentieth Century: the Economic and Political Task*, Appendix 2, quotation on 153.

Chapter 12: Pacifism

[1] *Christianity and War*, 3–4; *The Times*, 16 April 1924; *The Challenge*, 4 February 1916; Iremonger, 542–543.

[2] *Christianity and War*, 2; *The Challenge*, 4 February 1916; Iremonger, 540.

[3] CTP 69–71.

[4] LL 159.

[5] TWT 32; LL 178.

[6] RE 171–178.

[7] Iremonger, 542–543.

[8] KG 86–87, 91.

[9] *The Challenge*, 4 February 1916; TWT 28–29.

[10] RE 177.

[11] KG 38; *National Report of Proceedings of Church Assembly*, 4 February 1932; 'Education for Peace' at Birkbeck College, 18 June 1941.

[12] *Christianity and War*, 10–13.

[13] LL 131–138.

[14] CTP 74–75; Iremonger, 544; CLF 3.

[15] RE 178; TWT 9; *The Times*, 4 November 1935 (Raven's letter 31 October). On Raven and the varieties of Christian pacifism between the wars see Alan Wilkinson, *Dissent or Conform? War, Peace and the English Churches, 1900–1945*, Chapter 5. On Christian and non-Christian pacifism see Martin Ceadal, *Pacifism in Britain 1914–1945: The Defining of a Faith*.

[16] TWT 29, 31–35.

[17] TWT 55; CLF 46; *The Challenge*, 29 January 1915 and 2 April 1916.

[18] Speech at Birkbeck College, 18 June 1941.

[19] Iremonger, 543; *The Times*, 4 September 1939; LL 134; *The Challenge*, 4 February 1916; PTT 78; RE 177.

[20] PTT 78; J 322–323; *Is Christ Divided?* 24–31.

[21] *The Challenge*, 14 April 1916 and 30 November 1917. On conscientious objection see Alan Wilkinson, *The Church of England and the First World War*, 46–56, and *Dissent or Conform?* 50–53, 103–105, 290–292.

[22] G. H. C. Macgregor, *The New Testament Basis of Pacifism*, 11.

[23] Macgregor, NTBP, 63; cf. his *The Relevance of the Impossible*, 59–61.

[24] Macgregor, NTBP, 11–12, 32.

[25] Macgregor, NTBP, 24–26.

[26] v.s. 142–144.

[27] Quoted by Macgregor, *The Relevance of the Impossible*, 79; cf. above 144.

[28] Macgregor, *The Relevance of the Impossible*, 78–80.

[29] v.i. 181.

[30] v.s. 147.

[31] v.i. 160–161.

[32] ECP 36–37.

[33] v.s. 145–146.

[34] Macgregor, *The Relevance of the Impossible*, 72–74.

[35] v.s. 146, 152.

[36] Macgregor, NTBP, 88ff.
[37] Macgregor, NTBP, 74–75, 104.

Chapter 13: War

[1] Iremonger, 173–174; TWT 11–14.
[2] *The Challenge*, 26 November 1915; *The Contemporary Review*, July 1920, 65–66; CLF 81.
[3] *The Challenge*, 6 August 1915; SSTC 93; *Christianity and War: a Word to Teachers*, 14.
[4] HNW 10–13, 27.
[5] *The Challenge*, 15 November 1918; CLF 88–89.
[6] TWT 9; LL 102; *The Challenge*, 22 October 1915.
[7] TWT 84–90; *Christianity and War*, 7–10; LL 20–21, 145–146.
[8] LL 11–14.
[9] William Temple Papers, Vol. 57, Lambeth Palace Library. See also Alan Wilkinson, *Dissent or Conform? War, Peace and the English Churches, 1900–1945*, 265–272.
[10] 'The Freedom of Nations and of Men' at a reception given by the Anglo-Polish Christian Circle, 17 May 1944.
[11] Iremonger, 383–384; *The Times*, 19 December 1938 and 9 December 1943; H. L. Debates, Vol. 126, cols 811–821, 858–860 (23 March 1943).
[12] Sermon of 14 January 1943; Iremonger, 558; CLF 171.

Chapter 14: Peace

[1] *The Challenge*, 29 January 1915.
[2] *Christianity and War*, 14–16.
[3] *The Challenge*, 30 June 1916.
[4] *The Challenge*, 16 February 1917.
[5] *The Challenge*, 18 October 1918; cf. 25 October 1918.
[6] *The Contemporary Review*, July 1920, 69–70; *The Pilgrim*, April 1921, 241.
[7] *The Pilgrim*, July 1922, 463–464; Iremonger, 375–377.
[8] *The Pilgrim*, January 1922, 127 and July 1922, 466; *The Constructive Quarterly*, March 1919, 7; CS 164; TSPD 34–36.
[9] RE 124–135; CTP 91, 94.
[10] *The Times*, 25 March 1933.
[11] *The Times*, 20 August 1935 and 23 March 1937.
[12] *York Diocesan Leaflet*, October 1936, reported in *The Times*, 1 October 1936; *The Times*, 30 April, 8 May, 8 September 1937.
[13] *The Times*, 4 October 1938.
[14] TWT 60, 68–69; *The Daily Telegraph*, 4 and 6 December 1939; TWT 57; Iremonger, 560.
[15] HNW 35–45.

[16] = HNW 91–104.

[17] *H. L. Debates*, Vol. 130, cols 400–410 (16 December 1943).

[18] KG 86–87, 91; CLF 172–173.

Chapter 15: Love and Justice

[1] Temple's own alleged comment on Niebuhr in 1937, quoted by Nathan Scott, *Reinhold Niebuhr*, 30.

[2] TWT 29, 15; CLF 167–168.

[3] CC 68; TWT 15; *York Diocesan Leaflet*, quoted in *The Times*, 29 October 1935; RE 175–176.

[4] CFCL 48–49; CC 68.

[5] CFCL 50–53; HNW 45.

[6] CFCL 55; CTP 80–83.

[7] TWT 26–27; *The Times*, 4 November 1935; Iremonger, 542–543.

[8] TWT 16; CTP 76–78; CFCL 59.

[9] CTP 85–86; *The Times*, 4 October 1935; CFCL 60; CC 69.

[10] CTP 86–87, 78.

[11] CTP 78; CFCL 53; TWT 18; CC 70; RE 176–177.

[12] CFCL 59–61.

[13] CSO 38; *H. L. Debates*, 16 December 1943; CFCL 59–61; CTP 89, 91.

[14] HNW 46; TWT 27; CFCL 57–58.

[15] CFCL 52–54, 58.

[16] CFCL 59; CSO 38.

[17] EPA 22–39.

[18] CLF 168; HNW 40, 44–45.

[19] TWT 66–70; RE 132.

[20] G. H. Outka, *Agape: an Ethical Analysis*, 75, 88–91.

[21] e.g. HNW 46ff; CSO 14.

[22] CC 70; TWT 18–19; CFCL 53; CTP 94; HNW 46.

[23] TWT 29–30; RE 205; CFCL 61–62.

[24] J. C. Bennett, in Bretall and Kegley (eds.), *Reinhold Niebuhr*, 62–64.

[25] G. Harland, *The Thought of Reinhold Niebuhr*, 215–219.

[26] Harland, 217ff.

[27] Bennett, 62.

[28] R. Niebuhr, *The Nature and Destiny of Man*, I 17, II 75 (English edition). See Outka, 24–34; Harland, 4–13.

[29] For what follows see Harland, 22–29.

[30] R. Niebuhr, *The Nature and Destiny of Man*, I 313; *The Christian Faith and the Common Life*, 72; *The Nature and Destiny of Man*, I 302; *An Interpretation of Christian Ethics*, 150.

[31] CV 273.

[32] D. B. Robertson, *Love and Justice: Selections from the Shorter Writings of Reinhold Niebuhr*, 83–84.

[33] R. Craig, *Social Concern in the Thought of William Temple*, 99–103.

[34] G. H. C. Macgregor, *The Relevance of the Impossible*, Chapter III.

[35] Paul Ramsey, in Bretall and Kegley (eds.), *Reinhold Niebuhr*, 106ff. The quotations are from *The Nature and Destiny of Man*, II 86, 256.

[36] cf. F. I. Gamwell, in Nathan A. Scott (ed.), *The Legacy of Reinhold Niebuhr*, 63–84.

[37] Macgregor, *The Relevance of the Impossible*, 42–44.

[38] Roger Shinn, in Nathan A. Scott (ed.), *The Legacy of Reinhold Niebuhr*, 93.

[39] cf. Shinn, ibid.; on Niebuhr's life see June R. Bingham, *The Courage to Change*; Paul Merkley, *Reinhold Niebuhr: A Political Account*; and R. H. Stone, *Reinhold Niebuhr, Prophet to Politicians*. On Niebuhr's Christian realism see further Ruurd Veldhuis, *Realism versus Utopianism?*

Chapter 16: A Framework for Christian Social Ethics

[1] NMG 499–500.

[2] D. M. MacKinnon, 'Revelation and Social Justice' in *Malvern 1941*, 81ff.

[3] For what follows see Harland, *The Thought of Reinhold Niebuhr*, 111ff.

[4] Julius Gould, quoted by J. P. Wogaman, *Christians and the Great Economic Debate*, 10.

[5] N. H. G. Robinson, *The Groundwork of Christian Ethics*, 18–25, 94–100, 108–115, 119, 139–144, 170.

Appendix I

[1] See C. F. Evans, 'Difficulties in Using the Bible for Christian Ethics', *The Modern Churchman*, Vol. XXVI, No. 3, 1984, 27–34.

[2] *Picture Post*, 31 October 1942.

[3] E. R. Norman, *Church and Society in England, 1770–1970*, 258; *The Times*, 13 August 1926; J. Oliver, *The Church and Social Order*, 86.

[4] H. H. Henson, *Christian Morality*, 32, 305.

[5] Owen Chadwick, *Hensley Henson*, 170, 181; v.s. 202, 68. Even more unsatisfactory is J. D. Carmichael and H. S. Goodwin, *William Temple's Political Legacy*. Their understanding of Temple's social theology is wretched. They write explicitly from a liberal point of view. Their man is atomic man; they have little sense of man's corporate nature or of the depth of sin; the problem of the irresponsible society is resolved into the problem of the irresponsibility of some individuals, especially the workers.

[6] Norman, *Church and Society in England*, 10–11, 282–283, 228, 313.

[7] ibid., 320, 323–324, 341.

[8] ibid., 374, 377–378, 323–324, 391.

[9] See especially Chapter 6.

[10] Norman, *Church and Society in England*, 380ff.

[11] D. E. Jenkins, in C. Elliott and others, *Christian Faith and Political Hopes*, 139ff. See also the criticisms of M. Dummett, *Catholicism and the World Order*.

¹² For what follows see G. Hunsinger (ed.), *Karl Barth and the Radical Tradition*, especially the essays by Marquardt, Gollwitzer, Diem, Bettis and Hunsinger.

¹³ The three pieces are collected in *Community, Church and State*, with an introduction by Will Herberg; the analogies are in the third, sections XXII and XVII.

¹⁴ J. B. Metz, *Faith in History and Society*. The quotation is on 34.

¹⁵ J. Moltmann, *Theology of Hope, The Crucified God, Hope and Planning, The Experiment Hope, The Church in the Power of the Spirit, The Open Church, The Future of Creation*; G. Gutiérrez, *A Theology of Liberation*.

¹⁶ G. Gutiérrez, *A Theology of Liberation*, ix, 13; and his Introduction in H. Assmann, *Practical Theology of Liberation*, 17.

¹⁷ See J. Andrew Kirk, *Liberation Theology: An Evangelical View from the Third World*; for further critiques see Dennis P. McCann, *Christian Realism and Liberation Theology*, esp. 164, 180, and R. H. Preston, 'Reflections on Theologies of Change', in R. H. Preston (ed.), *Theology and Change: Essays in memory of Alan Richardson*, 143–166.

Appendix II

¹ Margaret Kane wrote about these groups herself in *Theological Development*, Occasional Paper Number 2 of the William Temple Foundation. The experience which prompted her to set up these groups can be read in *Theology in an Industrial Society* and *Gospel in Industrial Society*. See also her more recent *What Kind of God? Reflections on Working with People and Churches in North-East England*, esp. Chapter VII.

BIBLIOGRAPHY

A. *WORKS BY WILLIAM TEMPLE*

1. Archive material

Lambeth Palace Library:
  The William Temple Papers
  MS 1765: Letters of William Temple to his brother, presented
  by his nephew, F. S. Temple, in 1960
Repton School

2. Books

Christ in His Church. London: Macmillan, 1925
Christianity and Social Order. Harmondsworth: Penguin, 1942.
  New edition: Shepheard-Walwyn and S.P.C.K., 1976, with a
  Foreword by the Rt. Hon. Edward Heath and an Introduction
  by Professor R. H. Preston. Page references are to the 1942
  edition.
Christianity and the State. London: Macmillan, 1928
Christianity in Thought and Practice. London: SCM Press, 1936
Christ's Revelation of God. London: SCM Press, 1925
Christus Veritas. London: Macmillan, 1924
The Church and its Teaching Today. New York: Macmillan, 1936
Church and Nation. London: Macmillan, 1915
The Church Looks Forward. London: Macmillan, 1944
Citizen and Churchman. London: Eyre and Spottiswoode, 1941
Essays in Christian Politics and Kindred Subjects. London: Longmans
  Green, 1927
The Faith and Modern Thought. London: Macmillan, 1910
Fellowship with God. London: Macmillan, 1920
The Hope of a New World. London: SCM Press, 1940
The Kingdom of God. London: Macmillan, 1912
Mens Creatrix. London: Macmillan, 1917
Nature, Man and God. London: Macmillan, 1934

The Nature of Personality. London: Macmillan, 1911
Personal Religion and the Life of Fellowship. London: Longmans Green, 1926
Plato and Christianity. London: Macmillan, 1916
The Preacher's Theme Today. London: S.P.C.K., 1936
Readings in St. John's Gospel. 2 vols. London: Macmillan, 1939–40
**Religious Experience and Other Essays and Addresses.* London: Clarke, 1958
Repton School Sermons: Studies in the Religion of the Incarnation. London: Macmillan, 1913
Studies in the Spirit and Truth of Christianity. London: Macmillan, 1914
***Thoughts in War-Time.* London: Macmillan, 1940
Thoughts on Some Problems of the Day. London: Macmillan, 1931
The Universality of Christ. London: SCM Press, 1921

*includes 'Robert Browning' (an essay read at Balliol, 1904)
'Christ and the Way to Peace', SCM Press, 1935
'Christian Democracy', SCM Press, 1937
'A Conditional Justification of War', Hazell, Watson and Viney/Hodder and Stoughton, 1940
'Social Witness and Evangelism' (Beckly Social Service Lecture, 1943), Epworth Press, 1943
'Thomism and Modern Needs', *Blackfriars*, March 1944
'What Christians Stand for in the Secular World' (a supplement in *The Christian Newsletter*, February 1944)

**includes 'On the Eve of War' (an address broadcast on 27 August 1939)
A set of articles published by *The Guardian*
'The Spirit and Aims of Britain in the War' (an address broadcast on 3 October 1939)
'What is a Just Peace?', *The Spectator*, 3 November 1939
'Theology Today' in *Theology*, November 1939

3. **Pamphlets**
not included in the above books
Christianity and War (Papers for War Time, No. 1). London: Oxford U.P., 1914

Christianity and War: A Word to Teachers. London: S.P.C.K., 1915
Education for Peace. London: Birkbeck College, 1941
The Ethics of Penal Action. London: National Association of Probation Officers, 1934
The Freedom of Nations and of Men. London: Anglo-Polish Christian Circle, 1944
(Note: *Christian Democracy*, London: SCM Press, 1937, was reprinted in *Religious Experience.*)

4. Symposia and Introductions
'Chairman's Introduction' in *Doctrine in the Church of England, The Report of the Commission on Christian Doctrine Appointed by the Archbishops of Canterbury and York in 1922.* London: S.P.C.K., 1938
'The Chairman's Opening Address' and 'A Review of the Conference' in *Malvern, 1941: The Life of the Church and the Order of Society, Being the Proceedings of the Archbishop of York's Conference.* London: Longmans Green, 1941
'Christian Faith and the Common Life' in *Christian Faith and the Common Life*, Vol. IV of the Oxford Conference, 1937, on Church, Community and State. London: Allen and Unwin, 1938
'The Church', 'The Divinity of Christ' and 'Epilogue' in *Foundations: A Statement of Christian Belief in Terms of Modern Thought by Seven Oxford Men.* London: Macmillan, 1912
Competition: A Study in Human Motive. London: Macmillan, 1917. A corporate product of the Collegium, of which Temple was a member
'In Time of War' with C. E. Raven in *Is Christ Divided?* Harmondsworth: Penguin, 1943
'Introduction' to *Men Without Work. A Report made to the Pilgrim Trust.* Cambridge U.P., 1938

5. Articles, addresses and sermons
not included in the above
Four publications deserve special note:
The Challenge, of which Temple was editor from 1915 to 1918

The Pilgrim, of which Temple was editor for its duration, 1920 to 1927. Several of the articles he wrote for it are gathered in *Essays in Christian Politics*; others are listed below

The Highway, the monthly Journal of the Workers' Educational Association

The York Diocesan Leaflet and *The York Diocesan Quarterly*

'Christian Social Doctrine' in *The Spectator*, CLXVI, 24 January 1941, 83–84

'The Church and the Labour Party' in *The Economic Review*, XVIII, April 1908, 190–202

'The Church and the Social Crisis' in *The Christian Century*, LIX, 7 October 1942, 1209–1211

'Education and Religion among Working-men' in *The Constructive Quarterly*, II, March 1914, 188–196

'Members one of Another': sermon on the occasion of the Disarmament Conference at Geneva, 31 January 1932, in Beable, W. ed., *Celebrated and Historical Speeches*, 9–15. London: Heath Cranston, 1933

'The Moral Foundation of Peace' in *The Contemporary Review*, CXVIII, July 1920, 65–70

'The New Problem in Economics' in *The Contemporary Review*, CXLI, April 1932, 409–414

'Principles of Reconstruction' in *The Fortnightly*, CLIII, May 1940, 456–461. Later included in HNW

'Principles or Ideals?' in *The Pilgrim*, III, January 1923, 218–225

'The Problem of Power' in *The Listener*, XXXII, 2 November 1944, 489, 492

'The Relations Between Church and State' in *The Contemporary Review*, CXXXIV, August 1928, 154–160

'What Must Christians Do Now?' in *The Christian Century*, LVII, 9 October 1940, 1242–1244

6. *Letters*

Temple, F. S. ed., *Some Lambeth Letters 1942–1944*. London: Oxford U.P., 1963

Also in *The Daily Herald*, *The Daily News*, *The Daily Telegraph*, *The Times*.

See also under 'Archive material'

7. Reports of his speeches in:
Chronicles of Convocation
House of Lords Debates Reports
National Assembly Reports
Pan-Anglican Congress Report (1908)
The Reptonian
The Times

B. OTHER WORKS

Arnold, Thomas, *Principles of Church Reform*, with an introductory essay by M.J. Jackson and J. Rogan. London: S.P.C.K., 1962

Auer, A., *Autonome Moral und Christlicher Glaube*. Düsseldorf, 1971

Ayer, A.J., *Language, Truth and Logic*. London: Gollancz, 1936

Barth, K., *Church Dogmatics*, Vol. II Part 2, Vol. III Part 4, Eng. Tr. Edinburgh: T. and T. Clark, 1957, 1961

Barth, K., *Community, State and Church*. Three essays with an introduction by Will Herberg. Gloucester, Mass.: Peter Smith, 1968

Best, G. F. A., *Bishop Westcott and the Miners*. Cambridge U.P., 1967

Bettany, F. G., *Stewart Headlam*. London: John Murray, 1926

Bingham, J. R., *Courage to Change: an Introduction to the Life and Thought of Reinhold Niebuhr*. New York: Scribner's, 1961

Binyon, C. G., *The Christian Socialist Movement in England*. London: S.P.C.K., 1931

Böckle, F., *Fundamental Moral Theology*. Dublin: Gill and Macmillan, 1980

Bretall, R. W. and Kegley, C. W. eds., *Reinhold Niebuhr*. New York: Collier Macmillan, 1962

Brunner, E., *Justice and the Social Order*. London: Lutterworth, 1945

Carmichael, J. D. and Goodwin, H. S., *William Temple's Political Legacy*. London: Mowbrays, 1963

Carpenter, S. C., *Church and People, 1789–1889*. London: S.P.C.K., 1933

Ceadal, M., *Pacifism in Britain 1914–1945: The Defining of a Faith*. Oxford: Clarendon, 1980

Chadwick, W. O., *Hensley Henson*. Oxford: Clarendon Press, 1983

Christensen, T., *The Divine Order*. Leiden: Brill, 1973
Christensen, T., *Origin and History of Christian Socialism, 1848–1854*. Aarhus: Universitetsforlaget, 1962
Cole, G. D. H. and Postgate, R., *The Common People, 1746–1946*. 4th ed. London: Methuen, 1971
Craig, R., *Social Concern in the Thought of William Temple*. London: Gollancz, 1963
Curran, C. E., *Catholic Moral Theology in Dialogue*. Notre Dame U.P., 1976
——, *New Perspectives in Moral Theology*. Notre Dame U.P., 1976
——, *Themes in Fundamental Moral Theology*. Notre Dame U.P., 1977
——, *Transition and Tradition in Moral Theology*. Notre Dame U.P., 1979
Demant, V. A., *The Miners' Distress and the Coal Problem*. London: SCM Press, 1929
——, *The Religious Prospect*. London: Muller, 1939
——, *This Unemployment: Disaster or Opportunity?* London: SCM Press, 1931
d'Entrèves, A. P., *The Natural Law*. 2nd ed. London: Hutchinson, 1970
Dummett, M., *Catholicism and the World Order*. London: Catholic Institute for International Relations, 1979
Edwards, D. L., *Leaders of the Church of England, 1828–1978*. London: Hodder and Stoughton, 1978
Elliott, C. et al., *Christian Faith and Political Hopes*. London: Epworth, 1979
Evans, C. F., 'Difficulties in Using the Bible in Christian Ethics' in *The Modern Churchman*, Vol. XXVI, No. 3, 1984, 27–34
Finnis, J., *Natural Law and Natural Rights*. Oxford: Clarendon, 1980
Fletcher, J. F., *Situation Ethics*. London: SCM Press, 1966
——, *William Temple, Twentieth-century Christian*. New York: Seabury, 1963
Fuchs, J., *Personal Responsibility and Christian Morality*. Dublin: Gill and Macmillan, 1980
Goodfellow, I., *The Church Socialist League, 1906–1923: Origins, Development and Disintegration*. Unpublished Durham University Ph.D., 1983

Gutiérrez, G., *A Theology of Liberation*. London: SCM Press, 1974

Harland, G., *The Thought of Reinhold Niebuhr*. New York: Oxford U.P., 1960

Henson, H. H., *Christian Morality*. Oxford: Clarendon Press, 1936

——, *Quo Tendimus?* London: Hodder and Stoughton, 1924

——, *Retrospect of an Unimportant Life*. Vol. 3. London: Oxford U.P., 1950

Honecker, M., *Das Recht des Menschen*. Gütersloh: Gerd Mohn, 1978

Huber, W. and Tödt, H. E., *Menschenrechte*. Stuttgart: Kreuz Verlag, 1977

Hudson, C. E. and Reckitt, M. B., *The Church and the World*. Vol. 3. London: Allen and Unwin, 1940

Hughes, Gerard J.,S.J. *Authority in Morals*. London: Heythrop Monographs, 1978

Hunsinger, G. ed., *Karl Barth and Radical Politics*. Philadelphia: Westminster Press, 1976

Iremonger, F. A., *William Temple, Archbishop of Canterbury: His Life and Letters*. London: Oxford U.P., 1948

John XXIII, *Mater et Magistra* (1961). London: Catholic Truth Society, 1963

——, *Pacem in Terris* (1963). London: Catholic Truth Society, 1963

Jones, P. d'A., *The Christian Socialist Revival, 1877–1914*. Princeton, N.J.: Princeton University Press, 1968

Kane, M., *Gospel in Industrial Society*. London: SCM Press, 1980

——, *Theology in an Industrial Society*. London: SCM Press, 1975

——, *Theological Development*. Manchester: William Temple Foundation, 1980

——, *What Kind of God? Reflections on Working with People and Churches in North-East England*. London: SCM Press, 1986

Kirk, J. A., *Liberation Theology: An Evangelical View from the Third World*. Basingstoke: Marshall, Morgan and Scott, 1979

Leo XIII, *Rerum Novarum* (1891). London: Catholic Truth Society, 1910

Lowry, C. W., *William Temple: An Archbishop for All Seasons*. Washington: University Press of America, 1982

Lucas, J. L., *The Principles of Politics*. Oxford: Clarendon Press, 1966

McCann, D. P., *Christian Realism and Liberation Theology*. New York: Orbis Books, 1981

Macgregor, G. H. C., *The New Testament Basis of Pacifism*. London: Clarke, 1936

——, *The Relevance of the Impossible*. London: Fellowship of Reconciliation, 1941

MacKinnon, D. M., 'Revelation and Social Justice' in *Malvern 1941*, 81–116. London: Longmans Green, 1941

Macquarrie, J., *Three Issues in Ethics*. London: SCM Press, 1970

McSweeney, W., *Roman Catholicism: The Search for Relevance*. Oxford: Blackwell, 1980

Maritain, J., *The Rights of Man*. London: Bles, 1944

——, *Scholasticism and Politics*. London: Bles, 1940

——, *True Humanism*. London: Bles, 1938

Matthews, W. R. et al., *William Temple: An Estimate and an Appreciation*. London: Clarke, 1946

Merkley, P., *Reinhold Niebuhr: a Political Account*. Montreal: McGill-Queen's U.P., 1975

Mess, H. A., *Industrial Tyneside. A Social Survey made for the Bureau of Social Research for Tyneside*. London: Benn, 1928

Metz, J. B., *Faith in History and Society*. London: Burns and Oates, 1980

Mews, S. P., 'Neo-orthodoxy, Liberalism and War: Karl Barth, P. T. Forsyth and John Oman 1914–18' in Derek Barker, ed., *Renaissance and Renewal in Christian History*. Oxford: Blackwell, 1977

Mieth, D., *Dichtung, Glaube und Moral*. Mainz, 1976

——, *Moral und Erfahrung*. Freiburg: Universitätsverlag & Herder, 1977

Moltmann, J., *The Church in the Power of the Spirit*. London: SCM Press, 1977

——, *The Crucified God*. London: SCM Press, 1974

——, *The Experiment Hope*. London: SCM Press, 1975

——, *The Future of Creation*. London: SCM Press, 1979

——, *Hope and Planning*. London: SCM Press, 1971

——, *The Open Church*. London: SCM Press, 1978

——, *Theology of Hope*. London: SCM Press, 1967

Morris, M. ed., *The General Strike*. Harmondsworth: Penguin, 1976 (especially the essays by G. W. McDonald and S. Mews)

Niebuhr, Reinhold, *An Interpretation of Christian Ethics*. 3rd. ed. London: SCM Press, 1941

——, *The Nature and Destiny of Man*. 2 vols. London: Nisbet, 1941–1943

——, *Christian Realism and Political Problems*. New York: Scribner's, 1953

——, 'The Christian Faith and the Common Life' in *Christian Faith and the Common Life*, Vol. IV of the Oxford Conference, 1937, on Church, Community and State. London: Allen and Unwin, 1938

——, 'Dr. William Temple and his Britain' in *The Nation*, CLIX, 11 November 1944, 584–586

Noel, Conrad, *Socialism in Church History*. London: F. Palmer, 1910

Norman, E. R., *Christianity and the World Order*. Oxford U.P., 1979

——, *Church and Society in England, 1770–1970*. Oxford: Clarendon, 1976

O'Connell, T. E., *Principles for a Catholic Morality*. New York: Seabury, 1976

Oldham, J. H., in Visser't Hooft, W. A. and Oldham, J. H., *The Church and its Function in Society* (Preparatory volume for the Oxford Conference of 1937). London: Allen and Unwin, 1937

——, 'Introduction' in *The Churches Survey their Task, The Report of Conference at Oxford, 1937, on Church, Community and State*. London: Allen and Unwin, 1938

Oliver, J., *The Church and Social Order. Social Thought in the Church of England, 1918–1939*. London: Mowbrays, 1968

Outka, G., *Agape*. New Haven: Yale U.P., 1972

Outka, G. and Ramsey, P. eds., *Norm and Context in Christian Ethics*. London: SCM Press, 1969

Padgett, J. F., *The Christian Philosophy of William Temple*. The Hague: Nijhoff, 1974

Paul VI, *Humanae Vitae* (1968). London: Catholic Truth Society, 1968

——, *Populorum Progressio* (1967). London: Catholic Truth Society

Pius XI, *Quadragesimo Anno* (1931). London: Catholic Truth Society, 1960

Preston, R. H., *Church and Society in the Late Twentieth Century: The Economic and Political Task.* London: SCM Press, 1983
——, 'The Malvern Conference' in *The Modern Churchman*, April 1942, 15–22
——, 'Middle Axioms in Christian Social Ethics' in *Crucible*, January 1971, 9–15; reprinted in *Explorations in Theology 9*. London: SCM Press, 1981
——, 'William Temple as a Social Theologian' in *Theology*, September 1981
——, ed., *Theology and Change. Essays in Memory of Alan Richardson*. London: SCM Press, 1975
Ramsey, I. T. ed., *Christian Ethics and Contemporary Philosophy*. London: SCM Press, 1966
Ramsey, P., *Deeds and Rules in Christian Ethics*. New York: Scribner's, 1967
Reckitt, M. B. ed., *For Christ and the People*. London: S.P.C.K., 1968
Richter, M., *The Politics of Conscience*. London: Weidenfeld and Nicolson, 1964
Robertson, D. B. ed., *Love and Justice. Selections from the Shorter Writings of Reinhold Niebuhr*. Gloucester, Mass.: Smith, 1976
Robinson, N. H. G., *The Groundwork of Christian Ethics*. London: Collins, 1971
Rommen, H. A., *The Natural Law*. St. Louis and London: Herder, 1947
Sandford, E. G. ed., *Memoirs of Archbishop Temple* by Seven Friends. London: Macmillan, 1906
Scott, N., *Reinhold Niebuhr*. Minneapolis: University of Minnesota Press, 1963
——, ed., *The Legacy of Reinhold Niebuhr*. Chicago U.P., 1975
Stone, R. H., *Reinhold Niebuhr, Prophet to Politicians*. Nashville: Abingdon, 1972
Suggate, A. M., *William Temple's Christian Social Ethics: A Study in Method*. Durham University Ph.D. 1980 (unpublished)
——, 'Reflections on William Temple's Christian Social Ethics', in *Crucible*, October–December 1981, 155–163
——, 'William Temple and the Challenge of Reinhold Niebuhr', in *Theology*, November 1981, 413–420
——, 'William Temple and the Future of Christian Social Ethics',

in F. K. Hare ed., *The Experiment of Life*, 131–149. University of Toronto Press, 1983

Taylor, M. H. ed., *Christians and the Future of Social Democracy.* Ormskirk: G. W. and A. Hesketh, 1982

Thielicke, H., *Theological Ethics.* 2 vols. London: A. and C. Black, 1969

Thomas, O. C., *William Temple's Philosophy of Religion.* London: S.P.C.K., 1961

Veldhuis, R., *Realism versus Utopianism? Reinhold Niebuhr's Christian Realism and the Relevance of Utopian Thought for Social Ethics.* Assen: van Gorcum, 1975

Ward, K., *Ethics and Christianity.* London: Allen and Unwin, 1970

White, Victor, O.P., 'Tasks for Thomists' in *Blackfriars*, March 1944, 93–117

Wilkinson, A., *The Church of England and the First World War.* London: S.P.C.K., 1978

——, *Dissent or Conform? War, Peace and the English Churches, 1900–1945.* London: SCM Press, 1986

Winter, G., *Elements for a Social Ethic.* London: Collier Macmillan, 1966

Wogaman, J. P., *Christians and the Great Economic Debate.* London: SCM Press, 1977

Young, G. M., *Portrait of an Age.* Oxford: Oxford U.P., 1936, 1953

Christianity and Industrial Problems. The Report of the Archbishops' Fifth Committee of Enquiry. London: S.P.C.K., 1918

The Documents of Vatican II (ed. Abbott, W. M. and Gallagher, J.). New York: The America Press, 1966

Essays and Reviews (by F. Temple et al.). London: Longmans Green, 1860

Lux Mundi (ed. Charles Gore). London: Murray, 1889

Malvern, 1941. The Life of the Church and the Order of Society. Being the Proceedings of the Archbishop of York's Conference. London: Longmans Green, 1941

Conference on Christian Politics, Economics and Citizenship Commission Reports. 12 vols. London: Longmans Green, 1924

The Proceedings of COPEC. London: Longmans Green, 1924

The Economist   *Picture Post*
The Financial News   *Public Opinion*

SUGGESTIONS FOR FURTHER READING

There are several good books on Christian ethics. Among the simplest (though challenging) are:

Richard G. Jones, *Groundwork of Christian Ethics*. London: Epworth, 1984

George Newlands, *Making Christian Decisions*. London: Mowbrays, 1985

More extended and demanding are:

Edward LeRoy Long, Jr., *A Survey of Christian Ethics*. New York: Oxford U.P., 1967

now supplemented by *A Survey of Recent Christian Ethics*. Oxford U.P., 1983

J. Philip Wogaman, *A Christian Method of Moral Judgment*. London: SCM Press, 1976

Brian Hebblethwaite, *The Adequacy of Christian Ethics*. London: Marshalls, 1981

Stanley Hauerwas, *The Peaceable Kingdom*. Notre Dame: University of Notre Dame, 1983

Ian C. M. Fairweather and James I. H. McDonald, *The Quest for Christian Ethics*. Edinburgh: The Handsel Press, 1984

Robin M. Gill, *A Textbook of Christian Ethics*. Edinburgh: T. and T. Clark, 1985

James M. Gustafson, *Protestant and Roman Catholic Ethics*. Univ. of Chicago, 1978

Oliver O'Donovan, *Resurrection and Moral Order: An Outline for Evangelical Ethics*. Leicester: Inter-Varsity Press, 1986

A famous book which presents five types of response to the question of the relation of the Christian faith to the world is:

H. Richard Niebuhr, *Christ and Culture*. New York: Harper and Row, 1951

For those wishing to start out on some of the current issues mentioned in Appendix III the following should be helpful:

On *work and unemployment*:

Roger Clarke, *Work in Crisis: Dilemma of a Nation*. Edinburgh: St. Andrew Press, 1982

Michael Moynagh, *Making Unemployment Work*. Tring: Lion Publishing, 1985

For critiques of different *economic* systems, see:
J. Philip Wogaman, *Christians and the Great Economic Debate*. London: SCM, 1977
Ronald H. Preston, *Religion and the Persistence of Capitalism*. London: SCM, 1979

On *war and peace in a nuclear age*, see:
——, *The Church and the Bomb*. London: Hodder and Stoughton and CIO Publishing, 1982
F. Bridger (ed.), *The Cross and the Bomb*. London: Mowbray, 1983 and the response:
Robin M. Gill, *The Cross Against the Bomb*. London: Epworth, 1984
The pacifist position is well represented by:
J. H. Yoder, *The Politics of Jesus*. Grand Rapids, Michigan: Eerdmans, 1972
Kenneth G. Greet, *The Big Sin*. London: Marshalls, 1982

INDEX